·Buccleuch·

·Harden·

·Thirlestane·

1118

SCOTT

1923

★

·Hassendene·

·Whitslaid·

·Goldielands·

A·G·LAW·SAMSON

Arms of Buccleuch and his Principal Lieutenants
circa 1596

SCOTT
1118-1923

BEING A COLLECTION OF "SCOTT"
PEDIGREES CONTAINING ALL KNOWN
MALE DESCENDANTS FROM BUCCLEUCH,
SINTON, HARDEN, BALWEARY, ETC.

COMPILED AND ARRANGED
BY
Keith S. M. Scott
F.S.A. (Scot.)

WITH AN INTRODUCTION
BY
The Master of Polwarth,
Captain The Hon. W. T. Hepburne-Scott,
Younger of Harden

Illustrated by Mr. A. G. Law Samson, Writer to the Lyon Office

HERITAGE BOOKS
2025

HERITAGE BOOKS

AN IMPRINT OF HERITAGE BOOKS, INC.

Books, CDs, and more—Worldwide

For our listing of thousands of titles see our website
at
www.HeritageBooks.com

A Facsimile Reprint
Published 2025 by
HERITAGE BOOKS, INC.
Publishing Division
5810 Ruatan Street
Berwyn Heights, MD 20740

Previously published 1969;
Originally published 1923

Library of Congress Catalog Card No. 72-79269

International Standard Book Number
Paperbound: 978-0-7884-4702-0

INTRODUCTION.

TWO Hundred and Forty-two years have passed since that "Old Souldier and no Scholler," Captain Walter Scot of Satchells, published his inimitable rhyming history of the "Right Honourable Name of Scot," and now another historian of the family has arisen in the person of Captain Keith Scott, who also may be called an "Old Souldier," inasmuch as he played his part in the greatest war of all time.

Captain Scott has not followed the example of his predecessor and written his history in verse, but he has set forth his pedigrees in a much clearer and more concise form, adhering rigidly to genealogical details.

He has produced a book which is of very great interest, not only to all the families concerned, but also to all students of Border History, and to genealogists in general. The histories of the titled and principal land owning families are included in works such as Peerages and Burke's "Landed Gentry," and are accessible to the public, but there are numerous other families, with pedigrees just as long and as interesting, and it is in these that the great interest of this book lies.

Captain Scott has taken infinite pains in collecting and tracing such pedigrees back to the parent stems and it is greatly to be hoped that the publication of this book may lead to the tracing of other branches, and provide clues for connecting these with the older lines. The majority of Border Scotts are probably descended from one or other of the three main branches into which, as will be seen, the family is divided, and it is regrettable that, largely through lack of interest in the subject, the connecting links have in many cases been lost. It is hoped that any who can provide further information relative to the subject will send it to the compiler and thus provide material for the possible future publication of a supplementary volume.

Captain Scott has made a notable contribution to the list of Scottish Genealogical works, and sincere thanks are due to him for the thorough manner in which he has carried out his task.

Walter Scott.

Harden,
    January, 1923.

PREFACE.

A S its title implies this book is a collection of "Scott" pedigrees connected together in order of seniority, and intended to include as far as possible all male descendants of the founder of the family. The genealogies are taken from various editions of Burke, from Douglas, Satchells,* Dr. William Scott's "Scott of Stokoe," Mr. Winning's notes in the fifth edition of Satchells, Mr. Craig Brown's History of Selkirk, Major Tancred's "Annals of a Border Club," Mr. Grant's "Zetland Families," and from similar works of reference amplified by research into Parish Registers, in which I have been assisted by Mr. H. M. Paton of Edinburgh, and also in some cases by information supplied to me by members of the various families. I have also gratefully to acknowledge assistance and advice from Captain The Hon. The Master of Polwarth, and Mr. F. J. Grant, W.S., *Rothesay Herald*, both of whom have perused the collection in draft form and were instrumental in obtaining additional data.

Where the pedigrees contained in this collection differ from the works of reference mentioned above, I have only tampered with the latter when there has been no doubt that they have been wrong or incom-

---

* "A true history of several Honourable Families of the Right Honourable name of Scot," by Captain Walter Scott of Satchells. Original edition 1688, second edition Edinburgh 1776, third edition Hawick 1786, fourth edition 1892, fifth edition Hawick 1894, edited by Mr. John G. Winning.

plete. Note for instance that Walter Scott, tenant in Baillieknowe, did not marry Barbara Makdougal as stated in some editions of Burke.

Where possible, I have put into pedigree form the genealogies given by Captain Walter Scott of Satchells, and placed them in their proper place in this book. Many of these are necessarily sketchy and stop at the time of Satchells' book, namely 1688; where they are unsupported by other works they must be accepted with considerable reserve. There may be families living who can connect with these pedigrees, and for this purpose I propose leaving some blank pages at the end.

Before commencing the genealogy a few words are desirable on the general scheme and method of compiling; on the heraldry of the family; and also on the chieftainship of the Clan.

With regard to the general scheme, the method is the same as that adopted by Burke, except that every branch of over two male generations (in some cases of two generations only), has been given a separate heading. Male descent only is given, but when a family that has been traced for several generations in the male line becomes extinct the present representative (or representatives) where known in the female line are given; for example the Buccleuch line is given step by step to Mary and Anna, and then a brief note explains that this family is now represented in the female line by the present Duke.

Daughters are entered under each individual entry after sons as in the case of Burke's publications. Husband's names will be given where known, but not particulars of issue.

The Scott family naturally falls into three parts, and for the sake of convenience I have so divided these genealogies, with an additional part for families that are probably connected with the main branch but of which the exact connecting link is lost.

In the case of each family or cadet I have given the arms of the head of that branch where I know they have been matriculated.* Those families to which I have assigned no arms are probably without right in arms unless they have been matriculated since August, 1922.†

I have also in one or two cases entered the arms that are on record to extinct families.

With regard to the heraldry of the family, Sir Richard Scott's arms were, according to tradition, " or, two mullets in chief and a crescent in base azure," and on his marriage with the heiress of Inglis of Murdiestoun, whose arms were probably " or, a bend azure," he adopted her arms and displayed his stars and crescent on the bend, probably as in fig. II.‡

There was no very strict heraldic law in force in Scotland until early in the seventeenth century, and various members of the family seem to have rung the changes on the different methods of charging the bend. The clan arms given by Mr. R. Armstrong in his "History of Liddesdale" are as shown in fig. IV. The seals of six generations of the Buccleuch family from 1449 to 1568 are consistently as fig. III. In spite of this, however, a Scott of Buccleuch is noted in 1542 as bearing fig. VIII., in 1550 as fig. IV., and in 1562 as fig. V.; this latter was the father of the first Lord Scott of Buccleuch. The first Earl reverted to fig. III., and Francis, second Earl, adopted a star of six points between two crescents (fig. IX.) Anna, before marriage, bore as fig. VIII., and after marriage as an escutcheon of pretence, fig. III., and later, after the attainder of Monmouth, as fig. IX.

---

*Most readers will know that coat-armour of Scottish origin descends to the eldest son and that younger sons and their descendants are not armigerous until they matriculate at Lyon Office with "due and proper difference." The rule in England is different, all male descendants of the grantee being armigerous but in order to retain recognition of right in arms by the Heralds' College, pedigrees should be recorded and kept up to date by at least every second generation. A great grandson of a grantee or of a man whose arms were on record would not be officially recognised as armigerous without proof of descent being given and recorded.

†All descendants in the male line of the Rev. J. W. Napier-Clavering are armigerous, the arms having been exemplified at the Heralds' College, likewise all the male descendants of Mr. John Scott, Morpeth. and Mr. William Scott of Willsboro', Baron of the Exchequer, and the daughters of such male descendants according to the law of arms.

‡See next page.

PREFACE.

The Howpasleys and their descendants, including the Napiers, seem to have adopted a pierced mullet between two crescents, fig. VII.

The variation of étoile, mullet, and pierced mullet or spur-rowel has possibly arisen not so much out of deliberate differencing as from different artists' interpretation of " star," which was a loose term used in early heraldry for any kind of star.

As regards the second branch of the family, the Sinton family certainly bore the bend till towards the end of the sixteenth century, and quite possibly up to about 1672 if not later. William of Harden's seal in 1540 was as fig. V., and later his grandson, Auld Watt, bore as fig. VI., which continued to be the arms of the family till probably about 1820, after which they bore as fig. I. Cadet families of Harden prior to 1820 (with the exception of Scott of Abbotsford) bear a differenced version of fig. VI.

Possibly arising out of Satchells' views that Sinton branched from Buccleuch before the alliance with Inglis of Murdiestoun, the then Laird of Sinton or more possibly Archibald of Boonraw, altered his arms to the old pre-Murdiestoun Scott arms (fig. I). Boonraw made a deed of gift of his arms in 1700, twenty years before his death, to Sir William Scott of Harden, and the then Lord Lyon, Sir Alexander Erskine, made a grant of these arms to Sir William Scott (a doubtful procedure) which grant was not registered but lay in the Harden charter chest till 1820 when Sir Walter (then Mr.) Scott of Abbotsford presented it at Lyon Office and had it duly entered. The Lairds of Harden then, or about then, commenced to use the arms of Boonraw with a female figure bearing the sun and crescent for crest in lieu of the bend, star, crescents, and rose in their arms and the stag for crest.

This reversion is, in my opinion, to be regretted as being founded on a pedigree of Satchells which is most probably incorrect, and I should personally like

to see the old arms of Auld Watt of Harden reintro-
duced into Lord Polwarth's coat.

Whether this is ever done or not, to be consistent
all families descended from Sinton and Harden should
bear the arms (either fig. I. or fig. VI.) borne by the
father of the particular cadet from which they descend,
suitably differenced.

For instance, the Raeburn family do not appear to
have matriculated arms, and the present Laird of
Raeburn and Lessudden is, strictly speaking, non-
armigerous. The first Laird of Raeburn was the third
of five sons of Sir William Scott of Harden, the
Harden family bearing at that time " or, on a bend
azure an étoile between two crescents of the field
differenced by a rose gules "; the second, fourth, and
fifth sons matriculated their arms surmounting the
rose, by a crescent, a martlet, and an annulet respectively. The descendants of the second son eventually
succeeded to the representation of the family and to
Boonraw's arms; the other matriculations survive in
the arms of General Scott of Sunlaws and Mr. Scott-
Plummer. Although it is not the modern method of
matriculation, I respectfully suggest that the present
Mr. Scott of Raeburn, who is credited in some works
of reference as bearing the Boonraw arms undiffer-
enced, should matriculate his arms and ask for
permission to bear, " or on a bend, etc., etc., surmounting the rose by a mullet."

Sir Walter Scott of Abbotsford also transgressed
by bearing a differenced version of fig. I. instead of
fig. VI., he being descended from the Raeburn family;
and to emphasize the desirability of cadets bearing the
arms of the generation from which they spring unin-
fluenced by subsequent change in the senior arms,
compare the paternal quartering of His Grace the
Duke of Buccleuch, which contains the arms of France
as borne by Charles II., in spite of the fact that the
Kings of England have now discarded the fleur-de-lis
from their arms.

It is somewhat more difficult to deal with the heraldry of the third branch. The Scotts of Balweary were fairly certainly related to the Scotts of Buccleuch, but whether the connection is exactly as shown here is not so certain. The Scotts of Balweary may have adopted entirely different arms in order to distinguish themselves from the Buccleuchs when in armour, other methods of differencing not then having been thought of, or more possibly the arms borne by the Scotts of Balweary may have been the original arms of Balweary. At any rate the three lions' heads are equally as old as the crescents and stars.

With regard to the chieftainship of the family Lord Polwarth is undoubtedly universally recognized as the head of the Scotts, and the fact that there are many living members of the family appearing in these genealogies before Lord Polwarth, may give rise to some speculation.

The second Earl of Buccleuch, whose ancestors for many generations had been looked upon as heads of the family, died in 1651, and at that time there were living in probable order of seniority, Sir John Scott of Scotstarvit, Sir John Scott of Davington in an impoverished condition, George Scott of Boonraw (and several cadets such as Satchells, Whitslaid, Toderick) and Sir William Scott of Harden. These four families were all probably sprung from Buccleuch, but in no case has their pedigree been proved. Harden, being by far the most wealthy and influential Scott at that time, assumed the chieftainship on the Earl's death, and his heirs have held it ever since, although, as will be seen from the genealogies, he was far from even probably the senior Scott from a primogenital point of view, and was certainly junior to Boonraw.

As it is impossible to say with certainty in any, much less in all, genealogies exactly when the spelling of the name was altered from Scot to Scott (we find Scott in Parish Registers as early as 1630 and Scot as late as 1750), I have used the modern spelling throughout.

The names of sons who carry on the family in a particular genealogy are printed in small capitals—JOHN; names of sons whose descendants are given as a separate genealogy are printed in italics—*George*; names of sons who d. s.p. or of whose descendants there is no record, are printed in the same type as the body of the book.

Finally, the compiler apologizes for errors in dates and spelling which in spite of great care must have crept in in considerable numbers in a book almost entirely made up of dates and names, especially in the many cases where information is supplied in manuscript, or documents are lent and subsequently returned. There are many cases when it will appear to readers that a genealogy might have been corrected or amplified by the present representative. Every effort has been made to communicate with some member of each family before going to press, but in many cases without success. The courtesy and kindness of those who have helped me are here very gratefully acknowledged. Additions and corrections will be gladly received by the compiler after this edition is printed, and if possible either a supplement or a second edition will be printed at a later date.

The following usual abbreviations are used:

b.—born.	m.—married.
c.—about.	s.p.—without children.
d.—died.	unm.—unmarried.
dau.—daughter.	v.p.—during father's lifetime.

Keith Turnbull Scott

Newcastle-upon-Tyne,
  August, 1923.

CONTENTS.

CONTENTS.

Part I.—*Continued.*

CONTENTS.

Part II.

Being descendants of John Scott, brother to Robert Scott,
third of Rankilburn.

Part II.—*Continued.*

Part III.

Being descendants of Michael, brother to Richard, who married Alicia de Molla.

Part IV.

Being sundry families probably allied to families included in Parts I., II. and III., but of which the connecting link has been lost.

CONTENTS.

Part IV.—*Continued.*

*Illustrated.

NOTE.—Each family is inset from the family from which it springs, so that Melby comes from Gibbleston, Gibbleston from Scotstarvit, Scotstarvit from Allanhaugh, and Allanhaugh from Buccleuch (not from Wauchope).

Where it has not been convenient to give a territorial designation to any particular genealogy that genealogy is titled by the name of the present representative.

Part I.

Buccleuch.

The
Duke of Buccleuch ❖

THE reasonably authentic genealogy of this family
commences with Sir Richard Scott of Rankilburn and Murdiestoun (No. V. below), but I have
included the first four which are copied from a
pedigree in the hand of Sir Walter Scott of Abbotsford, now in the possession of Lord Polwarth.

I. UCHTRED FITZ-SCOTT was living in
1118 and was witness to two charters granted in 1128
and 1130 and is mentioned among the courtiers of
King David I.

II. RICHARD SCOTT was in all probability a
son of Uchtred. He witnessed a charter granted by
the Bishop of St. Andrew's to the Abbey of Holyrood

about the year 1158. According to Sir Walter Scott
of Abbotsford, Richard had two sons:

    1. RICHARD.
    2. *Michael*, ancestor of the Scotts of
       Balweary.

III. RICHARD SCOTT the elder m. Alicia,
dau. of Henry de Molla, with whom he received lands
in Roxburgh in the reign of Alexander II.; he was
succeeded in that property by his son,

IV. WILLIAM SCOTT, who also attended the
Court of Alexander II., and witnessed several of his
charters. His son,

V. SIR RICHARD SCOTT of Rankilburn and
Murdiestoun, swore fealty to Edward I. of England
in 1296. He acquired the lands and Barony of
Murdiestoun in Lanark by his marriage with the heiress
of Inglis of Murdiestoun, and d. in 1320, leaving a
son,

VI. SIR MICHAEL SCOTT, a gallant warrior
who distinguished himself at Halidon Hill 19th July,
1330. Sir Michael accompanied David II. to the
unfortunate battle of Durham, and fell in that engage-
ment on the 17th October, 1346. He left two sons:

    1. ROBERT his heir.
    2. *John*, ancestor of the Scotts of Sinton,
       Harden, Whitslaid, Toderick, Raeburn,
       Woll, Thirlestane, etc.

VII. ROBERT SCOTT, third of Rankilburn,
also of Kirkurd, succeeded his father, Sir Michael, in
1346; d. c. 1389, and was succeeded by his son,

VIII. SIR WALTER SCOTT of Rankilburn,
Murdiestoun, and Kirkurd. Sir Walter was killed at
the battle of Homildon Hill in 1402.

IX. ROBERT SCOTT succeeded his father, Sir Walter, and exchanged Glenkerry for the lands of Bellanden in 1415; he acquired half the lands of Branxholm from John Inglis of Manor in 1420, and d. 1426, leaving three sons:

    1. WALTER his heir.   2. *Stephen.*
    3. *Robert of Haining.*

X. SIR WALTER SCOTT, the eldest son, sixth Laird of Murdiestoun and Buccleuch, acquired the second half of the lands of Branxholm from Thomas Inglis in exchange for the lands of Murdiestoun. He m. Margaret Cockburn of Henderland and d. c. 1469, leaving three sons:

    1. DAVID his heir.
    2. *James* designed of Kirkurd and Hassendene, ancestor of the Scotts of Hassendene, Burnfoot, and Burnhead.
    3. *Sir Alexander of Howpasley,* ancestor of the Scotts of Thirlestane (Selkirkshire), Gilmanscleuch, Newburgh, Tushielaw, Horsleyhill, etc.

XI. SIR DAVID SCOTT, seventh Laird of Buccleuch, sat in Parliament as Lord of Buccleuch in 1487. He had, by a daughter of Thomas, Lord Somerville:

    1. Walter d. before 1471.
    2. DAVID.
    3. *Robert of Allanhaugh.*
    4. *William of Foulshiels.*
    1. Janet m. Sir James Douglas of Drumlanrig.
    2. Margaret m. James Haig of Bemerside.
    3. —— m. John Lindsay of Covington.
    4. Isabella m. Sir Symon Caruthers of Monswald.

NOTE.—Sir Walter Scott, sixth Laird of Buccleuch was the first of the family we find designated "of Buccleuch" but Rankilburn and Buccleuch being interchangeable names for the same place justifies him being described as sixth of Buccleuch.

XII. DAVID SCOTT, younger, of Buccleuch, m. 1472 Jane, dau. of George, fourth Earl of Angus, and dying 1488 in the lifetime of his father left an only son :

      1. WALTER, who succeeded his grandfather on the latter's death in 1491-2 and became

XIII. SIR WALTER SCOTT, eighth Laird of Buccleuch. This Sir Walter m. Elizabeth, dau. of Walter Kerr of Cessford, by whom he had two sons :

      1. SIR WALTER, who succeeded him.

      2. William of Whitehope, who d. s.p. 1523.

Sir Walter d. in 1504 at an early age, and was succeeded by his elder son,

XIV. SIR WALTER SCOTT, ninth Laird of Buccleuch, known as " Wicked Wat," was knighted at Flodden in 1513, defeated at Melrose 1526, defeated the English 1544 at the head of a large body of Scots at Ancrum Moor, and commanded a large force at the battle of Pinkie Cleuch in 1547. He was murdered by the Kerrs in the High Street of Edinburgh in 1552. Sir Walter m. three times : first Elizabeth Carmichael of the family who were afterwards Earls of Hyndford; secondly Janet, dau. of Andrew Kerr of Ferniehurst; and thirdly Janet, dau. of John Betoun of Creich, this last being the lady mentioned in the " Lay of the Last Minstrel." By the first marriage Sir Walter had :

      1. David (Sir) d. v.p.

      2. WILLIAM (Sir) of Kirkurd.

By the third marriage :

      3. Walter.   4. David of Stobiescot.

      1. Grisel m. William, seventh Lord Borthwick.

      2. Janet m. John Cranstoun of Cranstoun, and later Robert Scott of Haining.

      3. Margaret.

Sir Walter was also father of *Sir Walter Scott* of Goldielands.

XV. SIR WILLIAM SCOTT of Kirkurd, called "Whitecloak," younger of Buccleuch; m. Grisel, dau. of John Betoun above (sister to his stepmother), and d. 1552 during the lifetime of his father, leaving issue :

    1. WALTER.
    1. Janet m. Sir Thomas Kerr of Ferniehurst.
    2. Margaret m. Robert Scott of Thirlestane.
    3. Elizabeth m. John Carmichael of Meadowflat.
    4. —— m. Sir John Johnston of Johnston.
    5. —— m. Walter Scott of Headshaw.

XVI. SIR WALTER SCOTT succeeded his grandfather in 1552. He m. Lady Margaret Douglas, dau. of David, seventh Earl of Angus, and dying April, 1574, left issue with a dau. Mary, m. to William Elliot of Lariston, an only son,

XVII. SIR WALTER SCOTT, eleventh Laird of Buccleuch and first Lord Scott of Buccleuch. This chieftain, b. 1566, warden of the West Marches, was one of the bravest and most powerful barons of his time, and one of his exploits, known to all interested in the Scott family, was the rescue of one of his followers, William Armstrong, from Carlisle Castle (1596). He was elevated to the peerage in 1606, having m. Mary, dau. of Sir William Kerr of Cessford. Lord Scott d. December, 1611, aged about 45, leaving issue :

    1. WALTER, Master of Buccleuch.
    1. Margaret m. James, sixth Lord Ross.
    2. Elizabeth m. John, second Lord Cranstoun.
    3. Jean.

XVIII. WALTER SCOTT, the only son, was created, 16th March, 1619, Baron Scott of Whitchester and Eskdail and Earl of Buccleuch. Lord Buccleuch

m. October, 1616, Lady Mary Hay, dau. of Francis,
Earl of Erroll, and by her had issue :

1. Walter, Lord Scott, d. an infant.
2. FRANCIS, Lord Scott.
3. David of Canonbie d. July, 1648.
1. Elizabeth m. John, Earl of Mar.
2. Jean m. to the Marquess of Tweeddale.
3. Mary.

The Earl also had many illegitimate children, all
bearing the surname of Scott, of whom there were :

1. *Francis of Mangerton.*
2. *William* also of Mangerton.
3. *John of Gorinberrie,* legitimated by
   Cromwell, February, 1656.
1. Margaret m. John Pringle.
2. Janet m. Andrew Scott of Foulshiels.
3. Jane m. Robert Scott of Whitslaid.

The Earl of Buccleuch d. in 1636.

XIX. FRANCIS SCOTT, second Earl of Buccleuch, was b. 1626. By his marriage with Lady
Margaret Leslie, dau. of the sixth Earl of Rothes and
widow of Lord Balgonie, he left issue :

1. Walter d. young. 1. MARY.
2. A dau. d. young. 3. ANNA.

The Earl d. in 1651, and was succeeded by his
eldest daughter when she was but four years old.

XX. MARY SCOTT, Countess of Buccleuch,
m. at the age of eleven Walter Scott of Highchesters,
subsequently created Earl of Tarras. The Countess
d. on the 11th March at the age of thirteen, and was
succeeded by her sister,

XX. ANNA SCOTT, Countess of Buccleuch
and subsequently Duchess of Buccleuch and Monmouth. The Duchess m. April, 1663, James, Duke of
Monmouth, illegitimate son of Charles II., and the

Buccleuch family is now represented in the female line by her direct descendant, Sir Charles Montagu-Douglas-Scott, K.T., seventh Duke of Buccleuch and ninth Duke of Queensberry, etc., etc., etc.

Arms.—Quarterly : 1st and 4th, The Royal Arms of Charles II. (viz., quarterly : 1st and 4th quarterly France and England; 2nd Scotland; 3rd Ireland) debruised by a baton sinister argent; 2nd and 3rd or, on a bend azure an étoile between two crescents of the field, for Scott. Crest.—A stag, trippant, ppr., attired and unguled, or. Supporters.—Two females, richly attired in antique habits, vert., their under robes azure, the uppermost argent, and upon their heads plumes of three ostrich feathers, of the last. Motto.—Amo. Seats.—Dalkeith House, Dalkeith; Bowhill, Selkirk; The Lodge, Langholm; and Drumlanrig Castle, Thornhill, Dumfriesshire. Town House.—2 Grosvenor Place, S.W.

Note.—The above arms appear to be the only arms that have ever been exemplified, but arms as sketched at the head of this genealogy have been credited to the Duke in several publications, and His Grace is probably entitled to the extra quarterings by descent if not officially.

Mangerton.

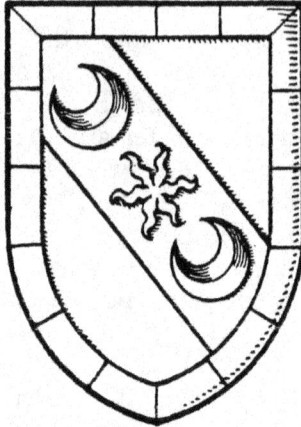

Scott
of Mangerton

XIX. FRANCIS SCOTT of Mangerton, natural son to Walter, Earl of Buccleuch, is the first of this family designed of Mangerton. He left a dau. m. to Sir John Scott of Ancrum, and Mangerton passed to

XIX. WILLIAM SCOTT of Mangerton, another natural son of the same Earl. This Laird was succeeded by

XX. SIR FRANCIS SCOTT of Mangerton, who was on the Commission for peace for Roxburghshire. He d. September, 1672, and was succeeded by his son,

XXI. FRANCIS SCOTT of Mangerton, who d. s.p. May, 1698, and was succeeded by his sister,

XXI. ELIZABETH SCOTT, of whom nothing is known.

Arms.—Or, on a bend azure an étoile between two crescents of the field. A bordure componée of the second and first.

⚙orinberrie.

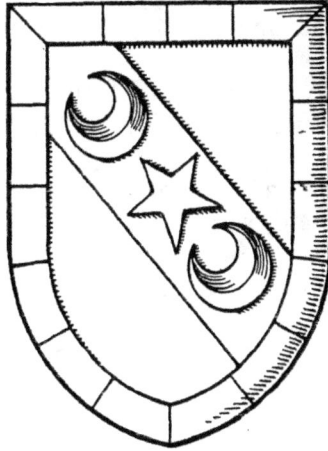

Scott of Gorinberrie

XIX. JOHN SCOTT of Gorinberrie, natural son of Walter, first Earl of Buccleuch, by Annas Drummond, cousin to the Earl of Perth, and subsequently legitimated by Cromwell, was one of the tutors to Mary, Countess of Buccleuch, during her minority. He m. a dau. of Sir John Riddell, having, so far as we know, only one son,

XX. FRANCIS SCOTT, Laird of Gorinberrie, living in 1688. Francis Scott m. Penelope, dau. of Sir John Wachop of Niddrie, by whom he had issue a dau. Anna, m. to Archibald Douglas of Cavers, a son Charles, witness to the wedding of Elliot of Tarras in 1731 and his successor

XXI.   JOHN SCOTT of Gorinberrie, who m. a
dau. of Charles Kerr, first of Abbotrule, and by her
had issue, probably among others:

    1. FRANCIS.
    2. James b. October-November, 1703.
    1. Ann, m. to the Hon. Walter Scott, 10th of
       Harden.
    2. A dau. m. to Douglas of Cavers.

XXII.   FRANCIS SCOTT succeeded his father,
but we have no further record of this family.

Arms.—Or, on a bend azure a star between two
crescents of the field, within a bordure componée gules
and argent.   Crest.—An anchor in pale, inwrapt by a
cable proper.   Motto.—Sperandum.

Wauchope.

Macmillan Scott ⁘
⁘ of Wauchope

MAJOR TANCRED gives in his "Annals of a Border Club" a different version of this family's descent, but I have been unable to discover whence he derived it.

The following is taken from an old lithographed pedigree kindly lent me by Captain A. F. Macmillan-Scott, and where it is at variance with Major Tancred's version, there seems little doubt that the family's version is more probably correct.

XV. SIR WALTER SCOTT of Goldielands, natural son of Walter Scott, ninth Laird of Buccleuch, was a man of considerable importance during the minority of his nephew, and led the Clan at the raid of the Reidswyre in July, 1575; he d. in November, 1596, leaving a son,

       1. WALTER, who succeeded him, and a natural son,

       2. Charles of Crumhaugh, who had a son, WALTER, successor to his cousin, also

       1. A dau. m. to Robert Scott of Glack.

XVI. WALTER SCOTT of Goldielands succeeded his father and m. Jean, dau. of Sir Andrew Riddell, by whom he had a son,

XVII. WALTER SCOTT of Goldielands, who also succeeded his father, but d. without issue in or before 1672.

XVII. WALTER SCOTT of Crumhaugh and afterwards of Goldielands, b. 1632, succeeded his cousin, but the estates of Goldielands passed back to the Buccleuch family. Walter Scott, however, retained a considerable estate inherited from his cousin. He m. Janet Glendinon and d. 1700, leaving:
1. CHARLES.
2. WALTER, whose line eventually succeeded to the representation of this family.

XVIII. CHARLES SCOTT, the elder son, b. 1664, m. Rachel, dau. of Langlands of that ilk, and d. v.p. October, 1698, leaving a son,

XIX. WALTER SCOTT of Crumhaugh and Howpasley, b. August, 1689, who succeeded his grandfather and m. Beatrice, dau. of Gideon Scott of Falnash, by whom he had a younger son, Gideon in Priesthope, father of Beatrice, who m. Walter Scott of Wauchope, and

XX. CHARLES SCOTT of Crumhaugh and Howpasley, b. 1719, m. Christian Anderson and d. 1757. Charles Scott had issue:
1. WALTER.
2. Gideon, from whom descended the Scotts in Priesthaugh, now extinct in the male line.
1. Henrietta, from whom descended the Erskines of Shielfield.

XXI. CAPTAIN WALTER SCOTT, b. 1741;
d. 1809 without issue.

XVIII. WALTER SCOTT in Goldielands,
second son of Walter Scott and Janet Glendinon, b.
1670, m. Christian, dau. of Robert Bennet of Chesters,
by whom he had issue:
1. Charles b. April, 1696, d. young.
2. WALTER.
3. Robert b. June, 1704, d. s.p.
4. Charles b. January, 1708, d. s.p.
1. Joan.

XIX. WALTER SCOTT of Wauchope and
Howcleuch, the eldest surviving son, b. July, 1700, m.
Rachel, dau. of Francis Elliott of Fenwick, and had
by her two sons,
1. Walter, b. 1726, m. 1768 Elizabeth, dau.
of David Rutherford, and second, 1789
Beatrice, dau. of Gideon Scott in
Priesthope, but d. s.p. 1796.
2. CHARLES.
Walter Scott purchased the estate of Wauchope in
the parish of Hobkirk, and Howcleuch and other lands
in the parish of Robertoun, and gave Wauchope to his
eldest son and Howcleuch to his second son. He died
in 1786.

XX. CHARLES SCOTT of Howcleuch, b.
1728, succeeded to Wauchope in 1796; m. August,
1776, Elizabeth, dau. of Archibald Dickson of
Hassendene Burn, and d. 1808, leaving
1. WALTER.
2. Archibald, succeeded to Howcleuch; m.
Charlotte Sibbald 1804, but d. s.p. 1874.
3. Charles b. November, 1782; d. unm.
July, 1856.
4. Robert b. November, 1786; d. unm.
April, 1833.
5. James b. July, 1789; d. unm. May, 1810.

6. William b. February, 1792; d. unm.
   September, 1828.
1. Rachel m. Hugh Mitchell.
2. Christian m. Archibald Dickson.
3. Agnes d. young.
4. Jessie m. John Cockburn.

XXI. WALTER SCOTT of Wauchope, b.
July, 1778, succeeded to Wauchope on his father's
death. He m. June, 1812, Marion, dau. of Thomas
Macmillan, Esq., of Shorthorpe, Co. Selkirk, and by
her left issue:

1. Charles b. 1st May, 1814; d. December,
   1817.
2. THOMAS his heir.
3. Walter, M.D., H.E.I.C.S., b. July, 1817;
   d. at Allahabad, Bengal, August, 1844.
4. Charles b. 24th March, 1819; m. 1862
   Margaret Amelia, dau. of Browne
   Roberts, Esq., of Ravensbourne Park,
   Kent. Succeeded his uncle Archibald to
   Howcleuch in 1874. He matriculated
   arms with a crescent counterchanged for
   difference.
5. Archibald b. November, 1822; d. at
   Malta, May, 1862.
1. Anna d. December, 1817, aged 4 years.

Mr Scott d. 24th May, 1857, and was succeeded by
his eldest surviving son.

XXII. THOMAS MACMILLAN-SCOTT,
Esq., of Wauchope and Pinnacle Hill, Writer to the
Signet, J.P., b. February, 1816, assumed the additional
surname and arms of Macmillan in accordance with the
conditions of the entail of his maternal grandfather's
estate of Shorthorpe; m. April, 1844, Katherine Jane,
dau. of Browne Roberts, Esq., of Ravensbourne Park,
Kent, formerly of the Bengal Army, and High Sheriff
of Calcutta, and had issue :

1. Walter b. December, 1846; d. April, 1847.
2. WALTER.
3. Arthur Francis, Advocate, Captain Reserve of Officers, b. October, 1854. Succeeded his uncle Charles to Howcleuch; m. Louisa Bryant.
   1. Edith Marion m. General Sotheby.
   2. Marion Maud. 3. Katherine.

Mr Macmillan-Scott d. June, 1862, and was succeeded by his eldest surviving son,

XXIII. WALTER MACMILLAN-SCOTT, Esq., of Wauchope and Pinnacle* Hill, J.P., late Captain Scottish Borderers Militia, and formerly Lieutenant 6th Dragoon Guards (The Carbineers), b. 1848; m. 1876 Antoinetta, eldest dau. of Theodore Henry Dury, Esq., of Bonsall, Co. Derby, and had issue:

1. THOMAS ALEXANDER FREDERICK.
1. A dau. m. to Rear-Admiral T. C. Tancred.

XXIV. THOMAS ALEXANDER FREDERICK MACMILLAN-SCOTT of Wauchope and Pinnacle Hill, Esquire, J.P., b. 1881; m. first 1912, Karin Anna, dau. of Peter Erichsen of Trondhjem, and secondly December, 1918, Enid Cynthia, dau. of C. H. Paine of Ivyhill, Essex.

Arms.—1st and 4th or, on a bend azure a mullet between two crescents of the first, a bordure componée of the second and first; 2nd and 3rd per pale or and argent a lion rampant sa., in chief three mullets az. Crests.—1. A stag's head erased gules. 2. A dexter and sinister hand issuing from the wreath brandishing a two-handed sword all proper. Mottoes.—Over the crests, Miseris Succuro; under the arms, Ardenter Amo. Seat.—Wauchope and Pinnacle Hill, Kelso, N.B.

Allanhaugh.

XII. ROBERT SCOTT of Allanhaugh and Whitchester, second son of David Scott, seventh Laird of Buccleuch, d. at an advanced age leaving issue three sons:

    1. ROBERT of Allanhaugh.
    2. *Alexander.*
    3. James, whose line is believed to be extinct.

XIII. ROBERT SCOTT of Allanhaugh signed a bond in 1525, and was father of

XIV. WILLIAM SCOTT designed " son and heir apparent of Robert Scott in Allanhaugh," who eventually (circa 1557) succeeded and seems to have had descendants living designed of Allanhaugh down to Satchells' time (1688), but we have no trace of any of this family living now. According to Sir Walter Scott of Abbotsford the estate was eventually destined to two sons: the elder was slain by the younger for the sake of succession, and the then Lord of Buccleuch executed the murderer and confiscated the property.

Scotstarvit.

lord
•Howard de Waldon ❖

✦ lord lascelles ✦

THIS family without doubt descends from Buccleuch, and the following is the generally accepted genealogy. Anything like proof of the early steps cannot, I believe, now be given, but Sir Walter Scott of Abbotsford speaks of General Scott of Balcomie as Chief of the Clan.

XIII. SIR ALEXANDER SCOTT, second son of the first Robert of Allanhaugh, and grandson of David, seventh of Buccleuch, was appointed by James V. Vice-Register of Scotland in 1534. He d. before the year 1540, leaving a son,

XIV. ROBERT SCOTT, who was young at his father's death, and was educated under the inspection of his uncle James. He acquired a considerable estate, particularly the lands of Knightspottie, which continued to be for some time the chief title in his family. He m. first Elizabeth Sandilands, by whom he had no issue. He m. secondly Elizabeth, a widow and mother of Sir William Scott of Ardross, by whom he had two sons and one daughter:

    1. ROBERT.
    2. James m. Marion, dau. of Laurence Scott of Harperrig and was designed of Vogrie; he had issue two daughters:
        (1) Elspeth. (2) Jean.

XV. ROBERT SCOTT, the elder son, m. Margaret, dau. of Alexander Aitchison of Gosford, and d. in the lifetime of his father, leaving an only son,

XVI. JOHN SCOTT of Knightspottie, afterwards Sir John Scott of Scotstarvit, who succeeded his grandfather in 1592 at the age of seven. He obtained a charter of the lands of Tarvit in the County of Fife, and afterwards called these lands Scotstarvit; this then

became the chief title of his family.   He was knighted
by James VI. in 1617, and appointed Privy Councillor.
He m. first Ann, dau. of Sir John Drummond of
Hawthorn Dene, by whom he had issue :·

    1. Robert baptised May, 1609 ; d. young.
    2. JAMES (Sir).
    3. *John* (Sir) baptised August, 1614.
    4. William baptised August, 1615.
    5. *Alexander* baptised 1620.
    6. Robert baptised September, 1625.
    7. Ludovic baptised September, 1627.
    1. Margaret.   2. Jean.   3. Helen.
    4. Eupham.   5. Anna.   6. Eliza.
    7. Rebecca m. Mr John Ellis of Ellistone.
    8. Elizabeth.   9. Margaret.   10. Janet.

Sir John m. secondly Margaret, dau. of Sir James
Melville of Hallshill, by whom he had one son,

    8. George of Pitlochie, from whom there was
       no succession.

He m. thirdly Eupham, dau. of Moneypenny of Pit
Milly, by whom he had :

    9. Cecil baptised January, 1647, from whom
       there was no male succession.
    10. Walter of Lethum, baptised January, 1650,
       who registered his father's arms with a
       martlet for difference, and left an only
       dau. and heiress m. to the Hon. Charles
       Erskine.

Sir John d. in the 84th year of his age anno 1670.

   XVII.   SIR JAMES SCOTT, heir apparent to
Sir John Scott of Scotstarvit m. Lady Marjorie
Carnegie, dau. of John, Earl of Ethie, by whom he had
two sons :

    1. JAMES, who became his grandfather's heir.
    2. DAVID, who succeeded his brother.

Sir James d. anno 1650, and his elder son,

XVIII. JAMES SCOTT, succeeded his grandfather, and he, dying without issue, was succeeded by his brother,

XVIII. DAVID SCOTT of Scotstarvit, who m. Nicholas, dau. of Sir John Grierson of Lagg, by whom he had one daughter,

   1. Marjorie m. to the fifth Viscount Stormont.

He m. secondly Elizabeth, dau. of John Ellis of Ellistone, by whom he had issue:

   1. DAVID.
   2. Marjorie m. Peter Ogilvie of Balfour.
   3. Elizabeth m. to the Earl of Balcarras.

David Scott the elder d. 1718, in the 73rd year of his age, and was succeeded by his son,

XIX. DAVID SCOTT, Advocate, M.P. Crail 1722; m. Lucy, dau. of Sir Robert Gordon of Gordonstoun, November, 1716, by whom he had two sons and two daughters:

   1. DAVID his heir. 2. JOHN.
   1. Elizabeth m. Peter Hay of Leys.
   2. Lucy d. unm.

XX. DAVID SCOTT of Scotstarvit we believe d. without issue.

XX. GENERAL JOHN SCOTT of Balcomie, last male of this family, m. Margaret, dau. of Henrietta Baillie of Lamington, and by her had three daughters:

   1. Henrietta m. August, 1795, to William Henry, fourth Duke of Portland.
   2. Lucy m. 1795 Francis Lord Doune, afterwards Earl Moray.

3. Joan m. 1800 the Right Hon. George
Canning, and was created in her own right
Viscountess Canning. She had issue a
son, Sir Charles Canning, K.G., etc., who
succeeded but d. s.p., and a dau. Harriet.

The representation of Henrietta, Duchess of Portland, devolves through her daughter, Lucy (the male
line failing and the Dukedom passing to a cousin), to
Thomas Evelyn Scott-Ellis, eighth Baron Howard de
Waldon.

Lucy, Countess Moray, had two sons, both of
whom became Earls Moray but d. s.p., and her share
in the representation of the Scotstarvit family is
extinct.

Viscountess Canning's daughter Harriet m. in 1825
the Marquis of Clanricarde, whose male line failed in
the second Marquis, but who is represented in the
descendants of his five daughters:

1. Lady Elizabeth Joanna m. to the fourth
Earl of Harewood and had issue.
2. Lady Emily Charlotte m. to Richard, ninth
Earl of Cork, and had issue.
3. Lady Catherine m. to John Weyland of
Woodeaton, Oxon, and had issue.
4. Lady Margaret Anne m. to Wentworth
Blackett Beaumont, now represented by
Lord Allendale.
5. Lady Harriet Augusta m. to Thomas
Vernon-Wentworth and had issue.

There would thus appear to be six co-representa-
tives of this family equally entitled to the representation. The following are the only arms I have
traced which quarter Scott of Scotstarvit:

Arms.—Of Henry George Charles Lascelles,
Esquire, D.S.O., commonly known as Viscount
Lascelles, quarterly of eight, 1, Lascelles: Sa., a cross
patonce within a bordure or; 2, de Burgh: Or, a cross

gu., in the first quarter a lion rampant sa.; 3, Canning : Arg. three Moors' heads, couped, profile ppr., wreathed around the temples arg., and az.; 4, Salman : Gu., three spear heads in fesse arg.; 5, Marshall : Sa., a goat salient or; 6, Newburgh : Or, three bendlets az., a bordure gu.; 7, Scott : Or, on a bend az. a mullet between two crescents of the first, in chief a crescent gules, all within a bordure engrailed also gules; 8, Lascelles: As No. 1, Over all a label of three points argent. Crest.—A bear's head, couped at the neck, arg., muzzled, gu., buckled, or, collared, of the second, rimmed and studded, gold. Motto.—In solo Deo salus. Seat.—Goldsborough Hall, Yorkshire.

Arms.—Of Thomas Evelyn Scott-Ellis, eighth Baron Howard de Waldon : 1st and 4th Ellis, Erminois on a cross sable five crescents argent; 2nd and 3rd Scott, or on a bend azure a star between two crescents of the field, in chief a crescent gules within a bordure engrailed of the last. Crests.—1. On a mount vert a goat's head erased arg. 2. A dexter hand holding an annulet or in which is set a carbuncle ppr. Mottoes.— 1. Non quo sed quomodo. 2. In tenebris lux. Seat. —Chirk Castle, Denbigh.

Gibbleston.

Scott of Gibbleston

XVII. SIR JOHN SCOTT of Gibbleston, Fife, second son of Sir John Scott of Scotstarvit and Anne Drummond, his wife, m. an heiress of Sir Alexander Gordon of Cluny and d. 1658, leaving two sons:
1. GEORGE. 2. JOHN.

XVIII. GEORGE SCOTT of Gibbleston, b. May, 1644, Steward of Orkney, acquired property in Shetland. He m. November, 1665, Elizabeth, dau. of William Maxwell of Springkell, but apparently d. without issue and was succeeded by his brother,

XVIII. JOHN SCOTT of Gibbleston, who m. Grisel, dau. and co-heiress of James Mitchell of Girlesta in Shetland, and left issue:

1. JAMES.

2. *John of Melby.*

1. Barbara m. first 1725 Hector Scott of Scotshall and secondly Alexander Innes of Laxforth, M.D.

2. Lillias.

3. Elizabeth m. Robert Ash, a skipper.

XIX. JAMES SCOTT, the eldest son, succeeded to Gibbleston, but we understand was never married.

Arms Reg. Lyon Office, 1686.—Quarterly 1st and 4th or, on a bend azure a mullet between two crescents of the field within a bordure engrailed gules; 2nd and 3rd azure three bears' heads couped or. Crest.—A boar's head, couped, or, holding in the mouth four arrows gu. headed and feathered arg. Motto.—" Do well and let them say."

𝔐𝔢𝔩𝔟𝔶.

Scott of Melby ❖

XIX. JOHN SCOTT of Melby, the second son of John Scott of Gibbleston and Grisel Mitchell, m. first January, 1736, Elizabeth, dau. of Charles Mitchell of Uresland, Shetland, and by her had :

    1. JOHN.   2. James b. January, 1738.
    1. Elizabeth d. young.
    2. Margaret m. 1766 John Thomas Henry, of Bayhall.

He m. secondly January, 1748, Anne, dau. and co-heiress of Robert Sinclair of Scalloway, and had issue,

    3. Philadelphia m. George Chalmers, tide waiter of the Customs, Lerwick.

He m. thirdly Mary, dau. of Archibald Henry of Bayhall, and had by her :

    3. James m. Elizabeth Tennant.
    4. Clementina m. April, 1782, John Scott of Scalloway.
    5. Mary.

Mr. Scott d. August, 1765.

XX. JOHN SCOTT of Melby, the elder son, was killed by a fall in Vaila 1764, leaving by Jane Henry, his wife, dau. of Archibald Henry of Bayhall,

XXI. JOHN SCOTT of Melby, b. 1760, m. December, 1780, his cousin, Elizabeth, dau. of James Scott of Scalloway, and d. at Edinburgh July, 1850, having had issue :

1. JOHN.
2. James, a surgeon R.N., m. January, 1810, Katherine, dau. of John Scott of Scalloway, and d. January, 1860, leaving issue :
    (1) John b. March, 1819.
    (2) Charles Archibald b. May, 1821.
    (1) Elizabeth.
3. Charles in Royal Marines.
4. Archibald.
5. William Pitt of St. John's, New Brunswick.
6. Robert.
1. Jane m. Captain Archibald Henry of Bayhall.
2. Clementina m. September, 1828, James Hewat, accountant, Edinburgh, and d. October, 1873.
3. Margaret d. unm. December, 1856.
4. Catherine m. June, 1804, Cassiles Wilson, Supervisor.

XXII. JOHN SCOTT, younger, of Melby, b. 1782, the eldest son was drowned in February, 1813. He m. December, 1801, Barbara, dau. of Arthur Nicolson of Lochend, and by her had :

1. JOHN.
1. Janet m. June, 1821, Thos. Gifford of Hillswick, H.E.I.C.S.

Mr. Scott m. secondly June, 1806, Mary, dau. of John Scott of Scalloway, and by her had :

2. Thomas d. young.

3. James b. March, 1809; d. abroad.
4. Charles b. October, 1810.
5. ROBERT THOMAS CHARLES heir to his brother.
6. Thomas d. young.

XXIII. JOHN SCOTT of Melby, the eldest son, b. April, 1804, succeeded his grandfather, and m. 1825 Elizabeth Jane, dau. of Lieutenant-Colonel William Walker, and dying s.p. December, 1850, was succeeded by his half-brother,

XXIII. ROBERT THOMAS CHARLES SCOTT of Melby, D.L. and J.P.; b. January, 1812; m. October, 1859, Agnes Catherine, dau. of Alexander Scott Watson, C.E., and by her had issue :

    1. ROBERT THOMAS CHARLES.
    1. Agnes Catherine m. June, 1882, John Fowlie.
    2. Florence Sobieski Stewart.

XXIV. ROBERT THOMAS CHARLES SCOTT of Melby, b. July, 1864, sold the estate to Mr. Herbert Anderton 1897; m. July, 1885, Agnes, second dau. of Laurence Georgeson Sandness, and has issue :

    1. ROBERT THOMAS CHARLES b. December, 1886.
    2. Alexander James b. April, 1888; d. January, 1901.
    3. Stuart d. in infancy.
    1. Agnes Robina Mary m. James Small, Blairgowrie, Perth.
    2. Edith Margaret. 3. Catherine Watson.
    4. Georgina Josephine.
    5. Ella Ethel Laura Jane.
    6. Florence Joan Kathleen.

Arms as Scott of Gibbleston with a crescent for difference. Residence.—99A Commercial Street, Lerwick, N.B.

Scottshall.

Scott
of Scottshall

SIR WALTER SCOTT of Abbotsford, who was
personally acquainted with Mr. John Scott of
Scalloway and stayed with him in 1814, states
definitely that this family is a branch of Scotstarvit,
but I know of no work of reference substantiating this.
It is possible that

XVII. ALEXANDER SCOTT, goldsmith in
Edinburgh, was fifth son of John Scott first of Scotstarvit.   He m. Agnes, dau. of George Wauchope,
merchant in Edinburgh, by whom he had issue:
    1. James, who was father of:
        (1) Alexander d. 1732.
        (2) William, shipmaster in Orkney.
    2. George, who followed his father's pro-
       fession; m. Grizel Sinclair and had two
       sons:
        (1) John, a merchant in Dundee.
        (2) Alexander.

3. JOHN of Scottshall.
4. William.
5. Robert b. April, 1675.
1. Henrietta m. Alexander Livingstone of Bedlormie.
2. Janet.

XVIII. JOHN SCOTT of Scottshall m. Margaret, dau. of Hector Bruce of Muness, and had issue :

1. HECTOR his heir. 2. Andrew.
3. George. 4. Arthur. 5. John.
6. Robert.
1. Grizel m. August, 1725, John Stewart of Bigton.
2. Margaret.
3. Barbara m. Rev. James Grierson of Tingivall.

XIX. HECTOR SCOTT of Scottshall m. first Janet, dau. of William Douglas, and had issue :
1. John.
1. Ursilla m. Robert Barclay.
He m. secondly October, 1725, Barbara, dau. of John Scott of Melby, and had issue :
2. ROBERT his heir.
3. *James of Scalloway.*
4. George. 2. Barbara.

XX. ROBERT SCOTT of Scotshall m. first Janet, dau. of Arthur Nicolson of Lochend, and had issue :
1. Hector.
He m. secondly Elizabeth, dau. of James Graham, and had issue :
2. WALTER his heir.
3. John, a merchant in London.
1. Henrietta.
2. Elizabeth m. John Murray.

XXI. WALTER SCOTT of Scottshall m. Isabel, dau. and co-heiress of Andrew Bolt, merchant, Lerwick, and had issue:

1. Robert b. May, 1771.
2. Walter b. November, 1774.
3. JOHN, a Major 18th Regiment, heir to his father.
4. James b. March, 1779.
5. Keith Stewart b. July, 1781.
6. Thomas Dundas b. April.
1. Elizabeth m. Duncan Campbell, Surgeon.
2. Isabel.   3. Janet.
4. Henrietta.   5. Grace.

Arms.—Or, on a bend az. a mullet of six points btw. two crescents, ar. in chief a boar's head, couped, gu.; a bordure of the last.   Crest.—A boar's head, couped, gu. holding in the mouth a sheaf of arrows ppr. Motto.—" Do well, and let them say."

Scalloway.

XX. JAMES SCOTT, merchant in Scalloway, third son of Hector Scott of Scottshall and Janet Douglas, m. March, 1750, Catherine, dau. and co-heiress of Robert Sinclair of Scalloway, and through her acquired part of that estate. He d. 2nd July, 1793, leaving issue:

1. JOHN his heir.
2. Robert b. August, 1757, d. young.
3. James b. August, 1758.
4. Charles b. July, 1760, Lieutenant R.M.
5. Robert b. November, 1762.
1. Barbara.
2. Philadelphia m. George Chalmers, tide waiter, Lerwick.
3. Ann.
4. Elizabeth m. December, 1780, John Scott of Melby.
5. Grizel m. Robert Robertson of Gossaburgh.
6. Mary.

XXI. JOHN SCOTT of Scalloway, b. 6th April, 1756, succeeded his father; m. April, 1782, Clementina, dau. of John Scott of Melby, and had issue:

1. James b. 17th February, 1785, d. s.p.
2. JOHN his heir.
3. Charles b. 22nd July, 1793.
4. Robert b. 14th August, 1798.
5. James b. 3rd May, 1800.
1. Mary d. young.   2. Mary d. young.
3. Katherine m. her cousin, James Scott, Surgeon R.N.
4. Mary m. John Scott of Melby.
5. Elizabeth.   6. Jacobina Charlotte.

XXII. JOHN SCOTT of Scalloway, b. September, 1791, m. May, 1814, Jessie, dau. of Gideon Gifford of Busta, and had issue:

1. John James b. April, 1816; d. November, 1844.
2. GIDEON ARTHUR THOMAS GIFFORD.
1. Grace Elizabeth Clementina Charlotte m. Charles Spence.
2. Harriette Jane Christina.

XXIII. GIDEON ARTHUR THOMAS GIFFORD SCOTT of Scalloway, b. 26th June, 1822, m. 1866 Isabella, dau. of Charles Spence, and had issue:

1. Grace Clementina Henrietta Isabella.
2. Beatrice Frances Mary Irvine.

Mr. Scott of Scalloway became embarrassed financially and parted with his estates; he d. at Edinburgh 12th March, 1873.

ffoulsbiels.

WILLIAM SCOTT, mentioned in a Charter dated 1532 as son to Sir Walter Scott, Knight of Buccleuch, obtained by that charter the lands of Foulshiels.

JOHN SCOTT of Foulshiels in 1593 subscribed to a deed of loyalty. It is impossible with the meagre information available to say that it is even probable that this John was son or grandson of William, but the property was owned by Scotts down to the end of the seventeenth century.

JAMES SCOTT of Foulshiels was in possession in 1600, and was definitely father of

ANDREW SCOTT of Foulshiels, who m. Janet, natural dau. of the Earl of Buccleuch, and in 1647

WALTER SCOTT of Foulshiels was served heir to his brother Andrew. He left two daughters, co-heiresses to his estates, one of whom, Elizabeth, m. James Scott of Bowhill.

Hassendene.

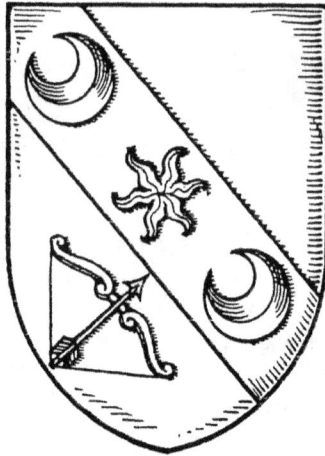

Scott of Hassendene

XI.   JAMES SCOTT of Kirkurd, second son of Sir Walter Scott of Kirkurd, was designed " of Kirkurd " for some considerable time.   He afterwards resigned Kirkurd to the Buccleuch family, and acquired the lands of Over and Nether Newhall in Roxburgh, now called Burnhead and Burnfoot, and also the lands of Hassendene in the same county. By Margaret, his wife, he had issue :

> 1. DAVID.   2. JOHN.   3. WILLIAM.
> 4. *Robert.*   5. *Adam of Clarilaw.*

XII.   DAVID SCOTT had a charter dated February, 1510, to Hassendene and both the Newhalls. He d. s.p. and was succeeded by his brother,

XII. JOHN SCOTT of Hassendene, of whom we know little except that he m. Agnes Scott and d. s.p.

XII. WILLIAM SCOTT of Hassendene succeeded his brother early in 1530. It is supposed that he had three sons:

    1. DAVID his heir.

    2. *Adam of Burnfoot.*

    3. Walter.

XIII. DAVID SCOTT, the eldest son, was murdered in 1564 by William Elliot of Horsleyhill with the connivance of his son James, and I gather that James was executed at Edinburgh in 1564 along with others who had a hand in the occurrence.

XV. ROBERT SCOTT of Hassendene is believed by Mr. Scott of Rodono to be David's grandson, and was followed by his son.

XVI. ADAM SCOTT is mentioned in 1637 as " younger of Hassendene " and son to Robert, and in 1669 he was served heir general to his father.

XVII. ROBERT SCOTT succeeded his father Adam and was living in 1691.

Arms of Scott of Hassendene.—Or, on a bend azure a star of six points between two crescents argent; in base a bow and arrow of the second. Crest.—A hand erect holding a pole-axe ppr. Motto.—" Trusty and True."

Burnfoot (In Teviot).

T HE first trace there is of a Scott owning
    Burnfoot is

XIII.   ADAM SCOTT of Burnfoot and Burnhead, who was nearly related to Hassendene and was
probably son to either William or Robert, sons of
James, first of Hassendene.

XIV.   WILLIAM SCOTT, younger, of Burnfoot
appears to have d. v.p. and

XV.   ROBERT SCOTT of Burnfoot was, in
1585, served heir to his grandfather Adam, and d.
December, 1612, leaving three sons:
            1. ADAM.   2. ROBERT.   3. *William*.

XVI.   ADAM SCOTT of Burnfoot succeeded
him, but d. s.p., and

XVI.   ROBERT SCOTT of Burnfoot followed.

XVII.   WALTER SCOTT of Burnfoot was
served heir in November, 1667, to his father Robert
and grandfather Robert in the lands of Burnfoot and
Burnhead.   He left a son,

XVIII.   ADAM SCOTT of Burnfoot, who sold
Burnhead to William Scott in Burnhead.

Burnhead.

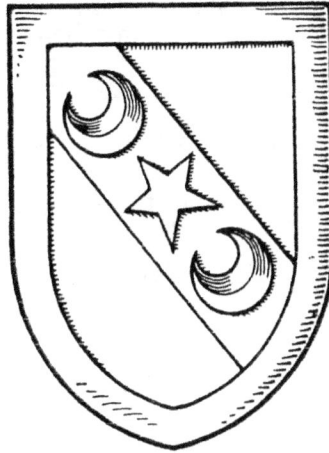

Scott of Burnhead.

MR. SCOTT of Rodono, in his Memorial categori-
cally denies the possibility of the correctness
of the first two or three generations of this
family as given by Burke, and mentions the
"undoubted" fact that John Scott, son of James of
Kirkurd, d. s.p. He also mentions that Burnhead
and Burnfoot were in the possession of the Burnfoot
family down to 1692. It would appear possible that

XVI. WILLIAM SCOTT, third son of Robert
Scott of Burnfoot, was tenant in Burnhead, and was
identical with William Scott, who m. Margaret, dau.
of Nicol Cairncross, by whom he had one son, ROBERT.
He d. about 1640.

XVII. ROBERT SCOTT in Burnhead m. first
1636 Marian, dau. of Ragnel Bennet of Chesters, by
whom he had two daughters. He m. secondly 1643
Elizabeth, dau. of Hector Turnbull of Clarilaw, by
whom he had four sons:

XVIII. ROBERT SCOTT of Lies.

XIX. WALTER SCOTT of Clarilaw was probably either son or nephew of the above. He purchased Ashieburn some time before 1700, and was father of

XX. WILLIAM SCOTT of Africa and Ashieburn, Portioner of Nether Ancrum. William Scott was succeeded in Ashieburn in 1733 by

XXI. THE REV. JAMES SCOTT, who left two sons:
      1. WILLIAM. 2. EBENEZER.

XXII. WILLIAM SCOTT the elder succeeded to Ashieburn in 1794 and d. 1807, and was succeeded by his son,

XXIII. HENRY ERSKINE SCOTT, who sold Ashieburn and d. in 1847.

XXII. EBENEZER SCOTT, surgeon in Dalkeith, younger son of the Rev. James Scott, left two sons:
      1. JAMES. 2. RALPH ERSKINE.

XXIII. JAMES SCOTT, the elder son, was an accountant in Edinburgh, and m. Mary, dau. of Wm. Scott of Jedburgh, and by her had issue,

XXIV. EBENEZER SCOTT, accountant in London, who m. Catherine Ann, dau. of Jas. Neish, Esq., of Dundee, and by her had two sons:
      1. Thomas d. s.p.
      2. Ebenezer d. s.p.

Clarilaw.

Scott of Linburn :

FROM Walter Scott of Clarilaw (XIX) downwards this pedigree is supplied to me by the family.

I have supplied the connecting link to the Burnhead family showing this Walter Scott of Clarilaw as grandson to Robert Scott in Burnhead.

I have placed this genealogy here rather than in Part IV, where, perhaps, it more rightly belongs, as there is reasonable ground to assume that if Walter Scott of Clarilaw No. XIX was not a grandson of Robert Scott in Burnhead, it is extremely probable he was related. We have the three points which independently do not perhaps amount to much, but together justify this assumption, namely—(a) The Lairds of Lies and Clarilaw were brothers in 1688 (Satchells); (b) Robert of Lies was son to Robert of Burnhead; (c) Clarilaw appears to have come into the Scott family by the marriage of Robert Scott in Burnhead and Elizabeth, dau. of Hector Turnbull of Clarilaw. The eldest son of this marriage succeeded to Burnhead, and the second was

      1. WILLIAM.
      2. *Robert Scott of Lies.*
      3. Adam.   4. Alexander.
Wm. Scott d. in 1677.

XVIII. WILLIAM SCOTT of Burnhead, who purchased Burnhead from his kinsman, Adam Scott of Burnfoot, m. Agnes, dau. of Archibald Wedderstain, by whom he had, with several daughters, of whom Eupham m. Thomas Watson, writer in Hawick, was one, three sons:

      1. ROBERT his heir.
      2. William.
      3. Peter.

XIX. ROBERT SCOTT, the eldest son, m. Agnes, dau. of Gideon Scott of Falnash, and by her had:

      1. WILLIAM his heir.   2. Walter.
      1. Agnes.   2. MARGARET.
Mr. Robert Scott d. 1755.

XX. WILLIAM SCOTT of Burnhead, the eldest son, succeeded, but d. in 1795 unm. and was succeeded by his sister,

XX. MARGARET SCOTT, who d. s.p. and was succeeded by her cousin,

XX. WILLIAM WATSON of Burnhead, son of Eupham Scott and Thos. Watson, and whose great-grandson is Mr. William Scott-Watson, now of Burnhead.

Arms (of Scott of Burnhead but not rematriculated by Mr. Watson's family).—Or, on a bend azure a star between two crescents of the first within a bordure of the last. Crest.—A buck's head erased ppr. collared azure charged as the bend. Motto.—Over the crest, " In recto decus," and below the arms, " Nemo sibi nascitur." Seat.—Burnhead, Roxburghshire, N.B.

XXIII. RALPH ERSKINE SCOTT, younger son of Dr. Ebenezer Scott, was C.A. in Edinburgh; b. August, 1804; m. Jane, dau. of John Dalziel, Earlston, and by her had issue:

1. EBENEZER ERSKINE.

1. Christian d. unm.
2. Mary Dalziel m. John Bruce of Sunburgh.

XXIV. EBENEZER ERSKINE SCOTT, also C.A. in Edinburgh, b. May, 1839; m. Anne Goddard, dau. of Robert Mackay, W.S., Edinburgh, and had issue:

1. HENRY ERSKINE.

1. Jean Dalziel.
2. Elinor Mary.
3. Annie m. Herbert Pearson, Indian Judge, son of Sir Charles Pearson.
4. Agnes Elizabeth.
5. Margaret Georgina m. A. E. Milne, W.S.

XXV. HENRY ERSKINE SCOTT b. May, 1881; m. Constance May, dau. of Jas. Murdoch Brown, M.D., Edinburgh, and dying January, 1910, left issue,

XXVI. RALPH ERSKINE SCOTT b. January, 1907.

Arms.—Parted per pale, or and azure on a bend between two stags' heads erased a star of six points between two crescents all counterchanged. Crest.—A stag trippant proper attired and unguled argent charged on the shoulder with a star of six points of the last. Motto.—"Amo." Residence.—Linburn, Midlothian.

Altoun.

___

XII. ADAM SCOTT of Clarilaw is mentioned in a charter dated 1521 as cousin to Sir Walter Scott of Buccleuch, and as this family is stated by Satchells to have sprung from Hassendene, Mr. Scott of Rodono suggests he may have been a son of James Scott of Kirkurd. He was succeeded by his eldest son,

XIII. ROBERT SCOTT of Clarilaw and Altoun. He lived to an advanced age and died about 1594, when he was succeeded by his son,

XIV. ADAM SCOTT of Altoun, who did not long survive his father. Adam appears to have had two sons:
    1. WALTER his heir.
    2. Robert "vocat de Altoun."
Adam Scott d. in September, 1604.

XV. WALTER SCOTT of Altoun served heir to his father in 1606, and also to his grandfather, Robert Scott of Clarilaw, otherwise called "of Altoun," appears to have had two sons:
    1. ROBERT "junior of Altoun."
    2. William "vocat de Altoun" in Hassendene.

XVI. ROBERT SCOTT of Altoun succeeded about 1638. He appears to have had a son, William, younger of Altoun, who d. v.p., for in 1653 Margaret, Bessie Isobel and Agnes are served heirs portioners to the late Robert Scott of Altoun.

⳩owpasley.

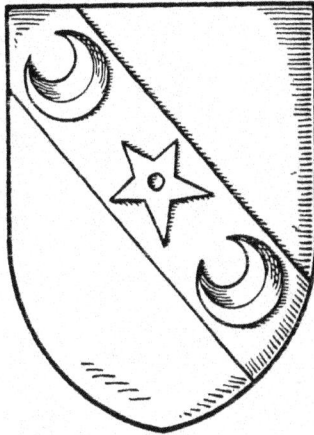

Scott of Howpasley.

XI. SIR ALEXANDER SCOTT, third son of Sir Walter Scott of Branxholm and Buccleuch, obtained a crown charter of the lands of Howpaslot dated 12th April, 1470. He fell at the battle of Sauchieburn on 11th June, 1488, and left issue:

1. WALTER.
2. Robert, Tutor of Howpasley.
3. William, Abbot of Melrose.
4. *David of Tushielaw.*

XII. SIR WALTER SCOTT of Howpasley is next found in occupation, and was almost certainly Sir Alexander's son. He is noted as tutor to Walter Scott of Branxholm in 1509, and nearest male relative. He m. a dau. of Elliot of Lariston, and was succeeded by his son,

XIII. ROBERT SCOTT of Howpasley, a minor under the tutory of his uncle Robert so late as 1530. He m. Isabel, dau. of John Murray of Falahill, and was succeeded by his son,

XIV. SIR WALTER SCOTT of Howpasley and Birkensyde. Sir Walter d. in 1580, and was succeeded by his son,

XV. WALTER SCOTT, served heir to Sir Walter in 1591. Walter Scott was, it is believed, succeeded by his son,

XVI. WILLIAM SCOTT of Howpasley, the last of the race. As will be mentioned elsewhere, Howpasley passed successively into the hands of Robert and Walter, cousins of Patrick Scott of Tanlawhill, and on their death without issue to Walter, Patrick's younger son, and on the latter's death without issue to the elder son, Sir Francis of Thirlestane, with whose family, I believe, it still remains.

Arms.—There are no arms on record to this family, but it seems highly probable that, in view of the arms of Thirlestane and Hundilshope, this family bore a pierced mullet between two crescents.

Tushielaw.

THE earliest record we have of Tushielaw is in
1502 when in the Records of Justiciary we
note William Scott was son of

XII. DAVID SCOTT of Tushielaw, and there
is little doubt that this David was brother to Sir Walter
Scott of Howpasley. Further it is more than probable
that this David is the David Satchells referred to as
" David of Howpasley with the Tod's Tail," Walter
and David having been known at different times by
both the name of Howpasley and Tushielaw. David
Scott left issue :

    1. ADAM his successor.
    2. *John of Thirlestane.*
    3. William.
    4. *Robert of Bowhill.*

XIII. ADAM SCOTT of Tushielaw was almost
certainly the eldest son, and received a charter of
Tushielaw in 1507. He earned for himself the name
of " King of Thieves," and was eventually hanged at
Edinburgh in May, 1530.

XIV. WILLIAM SCOTT is the next member of
this family mentioned in 1563, and he was in all
probability Adam's son. (The fact that Satchells
mentions a Robert intervening may be safely ignored
without corroborative evidence.) William Scott left
issue :

    1. Walter (Sir).
    2. *William of Midgehope.*
    3. *James of Hundilshope.*

XV. SIR WALTER SCOTT of Tushielaw m. Elizabeth, dau. of Gladstaines of Cocklaw and Hundilshope, and by her had issue:

1. ROBERT his heir.
2. *James of Boyken and Glenrath,* with his brother John in the Carlisle raid.
3. John of Mackersway, slayer of Walter Scott of Gamescleuch; m. Jeanne, dau. of Patrick Murray of Falahill, and had issue a son:
   (1) Walter.

Sir Walter d. between February, 1617, and January, 1628.

XVI. ROBERT SCOTT succeeded his father as Laird of Tushielaw, and d. in July, 1632, leaving:

1. WALTER his heir.
2. WILLIAM of Fawdshope, who succeeded his brother.

XVII. WALTER SCOTT of Tushielaw served heir to his father Robert in 1633, had a son James a Brigadier in the Life Guards, and a second son Robert. Walter Scott conveyed his estates to his brother in 1636, and is from then with his family entirely lost sight of.

XVII. WILLIAM SCOTT of Tushielaw was twice married. By his first marriage with Grizel, dau. of Robert Scott of Thirlestane, he had issue:

1. ANDREW, who, about the time of his father's purchase of Tushielaw, acquired Broadmeadows.
2. Walter in Caerabank.

William Scott m. secondly Margaret, dau. of John Govane of Cardrono, by which marriage he had one son:

3. *William of Broadmeadows.*

XVIII. ANDREW SCOTT obtained in 1663 a charter to Tushielaw in which he is described as eldest lawful son of the late William Scott of Tushielaw.

XIX. WILLIAM SCOTT, Andrew's son, succeeded during his minority, and was followed by his son,

XX. WALTER SCOTT, after which the family lapsed into obscurity.

𝔅roadmeadows.

XVIII. WILLIAM SCOTT, eldest son of William Scott of Tushielaw by his second marriage with Margaret Govane, obtained from his brother Andrew a charter to Broadmeadows. He m. Helen, dau. of Sir John Murray of Philiphaugh, by whom he had :

    1. ROBERT.

    1. Isabella m. John Balfour of Kailyie.

    2. Jean m. John Murray, Advocate, son of Sir John Murray of Philiphaugh and afterwards Lord Bowhill.

XIX. ROBERT SCOTT of Broadmeadows m. Agnes, dau. of Hugh Kelso, merchant of Edinburgh, but d. s.p., and in 1694 his sisters were served heirs portioners to their brother.

It should be noted that John Balfour's son, Charles, m. Jean, eldest dau. of William Plummer of Middlestead and his wife, Jean Kerr of Sunderland Hall, only child of William Kerr, the last male of the ancient house of Yair. By this marriage there were four daughters, of whom Jean Balfour of Broadmeadows m. William Scott of Woll, Advocate. She brought to her husband the lands of Broadmeadows, Midgehope, and Glenkerry.

Glenrath.

XVI. JAMES SCOTT of Glenrath, undoubted second son of Walter Scott of Tushielaw, d. April, 1619, leaving issue six children, all minors under the tutory of his brother John :

    1. WALTER.   2. William in Lintoun.

    3. James. 1. Mariot. 2. Elizabeth.

    3. Margaret.

XVII. WALTER SCOTT of Glenrath succeeded, but d. s.p., and was succeeded by his nephew,

XVIII. JOHN SCOTT, son of William in Lintoun, by whom the estate was sold to the Laird of Hundilshope.

F

horsleyhill.

Douglas
of Springwood Park

XV. WILLIAM SCOTT, Laird of Midgehope, was second son to William Scott of Tushielaw, and was followed by his son,

XVI. WILLIAM SCOTT of Midgehope, one of the rescuers of Kinmont Will.

XVII. ROBERT SCOTT, son to the second William, was Baillee and Portioner in Hawick. He was father of

XVIII. WILLIAM SCOTT, the first Scott noted as Laird of Horsleyhill. This William was father of

XIX. ROBERT SCOTT, Laird of Horsleyhill at the time of the Postral. This Robert was father of Eliza m. to Walter Scott of Woll, and

XX. FRANCIS SCOTT, who was father of

XXI. CAPTAIN ROBERT SCOTT of Horsleyhill, who registered arms at Lyon Office in 1742. He m. Agnes Douglas of Springbank, and had issue,

XXII. JOHN SCOTT of Horsleyhill and Belford, who left a daughter m. to Thomas Davidson, Surgeon in Kelso, and a son,

XXIII. HENRY SCOTT of Horsleyhill and Belford, the last male of this family. Henry Scott m. 1792 Catherine, dau. of John Hay of Newhall, and had by her an only daughter, Hannah Charlotte, who in 1822 m. Sir James Douglas, Bart., and subsequently William Scott-Kerr, Esq., of Sunlaws (q.v.). By her first husband she had issue, among others, Sir George Henry Scott-Douglas, and this family is now represented in the female line by her grandson, Sir George Brisbane Douglas, Bart., of Springwood Park, Roxburgh.

Arms.—1st and 4th arg., a human heart gu., imperially crowned or; on a chief az., three mullets of the first, all within a bordure nebuly of the fourth; 2nd and 3rd, or on a bend az., a star of six points, between two crescents of the first, and in chief a sword erect point upwards ppr. Crests.—1. A cubit arm erect, grasping a broken tilting-spear, all ppr. 2. A lion's head erased, holding in the mouth a thistle stalked and leaved, all ppr. Mottoes.—" Do or Die," for Douglas; " Pro Patria," for Scott.

Hundilshope.

Scott
- of Hundilshope

XV. JAMES SCOTT of Hundilshope is designated brother to Sir Walter Scott of Tushielaw in a charter dated 1596. He appears to have had four sons:

      1. JOHN.   2. James.

      3. Robert in Holly Arch.

      4. Thomas in Hundilshope.

XVI. JOHN SCOTT, Portioner of Hundilshope, appears on various documents 1607-1617.

XVII. JOHN SCOTT of Hundilshope was in 1619 served heir in general to his father, John, Portioner of Hundilshope.

XVIII. JAMES SCOTT of Hundilshope is the next Laird in 1648, but there is no evidence as to his relationship with John. He left two sons :

    1. John, who apparently d. v.p.

    2. DAVID.

XIX. DAVID SCOTT of Hundilshope succeeded, and was followed by his son,

XX. DAVID SCOTT of Hundilshope, who in January, 1737, resigned his lands and barony.

Arms.—Or, on a bend az. a mullet pierced, between two crescents of the first, all within a bordure of the second. Crest.—A right hand issuing, holding a lance, all ppr. Motto.—" I am ready."

Davington.

Scott of Davington

IN conjunction with this genealogy there are to be considered the several pedigrees given in Nisbett's Heraldry; Satchells' various genealogies of this family; and Mr. John Scott of Rodono's extensive notes on the subject wherein he denies the authenticity of the grant of arms by James V., and also the existence of the grantee.

Whilst I have not gone so far as to exclude the alleged mythical John Scott of Thirlestane I certainly concur that Satchells never intended to imply that Thirlestane and Howpasley were the same individual as is clearly proved in several parts of his work. He refers to the first Sir Walter of Howpasley, implying a second Sir Walter at a later date, as is the case, and we know that both Howpasley and Thirlestane signed the clan bond in 1589.

With regard to the arms, Lord Napier is in right of arms by the grant of 1700 from King William of England.   I have given a sketch of the same arms at the head of this genealogy, although the representative of the Davington family cannot be said to be in right of arms without registration.   I commend to those interested a careful study of Mr. John Scott's " Memoirs of Scott of Thirlestane."

XIII. JOHN SCOTT of Thirlestane, second son of David Scott of Tushielaw, is stated to have received a grant of a royal tressure to his arms from King James V. According to Satchells he m. a dau. of Scott of Allanhaugh, and left issue :

    1. ROBERT his heir.

    2. Philip of Kirkhope.

    3. Andrew d. s.p.

    4. *Simon of Newburgh.*   5. William.

He m. secondly Marion Douglas, and by her had a son,

    6. *James of Gilmanscleuch.*

XIV. ROBERT SCOTT, the eldest son, was tutor or curator to Sir Walter Scott of Branxholm and Buccleuch during the latter's minority, and was warden of one of the three marches. He m. c. 1563 Margaret, sister of his ward, and dying about 1576 left :

    1. ROBERT.

    2. *Walter of Gamescleuch.*

    3. William of Fingland and Merrilaw, in the Carlisle Raid with his brother of Gamescleuch. William left with an illegitimate son Symon living in 1609, two legitimate sons and two daughters :

(1) Robert, who acquired Howpasley, but d. s.p., and that
estate passed to

(2) Walter, who also d. s.p., and left
it to his cousin Patrick of
Tanlawhill.

XV. SIR ROBERT of Thirlestane, the eldest
son, was b., according to Satchells, in 1566. He m.
1590 Margaret, dau. of Sir John Cranstoun of Cranstoun, and by her had one son and two daughters:

1. Sir Robert of Cruxton, who m. Lady Mary
Lyon, dau. of the Earl of Strathmore,
and d. v.p. without legitimate issue 1619,
as appears from a portion of his tomb-
stone built into the new church at Ettrick.
He left a natural son, Peter, living in
1609.

1. Jean m. Robert Scott of Satchells.

2. Susannah m. Sir Walter Scott of Whitslaid.

Sir Robert m. secondly 1602 Katherine, dau. of
Sir Alexander Jardine of Applegarth, by whom he
had one son:

2. JOHN.

Sir Robert d. 1627.

XVI. SIR JOHN SCOTT of Thirlestane, only
son by the second marriage, succeeded to his father's
debts, the Thirlestane estates being virtually in the
hands of the Earl of Buccleuch and Sir William Scott
of Harden. He retired with his mother to Davington
in Eskdalemuir. Sir John m. Euphemia, widow of
Sir David Ogilvie of Clova, and by her had one son
and one daughter:

1. FRANCIS. 1. Katherine.

Sir John d. in 1666.

XVII.   FRANCIS SCOTT of Davington m. a
dau. of Robert Douglas of Auchintully, and had issue,
besides several daughters, six sons :

    1. John d. s.p. and v.p.   2. ·ROBERT.
    3. William of Beattock, father of
        (1) William in Moffatt, one of the
            parties to the 1773 litigation,
            see below.
    4. Francis m. and had one daughter,
        (1) Agnes, also a party to the same
            litigation.
    5. James of Coulfield m. Christian Stewart,
      and had issue :
        (1) Robert a litigant.
        (2) Francis b. August, 1739.
        (3) William b. April, 1741.
        (1) Agnes.
        (2) Katherine m. her cousin William.
        (3) Isabel m. her cousin John.
        (4) Jean m. David Muir, Provost of
            Annan.
    6. David.

XVIII.   ROBERT SCOTT, the second son,
succeeded to Davington, and had three sons and one
daughter :

    1. JAMES.
    2. John, a writer in Langholm, who m. his
      cousin Isabel, dau. of James Scott of
      Coulfield, and by her had :
        (1) John b. c. 1730, living in Canon-
            bie; unm. in 1810.
        (2) William b. 1735; m. Ann Little,
            and dying July, 1790, left issue :
        (i) Agnes. (ii) Susannah m. Chas.
        Boardman of Liverpool.

(3) Robert, who together with

(4) James, took part in the litigation respecting the Davington and Thirlestane estates.

(5) Francis b. 1743.

(1) Jane.　(2) Margaret.

3. WILLIAM OF MEIKLEDALE.

1. Margaret m. Gilbert Elliot of Newcastle, father of General William Elliot of Lariston.

XIX. JAMES SCOTT, the eldest son, a surgeon in Carlisle, succeeded to Davington in 1764 and d. 1770, having m. Mary Rae, and by her left an only son, JAMES, and six daughters; the daughters were :

1. Elizabeth m. James Cairns, Carlisle.

2. Mary m. John Hownam, shoemaker, Carlisle.

3. Susanna.　4. Charlotte.　5. Anne.

6. Margaret m. John Park, tenant in Davington.

XX. JAMES SCOTT, the only son, succeeded to Davington on a warrant by the tutors of Henry, Duke of Buccleuch, dated 7th February, 1770. He d. apparently without issue in 1772, and a warrant was granted by the Duke, dated 20th March, 1772, to " Eliza, Mary, Susanna, Charlotte, and Anne, sisters of deceased James Scott, and to James Park, the eldest son of Margaret Park, another sister of James Scott." The succession of the estate was, however, disputed in 1772-3 by various grandchildren and great-grand-children of Francis of Davington as indicated above, and after lengthy litigation the estate was sold. It would appear from a pedigree compiled in 1833 for Lord Napier by Francis Martin, *Windsor Herald*, that the descendants of John Scott, writer in Langholm, failed at any rate in the male line. The representation of this family must therefore fall on the descendants of

XIX. WILLIAM SCOTT of Meikledale, third son of Robert Scott of Davington. Mr. Scott of Meikledale, b. 1694, m. his cousin Katherine, another dau. of James Scott of Coulfield, and dying 1772 left an only son and four daughters:

1. JAMES.
1. Elizabeth m. Thomas. Bell of Burnscleugh, Canonbie.
2. Susanna m. Gilbert Richardson, Langholm, whose son Gilbert m. his first cousin Catherine.
3. Catherine m. John Caruthers of Billmansknowe, Canonbie.
4. Mary d. unm.

XX. JAMES SCOTT of Forge, Canonbie, J.P., m. Phœbe, dau. and co-heiress of James Dixon of Bath, and sister of Lady Harris. He d. October, 1799, leaving issue:

1. William d. at Bhurtpore.
2. Charles, A.D.C. to Lord Harris at Seringapatan, d. 1822, leaving a dau., Anne Harris.
3. GEORGE FRASER.
1. Catherine Eliza m. her cousin, Gilbert Richardson.
2. Phœbe.
3. Jemima m. Major-General Robert Bell (E.I.C. Artillery).
4. Sybilla m. Captain Charles Johnston. R.N., of Cowhill.

XXI. GEORGE FRASER SCOTT-ELLIOT, the third son, took the name of Elliot on succeeding his father's cousin, General Elliot, of Lariston. He sold this estate in 1843, and d. at his residence of Woodslea, near Canonbie. He m. February, 1818, Ann Margaret, dau. of James Bell, and had issue:

1. WILLIAM.
2. George, a Lieutenant in the Indian Army; d. unm. 1850-60.
3. *James.* 4. *Charles.*
1. Anne m. Andrew Walker of Fyndgate, a Calcutta merchant.
2. Elizabeth m. Captain Conolly.
3. Marion m. first John Dougal, a Calcutta merchant, and secondly Dr. Collville, E.C. minister of Canonbie.

XXII. WILLIAM SCOTT-ELLIOT, the eldest son, m. Jessie, dau. of —— Brown, an E.C. minister in Renfrewshire, and left issue:

1. WILLIAM. 1. Georgina.
2. Netta. 3. Marion. 4. Anne.

XXIII. WILLIAM SCOTT-ELLIOT, the only son and apparent heir-male of John Scott of Thirlestane.

Arms.—Not exemplified by any recent members of this family, but the arms said to have been granted by James V. to John Scott of Thirlestane were " or, on a bend azure, a mullet pierced, between two crescents of the field, all within the double tressure flory-counter-flory of Scotland of the second." Crest.—The top of an embattled tower arg., masoned sa., issuing therefrom six lances disposed saltireways, three and three with pennons, az. Motto.—" Ready, aye ready." Residence.—5 Afton Terrace, Edinburgh.

Drumwhill.

XXII. JAMES SCOTT-ELLIOT, a Calcutta merchant, third son of George Fraser Scott-Elliot and Ann Bell, m. Francisca May Durand of an old Huguenot family, and dying 1880, left issue:

1. GEORGE FRANCIS.
2. William, Lieutenant-Colonel, D.S.O., b. March, 1873; m. January, 1902, Theresa, dau. of Captain George Francis Lyon, R.N., of Kirkmichael, and has issue:
   (1) James b. November, 1902.
   (1) Eva.
   Address.—" The Prelude," Coleman's Hatch, Sussex.
3. Charles d. young.
1. Edith May m. Joseph Gillon Fergusson.
2. Annie Emilia, M.B.E., m. first Captain Arthur Ripley Pott of Toderick and Borthwickshiels, and secondly Captain J. A. Doig, K.O.S.B.
3. Lilian m. Eric Tayleur.
4. Ethel d. young. 5. Eliza d. young.

XXIII. CAPTAIN GEORGE FRANCIS SCOTT-ELLIOT, K.O.S.B., F.R.S.E., F.R.G.S., author and explorer, m. Annie Hathorn, dau. of R. H. Johnston Stewart of Physgill and Glasserton.

Seat.—Drumwhill, Mossdale, Kirkcudbrightshire.

Reginald Scott-Elliot.

XXII. GENERAL CHARLES SCOTT-ELLIOT, fourth son of George Fraser Scott-Elliot and Ann Bell, m. Mary, dau. of —— Vertu, and left issue :

  1. CHARLES REGINALD.
  1. Constance m. Rev. F. Hartley, R.N.
  2. Amy m. Brigadier-General Loch, D.S.O.
  3. Annie m. Major Angus Fraser, K.O.S.B.

XXIII. LIEUT.-COL. CHARLES REGINALD SCOTT-ELLIOT b. September, 1873, m. September, 1903, Elizabeth, dau. of R. E. Walker, Esq., and has issue :

  1. Elizabeth Noel. 2. Ruby.

Address.—C/o H. S. King & Co., 9 Pall Mall, London.

Thirlestane.

Lord Napier ❖

XV. WALTER SCOTT of Gamescleuch, second son of Robert Scott, tutor to Buccleuch, and Margaret Scott of Buccleuch, his wife, m. a dau. of Sir Patrick Porteous of Hackshaw, and was slain by John Scott, third son of Sir Walter Scott of Tushielaw, in 1609, leaving issue:

  1. PATRICK. 2. Simon.
  1. Marion. 2. Margaret.

XVI. PATRICK SCOTT of Tanlawhill and afterwards of Thirlestane is the Patrick who brought the Earl of Buccleuch's body from London to Leith; he purchased the wadsets of Thirlestane and m. Isobel, dau. of Sir John Murray of Blackbarony, Bart., and, dying 1666, left:

1 FRANCIS (Sir).

2. David d. young.

3. Walter of Howpasley d. s.p. before 1663.

1. Jean m. to Sir James Hay of Linplum.

2. Margaret m. to Sir Alexander Bannerman of Elswick.

3. Mary m. to Sir Wm. Primrose of Caering.

XVII. SIR FRANCIS SCOTT, first Baronet of Thirlestane, b. May, 1645, and created a Baronet of Nova Scotia on 22nd August, 1666, m. 1673 Lady Henrietta Kerr, sixth dau. of William, third Earl of Lothian, and had issue:

1. WILLIAM (Sir).

2. Patrick d. young.

3. Francis d. young.

4. Robert d. young.

5. Charles d. young.

6. James d. young.

1. Anne d. young.

2. Henrietta m. to Wm. Lord Ross.

3. Isabel Lilias d. young.

Sir Francis d. March, 1712, and was succeeded by his eldest son,

XVIII. SIR WILLIAM SCOTT, the second Baronet of Thirlestane. Sir William was twice m.; firstly in 1699 to Elizabeth, Mistress of Napier, the only surviving child of Margaret, Baroness Napier of Merchiston. By this marriage he had an only son, Francis. Lady Scott d. in 1705, and in 1710 Sir William m. secondly Jean, dau. of Sir John Nisbet of Dirleton and relict of Sir William Scott of Harden, but there was no issue of this marriage. Sir William d. October, 1725, and was succeeded by his son,

XIX. SIR FRANCIS SCOTT, sixth Baron Napier of Merchiston and third Baronet of Thirlestane, who inherited the Barony of Merchiston on the death of his grandmother in 1705 and assumed the name of Napier in lieu of that of Scott. Lord Napier m. first Henrietta, dau. of Charles, Earl of Hopetoun, and by her had five sons :

1. WILLIAM, seventh Baron.
2. *Charles of Merchiston Hall, Co. Stirling.*
3. Francis, Lieutenant-Colonel of Marines, m. Elizabeth, dau. of John Greenway of Portsmouth, and d. in 1779.
4. John d. unm. in 1759.
5. *Mark.*

Lord Napier m. secondly in 1750 Henrietta Maria, dau. of George Johnson of Dublin, and had by her:

6. *George.* 7. James d. 1760.
8. Patrick, Captain R.N., d. June, 1801.
9. James John killed in the "Fox" 1776.
10. Stewart d. 1778.
1. Henrietta m. William, twelfth Lord Ross.
2. Hester m. Alexander Johnson of Carnsalloch.
3. Mary d. 1765.

Lord Napier d. in 1773 and was succeeded by his eldest son,

XX. SIR WILLIAM NAPIER, seventh Baron Napier, a Lieutenant-Colonel in the Army, and Deputy-Adjutant-General of the forces in Scotland. He m. December, 1754, Mainie Anne, dau. of Charles, eighth Lord Cathcart, and, dying in 1775, was succeeded by his only son,

XXI. SIR FRANCIS NAPIER, eighth Baron, D.C.L., b. February, 1758. He m. April, 1784, Maria Margaret, eldest dau. of Lieutenant-General Sir John Clavering, K.B., and by her left:

1. WILLIAM JOHN, ninth Baron.
2. *Charles*.
3. Henry Alfred (Rev.) b. June, 1797; d. November, 1871.
1. Maria Margaret m. Rev. Orfeur William Kilvington of Hatfield, Vicar of Brignall, Co. York.
2. Anne m. Sir Thomas Gibson-Carmichael, tenth Baronet.
3. Sophia d. unm.
4. Caroline m. Nevile Reid.

Lord Napier d. August, 1823.

XXII. SIR WILLIAM JOHN NAPIER, ninth Baron, b. October, 1786, Captain R.N., m. March, 1816, Elizabeth, only dau. of Hon. Andrew James Cochrane Johnstone, and dying October, 1834, left issue:

1. FRANCIS, tenth Baron.
2. *William*.
1. Maria Margaret m. John, first Baron Addington.
2. Georgina Louisa d. unm.
3. Eliza m. Adm. The Right Hon. Sir John Charles Dalrymple Hay, third Baronet, G.C.B.
4. Anne Carmichael m. The Hon. George Hope, Captain R.N., fifth son of John, Earl of Hopetoun.
5. Ellinor Alice m. The Hon. George Grey Dalrymple.
6. Lucy Matilda.

XXIII. SIR FRANCIS NAPIER, tenth Baron, K.T., P.C., LL.D., created .Baron Ettrick of Ettrick, in the peerage of the United Kingdom, July, 1872 ; b. September, 1819 ; m. September, 1845, Anne Jane Charlotte, only dau. of Robert Manners Lockwood, and left issue:

1. WILLIAM JOHN GEORGE, eleventh Baron.
2. John Scott, C.M.G., Colonel late Gordon Highlanders (3 Halkin Street, S.W.), b. November, 1848, m. April, 1876, Isabella, youngest dau. of Thomas Shaw of Ditton, Co. Lancaster, and widow of Major James Leith, V.C., and has a daughter,
      (1) Lilias Dorothea Scott m. Reginald Evan Wynne-Roberts.
3. Basil, Lieutenant R.N., b. July, 1850; d. February, 1874.
4. *Mark Francis.*

Lord Napier and Ettrick d. December, 1898.

XXIV. SIR WILLIAM JOHN GEORGE NAPIER, eleventh Baron, D.L. Co. Selkirk, b. September, 1846, m. first, January, 1876, Harriet Blake Armstrong, youngest dau. of Edward Lumb of Wallington Lodge, Surrey, and by her had issue:

1. FRANCIS EDWARD BASIL, twelfth and present Baron.
2. Frederick William Scott, late Lieutenant 6th Battalion the Royal Fusiliers, b. May, 1878.

His.Lordship m. secondly, July, 1898, Grace, third dau. of James Cleland Burns, and had issue:

3. Archibald Lenox Colquhoun William John George. Sub-Lieutenant R.N., b. December, 1899.

Lord Napier and Ettrick d. December, 1913.

XXV. SIR FRANCIS EDWARD BASIL NAPIER, twelfth Baron Napier of Merchiston in Scotland, and Baron Ettrick of Ettrick, Co. Selkirk, in the United Kingdom, a Baronet of Nova Scotia, J.P., Selkirkshire, Captain 7th King's Royal Rifle Corps and R.A.F., and served in the Great War; b. November, 1876; m. December, 1899, the Hon. Clarice Jessie Evelyn, dau. of James, ninth Baron Belhaven and Stenton, and has issue:

1. WILLIAM FRANCIS CYRIL JAMES HAMILTON, Master of Napier, b. September, 1900, Lieutenant King's Own Scottish Borderers.
2. Neville Archibald John Watson Ettrick b. January, 1904, Midshipman, R.N.
3. Alastair John George Malcolm b. June, 1909.
1. Augusta Caroline Harriet Georgina Mary m. Captain Martin Frobisher.

Arms.—Quarterly: 1st and 4th, arg., a saltier, engrailed, between four roses gules, the roses barbed vert for Napier; 2nd and 3rd or, on a bend az., a mullet, pierced, between two crescents of the field, within a double tressure, flory-counterflory, of the second, for Scott of Thirlestane. Crests.—1. A dexter arm erect, couped below the elbow, ppr., grasping a crescent arg., over it the motto " Sans tache." 2. The top of an embattled tower arg., masoned sa., issuing therefrom six lances disposed saltireways, three and three, with pennons, az., over it the motto " Ready, aye ready." Supporters.—Dexter, an eagle, wings expanded, ppr. ; sinister, a chevalier in a coat of mail, with a steel cap, all ppr., holding in the exterior hand a spear with a pennon. Seat.—Thirlestane Castle, Co. Selkirk.

Cadets of Napier.

Claude Inverness Napier.

XXIV. THE HON. MARK FRANCIS NAPIER, fourth son of Francis, tenth Baron Napier, b. January, 1852, m. May, 1878, Emily Jones, and d. August, 1919, leaving issue:

1. Basil b. March, 1879. Killed in action S. Africa.
2. CLAUDE INVERNESS.
3. Philip Henry b. April, 1884, m. September, 1909, Gabrielle Jean, dau. of Sir Charles Harvey, Bart., and has issue :
   (1) Basil Mark b. February, 1911.
   (2) Nigel Claude Oliver.

XXV. CLAUDE INVERNESS NAPIER b. April, 1880, m. January, 1917, Lilian, dau. of Lieutenant-Commander Alfred Francey, R.N., and has issue,

1. Margaret Emily.

Francis Horatio Napier.

XXIII. THE HON. WILLIAM NAPIER, second son of William John, ninth Baron Napier, b. July, 1821 ; m. May, 1854, Louisa Mary, dau. of John H. Lloyd, Q.C. ; d. January, 1876, leaving issue:

1. FRANCIS HORATIO.
2. Charles Frederick, B.A., Oxford, Barrister-at-Law, Judge of the High Court of Judicature, Madras (82 Mount Road, Madras), b. February, 1862.

3. *William John.* 4. *Archibald Scott.*
1. Mary Eliza. 2. Beatrice.
3. Lilias m. first July, 1881, William Rose
   Robinson, eldest son of Sir William Rose
   Robinson, K.C.S.I. She m. secondly
   October, 1893, Henry Alfred Constant
   Bonar, C.M.G.

XXIV. FRANCIS HORATIO NAPIER,
M.B., F.R.C.S.E., b. February, 1861, m. April, 1893,
Margaret Elizabeth Horatia, dau. of Lieutenant-
Colonel William Hope, V.C., and has issue:

1. Archibald John Robert, Lieutenant
   Cheshire Regiment, served in Great War
   1914 (wounded); b. March, 1894.
2. Lawrence Egerton Scott, D.S.O. (1920),
   Lieutenant R.N., b. 1896.
3. Basil Hope b. August, 1911.

General William John Napier.

XXIV. GENERAL WILLIAM JOHN
NAPIER, C.B., C.M.G., Major-General R.A., third
son of the Hon. William Napier and grandson of
William John, ninth Baron Napier, served in South
Africa and in the Great War; b. November, 1863; m.
September, 1889, Maude Denison Gooch, dau. of
Colonel E. N. W. Holbrook, R.M.L.I., and has issue:

1. Arthur Francis Scott, Captain R.F.A.,
   served in the Great War; b. September,
   1890; m. November, 1915, Phyllis, eldest
   dau. of the late Edward Fleming, and has
   issue:

   (1) Charles John Scott b. October,
       1917.
   (1) Margaret Esmé Scott.

Archibald Scott Napier.

Archibald ❖
❖ Scott Napier

XXIV. ARCHIBALD SCOTT NAPIER, M.I.C.E., fourth son of the Hon. William Napier and grandson of William John, ninth Baron Napier, b. June, 1865, m. March, 1889, Katherine Edith, eldest dau. of Robert Liveing, M.D., and has issue:

1. CHARLES SCOTT, Lieutenant R.E., b. February, 1899.

2. Alexander b. September, 1904.

Arms.—Matriculated L.O. May, 1901. The arms of Lord Napier, namely quarterly Napier and Scott within a bordure indented gules, with crest and motto of Napier only. Address.—5 Stafford Mansions, Buckingham Gate, London.

Axwell Park.

Napier-Clavering.
.·.   of Axwell Park

XXII. MAJOR THE HON. CHARLES NAPIER, second son of Francis, eighth Baron Napier, b. October, 1794, m. first 1824 Alce Emma, dau. of Roger Barnston, and by her had issue:

1. Francis Roger Barnston b. October, 1828; d. November, 1849.
2. Charles Donald b. November, 1830; d. November, 1846.
3. JOHN WARREN of Axwell Park.
   1. Anne d. unm.   2. Alce Emma d. unm.

Major Charles Napier m. secondly July, 1840, Annabella Jane, only dau. of Edward Gatacre, Salop, D.L., and d. December, 1874, leaving by her:

4. *Edward*.   5. *William Archibald*.
6. *Lenox*.   7. *Alfred*.
3. Annabella m. the late Thos. W. A. Gill of Trewerse, Oswestry.
4. Lilias m. Sir T. W. P. Blomefield, fourth Baronet.
5. Louisa Augusta.

XXIII. REV. JOHN WARREN NAPIER-CLAVERING of Axwell Park, Durham, b. September, 1832, assumed, by Royal Licence February, 1894, the additional surname and arms of Clavering; m. September, 1857, Anna Maria Margaret Helen, dau. of Colonel Francis Hunter, H.E.I.C.S.; d. June, 1906, leaving issue :

1. CHARLES WARREN (NAPIER-CLAVERING).
2. *Francis (Napier-Clavering).*
3. Henry Percy (Napier-Clavering) (Rev.) b. July, 1861; m. February, 1909, Clarissa Katie Elizabeth, dau. of Francis Gedge of Redhill, Surrey.
4. *Arthur Lenox (Napier).*
5. Alan Bertram (Napier), I.C.S., b. October, 1867.
6. *Claude Gerald (Napier-Clavering) of Harborne.*
1. Edith Elizabeth Alice.

XXIV. CHARLES WARREN NAPIER-CLAVERING of Axwell Park, Co. Durham, Colonel (retired) late Somersetshire L.I., b. August, 1858, m. October, 1899, Margaret Nevile, fifth dau. of Nevile Reid of The Oaks, Hanworth and Shandwick, Ross-shire, and has issue :

1. Héléne Margaret b. October, 1900.

Arms.—Quarterly, 1st and 4th quarterly or and gules, over all a bend sable, for Clavering; 2nd and 3rd quarterly Napier and Scott, in the centre of the quarters a crescent sable for difference. Crests and mottoes.—Napier and Scott as those of Lord Napier, and in addition under the arms the motto, " Nil actum si quid agendum." Seat.—Axwell Park, Co. Durham.

Francis Napier-Clavering.

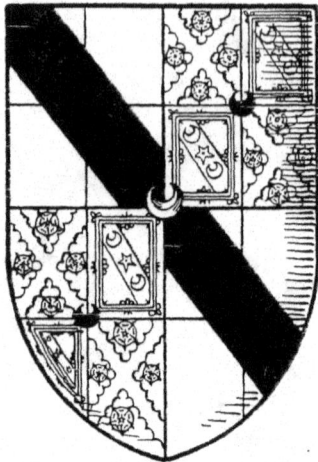

Francis
∴ Napier-Clavering ∴

XXIV. FRANCIS NAPIER-CLAVERING, M.A., second son of the Rev. John Warren Napier-Clavering of Axwell Park, Co. Durham, b. November, 1859, m. January, 1888, Elizabeth, dau. of Thomas Cowan, and has issue :

1. Noel Warren, D.S.O., Captain and Brevet Major R.E., served in Great War; b. December, 1888; m. July, 1921, Margaret, only dau. of T. Viqers of Montville, St. Peter's Port, Guernsey.

2. Francis Donald, M.C., Captain R.E., Special Reserve, served in Great War; b. April, 1892; m. September, 1920, Dorothy Avison, only dau. of Victor A. Holyroyd.

1. Edith Margaret m. Major William Hamilton Kenrick, I.M.S.

Arms.—As Napier-Clavering of Axwell Park, with a crescent for difference. Residence.—Branxholm, Minchin Hampton, Co. Gloucester.

Arthur Lenox Napier.

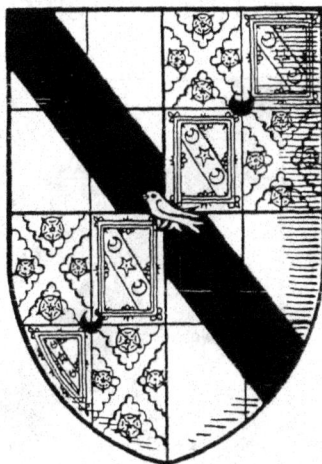

Arthur
Lenox Napier

XXIV. ARTHUR LENOX NAPIER, O.B.E.,
D.L., Captain late Yorkshire Regiment, Secretary
Terr. Force Association, Northumberland, fourth son
of the Rev. John Warren Napier-Clavering of Axwell
Park, Co. Durham, b. December, 1863, m. October,
1890, Marianne, dau. of Louis Valentine, and has
issue :

1. John Lenox Clavering, Lieutenant
R.H.A., served in Great War; b.
December, 1898.
1. Lilias Edith m. Eyre Gordon, I.C.S.,
Central Provinces, India.
2. Marian Ellen m. Captain James Westoll,
late Durham L.I. (T.F.).

Arms.—As Napier-Clavering of Axwell Park, with
a martlet for difference.   Residence.—Abbey Cottage,
Alnwick.

Claude Gerald Napier-Clavering.

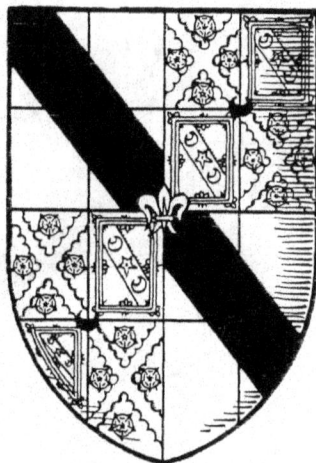

Claude Gerald
Napier-Clavering

XXIV. CLAUDE GERALD NAPIER-
CLAVERING, sixth son of the Rev. John Warren
Napier-Clavering of Axwell Park, Co. Durham, b.
February, 1869, m. Millicent Mary, dau. of the Right
Hon. William Kenrick, and has issue :

  1. Mark m. Elizabeth Miriam Squire, dau.
    of Sir Samuel Squire Sprigge, and has
    issue a dau. Julian.

  2. Alan William b. 1903.

  1. Mary Helen.

Arms.—As Napier-Clavering of Axwell Park, with
a fleur-de-lis for difference. Residence.—Tennal
Grange, Harborne.

Colonel Edward Napier.

XXIII. COLONEL EDWARD NAPIER, fourth son of Major the Hon. Charles Napier and grandson of Francis, eighth Baron Napier, b. June, 1841, m. June, 1866, Marthe Louise, eldest dau. of W. B. Buddicom of Penbedw Hall, Flintshire, and dying April, 1922, by her left issue :

1. Egbert, Major (retired) 3rd Battalion Gordon Highlanders, Chief Constable of Norfolk 1909-16, b. August, 1867, m. September, 1901, Evangeline Senechal, dau. of J. F. Dreyer of Valsschrivierdrift, Orange River Colony, and was killed in action November, 1916, leaving issue :
    (1) Evangeline Mary.
    (2) Esmé Georgina.
2. OWEN LLOYD HOWNAM.
3. George Charles b. August, 1873.
1. Phyllis Louise m. Henry Staveley Lawrence, C.S.I., I.C.S.
2. Annabella Mary Elizabeth.
3. Diana Caroline Marie m. Rev. Arthur Nesham Bax, M.A.
4. Jane Rosamond m. her dec. sister's husband, Henry Staveley Lawrence, C.S.I., I.C.S.

XXIV. OWEN LLOYD HOWNAM NAPIER, India Forest Service, b. August, 1869, m. October, 1898, Eliza Davison, dau. of General David Pott, C.B.

Residence.—Belle Vue, Sellack, Ross-on-Wye.

Clarence Napier.

***

XXIII. WILLIAM ARCHIBALD NAPIER, fifth son of Major the Hon. Charles Napier and grandson of Francis, eighth Baron Napier, b. March, 1845, m. April, 1879, Mabel, youngest dau. of William Edward Royds of Greenhill, Rochdale, and d. August, 1901, leaving issue :

    1. CLARENCE.

    2. Alan, H.B.M. Vice-Consul at Naples, b. July, 1881 ; m. November, 1911, Dorothy Emily Austin, younger dau. of James Robertson-Walker, J.P., of Gilgarran, Distington, Cumberland.

    3. Lenox, C.E., Captain R.E., b. 1887 ; m. November, 1916, Florence Kathleen, third dau. of —— Abercrombie of Tolcarne, Rusholme, Lancashire.

    1. Esmé m. Frank Douglas Montgomerie of Effingham, Surrey.

XXIV. CLARENCE NAPIER b. February, 1880, m. 1909 Lillie, dau. of J. Mills of Frome, Somerset, and has issue :

    1. Marcella.

Residence.—22 St. Quintin Avenue, North Kensington, W.

William Rawdon Napier.

XXIII. COMMANDER LENOX NAPIER, R.N., sixth son of Major the Hon. Charles Napier and grandson of Francis, eighth Baron Napier, b. September, 1846, m. June, 1873, Ellin, second dau. of W. B. Buddicom of Penbedw Hall, Flintshire, and d. January, 1886, leaving issue:

1. Henry Lenox, Major 11th Battalion Sherwood Foresters, Notts and Derbyshire Regiment, served in South African War 1900-2; b. June, 1876; m. February, 1911, Dorothy Alyn Louise, youngest dau. of the late James Mathias. He was drowned in the hospital ship *Anglia*, on active service November, 1915.

2. WILLIAM RAWDON.

3. Patrick Ronald, Captain A.S.C., b. April, 1879; m. October, 1903, Kathleen Hilda Mary, second dau. of the late James O'Reilly Nugent of Fareham, Hants. He d. May, 1911, leaving issue:
   (1) Patricia Marion Barbara.

1. Barbara.

2. Ellin Winifred.

XXIV. CAPTAIN WILLIAM RAWDON NAPIER, R.N., C.M.G., D.S.O., served during Great War; b. June, 1877; m. July, 1902, Florence Marie, eldest dau. of the late James O'Reilly Nugent of Fareham, Hants., and has issue:

1. MARK b. May, 1911.   2. Donald Charles.

1. Ellin Ruth Veronica.

Donald Charles Napier.

XXIII. ALFRED NAPIER, seventh son of Major The Hon. Charles Napier and grandson of Francis, eighth Baron Napier, b. May, 1848; m. July, 1886, Mary Louisa, dau. of the late General Charles Vanbrugh Jenkins, of Cruckton Hall, Salop; d. January, 1916, leaving issue:

1. DONALD CHARLES.
1. Mary Catherine.

XXIV. DONALD CHARLES NAPIER.

Cape St. Vincent.

XX. CAPTAIN THE HON. CHARLES NAPIER of Merchiston Hall, second son of Francis, sixth Baron Napier, b. November, 1731, m. first, December, 1763, Grizel, dau. of Sir John Warrender, Bart., of Lochend; she d. November, 1774. He m. secondly July, 1777, Christian, dau. of Gabriel Hamilton of Westburn, Co. Lanark, and dying December, 1807, left issue by the latter:

1. CHARLES (SIR).
2. Thomas Erskine (Sir), General in the Army, K.C.B., Colonel 71st Foot, and Governor of Edinburgh Castle; b. May, 1790; m. Margaret, dau. and co-heir of Alexander Falconer of Woodcot, and d. July, 1863, having by her had a daughter, (1) Matilda.
1. Henrietta Hope m. George Gordon of Hall Head, Co. Aberdeen.
2. Agnes Dundas.
3. Christian Graham m. Charles Campbell of Combie.

XXI. ADMIRAL SIR CHARLES NAPIER, K.C.B., of Merchiston House, Hants., Admiral of the Blue, Count of Cape St. Vincent, and grandee of the first class of Portugal, M.P., and distinguished British seaman; b. March, 1786; m. Eliza, dau. of George Younghusband and widow of Edward Elers, Lieutenant R.N., and d. November, 1860, leaving by her an only child,

> 1. Eloise Fanny, Countess of Cape St. Vincent, m. the Rev. Henry Jodrell, M.A., and by him had five daughters, of whom
>> (1) Heloise m. Colonel Tafford and had issue :
>> (i) Charles. (ii) Napier.
>> (iii) Claude, of whom Napier married and had issue.
>> (2) Cecilia Cator m. to Rev. Lewis R. C. Bagot, having issue:
>> (i) Caryl Ernest Bagot, presumably eventual co-representative of this branch with his cousin above.

ᚠrancis Ĵ. Ḣ. Scott Ṇapier.

XX. GENERAL THE HON. MARK NAPIER, fifth son of Francis, sixth Baron Napier, b. December, 1738, m. first, February, 1761, Anne, dau. of John Nelson of Craighcaffie; and secondly, Margaret, dau. of Alexander Simpson of Concraig, and d. 10th June, 1809, leaving issue by the latter:

     1. FRANCIS.
     2. Mark, Lieutenant-General in the Army, b. February, 1779; d. in 1843.
     1. Isabella m. Charles Maitland.
     2. Katherine Douglas d. unm.
     3. Marcia Anne Sympson m. Alexander Ogilvy.
     4. Marie m. June, 1823, the Rev. Thomas Henry Yorke.

XXI. FRANCIS NAPIER b. August, 1770, m. March, 1796, Mary Elizabeth Jane Douglas, dau. of Colonel Archibald Hamilton, and left issue:

     1. MARK.
     1. Alicia Coldon.

XXII. MARK NAPIER, Sheriff of Dumfries and Galloway, b. July, 1798, m. December, 1842, his cousin Charlotte, dau. of Alexander Ogilvy and widow of W. D. Macfarlane, and d. November, 1879, leaving by her:

     1. FRANCIS JOHN HAMILTON SCOTT.
     1. Marcia Charlotte.
     2. Alice Jane Douglas.
     3. Frances m. Lieutenant-Colonel Cecil Rice, late 72nd Highlanders.

XXIII. FRANCIS JOHN HAMILTON SCOTT NAPIER, Lieutenant (retired) R.N., b. December, 1850; m. 1909 Anne, dau. of William Ward.

Charles James Napier.

XX. COLONEL THE HON. GEORGE NAPIER, sixth son of Francis, sixth Lord Napier, Comptroller of army accounts in Ireland, b. March, 1751, m. first, January, 1775, Elizabeth, dau. of Captain Robert Pollock, and by her left an only daughter,

    1. Louise Mary.

He m. secondly, August, 1781, Sarah, seventh dau. of Charles, second Duke of Richmond, and d. October, 1804, leaving issue by her:

    1. Charles James (Sir), G.C.B., b. August, 1782, a Lieutenant-General in the army, and Colonel of the 22nd Regiment; a very distinguished officer, at one time Commander-in-Chief in India; m. April, 1827, Elizabeth, dau. of Thomas Oakeley and widow of Francis John Kelly, and secondly 1835, Frances, dau. of William Phillips of Court Henry, Co. Carmarthen, and relict of Richard Alcock, R.N. He d. s.p. August, 1853.

    2. GEORGE THOMAS (Sir), K.C.B.

    3. *William Francis Patrick* (Sir), K.C.B.

    4. Richard, barrister, b. 1787; d. January, 1868; m. 1817 Anne Louise, dau. of Sir J. Stewart, Bart., and widow of Captain Staples, R.N.

    5. *Henry Edward.*

    2. Emily Louisa Augusta.

    3. Caroline. 4. Cecilia.

XXI. GENERAL SIR GEORGE THOMAS NAPIER, K.C.B., b. June, 1784, m. first, October, 1812, Margaret, dau. of John Craig of Glasgow, and secondly, 1839, Frances Dorothea, eldest dau. of R. W. Blencowe and widow of William Peere Williams Freeman of Fawley Court, Co. Oxford. He d. September, 1855. By his first wife he had:

1. George Thomas Conolly, C.B., Major-General in the Army, Colonel of the 96th Foot, b. 1816, and d. May, 1873, leaving a daughter,
   (1) Maria Aletta m. John F. Mell.
2. John Moore, Captain 62nd Foot, b. 1817, m. July, 1843, Maria, dau. of Captain Richard Alcock, R.N., and d. in Scinde July, 1846, having by her had a daughter,
   (1) Sarah m. Lord Albert Seymour.
3. WILLIAM CRAIG EMILIUS.
1. Sarah m. Thomas Clarke.
2. Cecilia m. Colonel H. W. St. P. Bunbury, C.B.

XXII. GENERAL WILLIAM CRAIG EMILIUS NAPIER, Knight of the Medjidie, Colonel King's Own Scottish Borderers, late 3rd Buffs, and Governor Roy. Mil. College, Sandhurst, 1875-82, J.P., Hants.; b. March, 1818; m. April, 1845, Emily Cephalonia Napier; d. September, 1903, leaving issue:

1. Charles James b. 1850; d. 1851.
2. CHARLES JAMES.
1. Cecilia Margaret.
2. Susan Frances m. Colonel Cecil Bunbury.
3. Georgina Anne Emily m. Henry James Lionel Oakes, eldest son of Lieutenant-Colonel Orbell Henry Oakes of Nowton Court, Suffolk.
4. Hester Johnston.
5. Emily Caroline, M.B.E.
6. Margaret Cephalonia.   7. Sarah Lennox.
8. Violet Bunbury.

XXIII. CAPTAIN CHARLES JAMES NAPIER, O.B.E., b. August, 1858, m. Ellen Frederica, dau. of the late Frederick Thompson, and has a son,

1. Cecil Charles James b. 1890; m. March, 1907, Marie de Geneville Goodbirn.

William Charles Napier.

XXI. GENERAL SIR WILLIAM FRANCIS PATRICK NAPIER, K.C.B., third son of Colonel the Hon. George Napier and grandson of Francis, sixth Lord Napier, b. December, 1785, m. March, 1812, Caroline Amelia, second dau. of General the Hon. Henry Edward Fox, third son of Henry, Lord Holland, and d. February, 1860, having had issue:

1. JOHN MOORE.
1. Emily Anne.
2. Elizabeth Marianne m. the fourth Earl of Arran, K.P.
3. Louisa Augusta m. Colonel Patrick Lennard McDougall.
4. Caroline Jane.
5. Pamela Adelaide m. Philip William Skynner Miles of Kingsweston, Co. Gloucester, M.P. for Bristol.
6. Nora Creina Blanche m. first Lord Aberdare, G.C.B.

XXII. JOHN MOORE NAPIER b. November, 1816, m. June, 1847, Elizabeth Amelia Henrietta, third dau. of Colonel Charles Alexander, R.E., and d. April, 1867, having had issue:

1. WILLIAM CHARLES. 2. Chas. Arthur W.
1. Louisa Blanche m. Arthur Gordon Schneider.
2. Rose Leslie m. Edward Robert Portal, only son of W. T. Portal of Springfield, Northampton.
3. Geraldine Hester Mary.

XXIII. WILLIAM CHARLES NAPIER b. April, 1854.

Charles Lee Napier.

XXI. CAPTAIN HENRY EDWARD NAPIER, R.N., F.R.S., b. March, 1789, fifth son of Colonel the Hon. George Napier and grandson of Francis, sixth Lord Napier, m. Caroline Bennett, and by her left at his decease, October, 1853,

    1. CHARLES GEORGE.

    2. Richard Henry (ret.) Vice-Admiral R.N., b. March, 1836, m. first 1861 Mary, dau. of Frederick Dyer, and secondly 1883 Terese, eldest dau. of Robert Priest. He d. March, 1903.

    1. Augusta Sarah m. F. P. Williams Freeman.

XXII. CHARLES GEORGE NAPIER, F.G.S., C.E., b. July, 1829, m. December, 1860, Susanne, dau. of Samuel John Carolin, and d. September, 1882, leaving issue :

    1. HENRY EDWARD.

    1. Lilias Juliana m. Ernest Stork.

    2. Mabel Christiana m. John Peere Williams Freeman, M.D., of Weyhill, Andover.

XXIII. COLONEL HENRY EDWARD NAPIER, temporary Brigadier-General, late commanding 2nd Battalion Royal Irish Rifles, formerly 1st Battalion Cheshire Regiment. Served in South African War and in the Great War; b. September, 1861; m. 1887 Mary Ada, dau. of the late Captain W. F. Stewart, B.S.C., and d. of wounds received in action in the Dardanelles, April, 1915, leaving issue :

    1. CHARLES LEE.

    1. Lilias Mary.   2. Hester Caroline.

XXIV. CHARLES LEE NAPIER b. February, 1895.

Newburgh.

XIV. SIMON SCOTT, fourth son of Sir John Scott of Thirlestane, was, according to Satchells, tutor to his nephew, Robert Scott of Thirlestane, and father of

XV. ARTHUR SCOTT of Gamescleuch and afterwards of Newburgh, about whom we know little except that he was in the Carlisle Raid of 1596, and that he was a learned man. On succeeding his father to Newburgh he disposed of Gamescleuch to his cousin Walter, ancestor of Lord Napier. Mr. Arthur left, besides a second son, Arthur, and an illegitimate son, Robert, his heir,

XVI. SIR JOHN SCOTT of Newburgh, described by Satchells as "that Prince of Poets than whom Chaucer, Glovet, Sir Thomas More and Sir Philip Sidney never had a more Poetic Vein." Sir John had issue a dau. m. to Sir Walter Scott of Whitslaid and a son and heir,

XVII. SIR JOHN SCOTT of Rennalburn and Newburgh, who m. Margaret Canide, and had issue:
1. JOHN. 2. James b. August, 1623.
1. Janet. 2. Marie.

XVIII. JOHN SCOTT, Squire of Newburgh Hall "alias of Rennalburn," was b. September, 1620, and was living at the time of Satchells' book (1688).

XIX. JAMES SCOTT, son of the above, m. November, 1721, Philadelphia, dau. of William Ballentine of Crookdyke, Esquire, in the parish of Aerby, Cumberland (Parish Register of Langholm).

Gilmanscleuch.

XIV. JAMES SCOTT, according to Satchells, was the youngest son of John Scott of Thirlestane; he signed the clan bond in 1589, and was father of

XV. ROBERT SCOTT of Gilmanscleuch, called Truth, one of the rescuers of Kinmont Will. Robert had three sons:

1. JOHN, who succeeded him.
2. William.
3. Adam in Schaws, father of
    (1) Francis, a shepherd mentioned in the Postral.

XVI. JOHN SCOTT of Gilmanscleuch was entered as owner of the lands in 1628; in 1643 he was made Hon. Burgess of Selkirk; he was father of

XVII. FRANCIS SCOTT of Gilmanscleuch, appointed Commissioner of Supply in 1685.

XVIII. JOHN SCOTT and

XIX. JOHN SCOTT younger, of Gilmanscleuch, are mentioned in various Acts 1685-90 in connection with County Administration, and in or before 1728 :

XX. WILLIAM SCOTT of Gilmanscleuch sold the property to the Duchess of Buccleuch.

Bowhill.

SATCHELLS is very indefinite about this family and the records of the time are complicated by there being two distinct families styling themselves Scott of Bowhill. According to Satchells the founder of this family was

XIII. ROBERT SCOTT, a younger brother of John Scott of Thirlestane. In 1592 he had a son living styled

XIV. WALTER SCOTT of Bowhill. This Laird had two brothers, William and James, the first of whom was in the Carlisle Raid.

XV. ROBERT SCOTT of Bowhill was eldest son and heir to Walter above, and mention is made of three brothers, Walter, James and William. In 1625 we note

XVI. ROBERT SCOTT succeeded to Bowhill as heir to his father, and had two sons, Andrew and James, both of whom succeeded to Bowhill.

XVII. ANDREW SCOTT of Bowhill appears as witness to several documents 1661-8, and in 1668

XVII. JAMES SCOTT succeeds as second lawful son to Robert. It is considered probable that he purchased Bowhill in his father's and brother's lifetime.

XVIII. JOHN SCOTT of Bowhill was probably James's son and last male of this family. He sold the estate to Adam Scott in Deloraine, brother german to Francis Scott of Grassyards.

Roberton.

SCOTT of Roberton was one of the earliest Houses of Scott established on the border, and was in all probability an offshoot of Buccleuch.

X. STEPHEN SCOTT obtained in May, 1450, a Crown Charter to the lands of Murhous, and it is offered as a suggestion that this Stephen was a brother of the second Sir Walter Scott of Buccleuch. This Stephen also had a charter of the lands of Castlecary and of Weltoun.

XI. JOHN SCOTT of Weltoun was almost certainly a son of the above Stephen, and having disposed of Weltoun he appears later (1501) under the name of John Scott of Valis. He subsequently acquired (1502) Roberton and was afterwards designed " of Roberton." He was probably father of a younger son, Stephen of Valis, and

XII. WALTER SCOTT of Roberton, apparently d. s.p., for in 1535 we have

XII. STEPHEN SCOTT in Valis, afterwards of Roberton and Howcleuch, undoubtedly his brother.

XIII. JOHN SCOTT is mentioned as son and heir to Stephen Scott of Roberton, after which we have no further record till 1596, when

XIV. JOHN SCOTT of Roberton represents the House at the rescue of Kinmont Will. John may well have been the previous John's son. He d. in May, 1606, and was succeeded by his son,

XV. WILLIAM SCOTT of Roberton. William d. February, 1625, as appears from the Retour of his son,

XVI. JAMES SCOTT of Roberton, the last of his race in possession of Roberton. In 1627 he sold Roberton to Sir William Scott of Harden.

Haining.

X. ROBERT SCOTT of Haining was in all probability third son of Robert Scott, fifth Laird of Buccleuch, although there is no documentary evidence available to prove it. In 1477 he sold the lands of Haining, the deed being attested by David and Alexander, sons to Sir Walter Scott, sixth of Buccleuch. The Haining lands passed out of Robert Scott's hands to Murray of Philiphaugh, but the lands were eventually regranted by the King to his son,

XI. JOHN SCOTT of Haining, who fell at Flodden, and by deed (1514)

XII. ROBERT SCOTT, his son, was served heir. This Robert m. Janet, dau. of Sir Walter Scott, ninth of Buccleuch, and widow of John Cranstoun of Cranstoun; he d. before 1532, at which time his brother Walter was acting as tutor to Haining in the minority of the young Laird,

XIII. THOMAS SCOTT, who is mentioned as of Haining in 1538.

XIV. ROBERT SCOTT of Haining is mentioned in an action dated 1576 as son to the deceased Thomas, and in 1589 he signed the Scott bond. He had besides a younger son William, one of the rescuers of Kinmont Will, an elder son,

XV. SIR ROBERT SCOTT, who was entered heir in 1611. Sir Robert parted with Haining about 1625, but continued to be styled " of Haining." He had two sons, the younger, Walter, portioner of Guilan, and the elder,

XVI. ROBERT SCOTT " of Haining," with the second Earl of Buccleuch in 1643.

XVII. LIEUT.-COL. ROBERT SCOTT, son to Walter Scott, portioner of Guilan, is the last male of this family of whom there is any record.

Oakwood.

The first mention of the Oakwood family is

XI. ROBERT SCOTT of Oakwood, living in 1503 and suggested by Mr. Scott of Rodono to have been a son of the first Robert Scott of Haining. He left an elder son, Michael, and a younger son, Robert, who was possibly the grandfather of the well-known Simon of Bonnington.

XII. MICHAEL SCOTT was served heir to his father, the deceased Robert Scott of Oakwood, about 1516. He m. Isabella Ker and left a son,

XIII. WILLIAM SCOTT, who was confirmed by charter in this property in 1541. The mutual Scott clan bond was signed in 1589 by

XIV. ROBERT SCOTT of Oakwood, and in 1592 he witnessed a deed. In 1602 he built the present tower; he d. October, 1615, and in 1616

XV. ANDREW SCOTT of Oakwood was returned heir to his father Robert.

XV. PHILIP SCOTT of Oakwood in 1627 was possibly a brother of Andrew. Philip, however, does not appear to have held the property long, for in 1630 it was in the hands of a Murray, possibly of the Elibank family, and Elibank at that time was brother-in-law to the first Sir William of Harden, to whom the place eventually belonged.

The second Sir William of Harden was in his father's lifetime Sir William of Oakwood, and Oakwood has remained with this family ever since.

Bonnington.

XII. ROBERT SCOTT m. between 1514 and 1524 Katherine, dau. and heiress of John Boyle of Wamphray and Rysholme and widow of John Johnstone. Robert Scott assumed the designation "of Wamphray and Rysholme," but became a traitor and a spy during the invasion of 1545, and probably on this account the family parted with Wamphray in 1548 and Rysholme in 1550. At the time of this invasion he took refuge with the Laird of Oakwood, who was probably a kinsman.

This Robert Scott left three sons:

1. ROBERT, who was infest in the superiority of Rysholme in 1541.
2. ADAM, who was served heir to his brother in 1547.
3. Robert, an illegitimate son legitimatized in 1547.

Nothing is known of

XIII. ADAM SCOTT, but there is no doubt that he was father of John, present at the Carlisle Raid, and

XIV. SIMON SCOTT of Bonnington, Midlothian (not to be confused with Scott of Bonnington, W. Lothian, descended from a brother of Lord Clerkington). This Simon signed the clan bond in 1589, and is mentioned as son of Adam in a sasine dated 1594-5 and as grandson of Robert Scott and Katherine Boyle in 1611. That same year Simon Scott of Bonnington was served heir general to his grandmother, Katherine Boyle.

XV. ROBERT SCOTT, Simon's son, probably predeceased his father, for on 18th December, 1624, his uncle, the above mentioned

XIV. JOHN SCOTT of Bonnington, brother german to Simon of Bonnington, was served heir to his nephew in the lands of Ernsheuch and Singlie.

XV. ROBERT SCOTT of Bonnington was in possession in 1670, and was son to John and was father or elder brother of

XVI. JAMES SCOTT of Bonnington.

XVII. GILBERT SCOTT of Bonnington was served heir to James, his father, in 1675.   He d. shortly after, and was succeeded by his immediate younger brother,

XVII. CHARLES SCOTT of Bonnington, a commissioner of supply for Edinburgh in 1678.

Satchells mentions the Laird of Carnwathmills as being the representative of this family in 1688.

Woll.

THIS property was owned by Scotts in the seventeenth century, probably cadets of Haining, but how it is not now possible to say.

WALTER SCOTT of Woll is noted in 1606, and in 1608 John, brother to Walter of Woll, attacked and maltreated some people in Selkirk. He had by a first marriage :

    1. ROBERT his heir.   2. Francis.

And by a second marriage with Catherine Ormiston :

    3. George.   1. Katherine.

ROBERT SCOTT of Woll succeeded his father, and is noted in December, 1617, as guardian to his half-brother and sister. Robert apparently had four sons :

    1. FRANCIS.   2. JAMES.

    3. GEORGE.   4. John.

FRANCIS SCOTT was " of Woll " in 1627, and was succeeded by his brother,

JAMES SCOTT of Woll (1643), who also d. s.p. male, but is noted in the Parish Register of Ashkirk as father of three daughters between 1642 and 1645. He sold the estate to Sir William Scott of Harden.

GEORGE SCOTT, surgeon in Edinburgh, was in 1670 returned heir to his father, Robert Scott of Woll.

I

Part II.

—

Sinton.

Scott of Boonraw ❖

A GAIN I commend to those interested in this controversial genealogy Mr. John Scott of Rodono's
extensive notes on the subject.   Before they came into
my hands I had already made up my mind that the
Whitslaid family was senior to Harden, and Mr. Scott
of Rodono had apparently come to the same con-
clusion.

Mr. Scott says that the commonly accepted
genealogy from John, son of Sir Michael Scott of
Murdiestoun, down to Robert, murdered in 1509, is
entirely mythical and evolved from the fertile imagina-
tion of Satchells.   Whilst not concurring absolutely
in so sweeping a statement, it must be admitted that
there is no documentary proof to substantiate the

pedigree, and also that Sinton was not owned by Scotts during the fourteenth and part of the fifteenth centuries.

The following is the generally accepted pedigree of the family, but it can only be taken as authentic from Robert of Sinton (1509) onwards.

[1111 2] VII. JOHN SCOTT, younger son of Sir Michael Scott of Murdiestoun, sixth in the Buccleuch genealogy, had a son,

VIII. WALTER SCOTT of Sinton, who m. a dau. of Shortread of Headshaw, by whom he had :

    1. GEORGE, who succeeded to Sinton.
    2. John of Headshaw.
    3. Walter of Ashkirk.
    4. William of Glack.

IX. GEORGE SCOTT m. a dau. of Sir John Turnbull of Falshope, by whom he had a son,

X. WALTER SCOTT of Sinton, who m. in the reign of James II. a dau. of Scott of Hassendene, and left two sons :

    1. JOHN.   2. WALTER his brother's heir.

XI. JOHN SCOTT of Sinton m. a dau. of Quintin Riddell, but d. without issue.

XI. WALTER SCOTT, fifth of Sinton, m. a dau. of Sir John Johnston, and left a son,

XII. GEORGE SCOTT of Sinton, who m. a dau. of Scott of Roberton, and left a son,

XIII. WALTER SCOTT, mentioned in the writs of the family in 1487. He flourished in the reign of James IV., and left a son,

XIV. ROBERT SCOTT, designed of Strick-shaws during his father's lifetime. He was murdered by Andrew Crosser in 1509, at which time he was described as Robert Scott of Sinton. He left three sons:

1. WALTER.
2. *William of Harden.*
3. David living in 1526.

XV. WALTER SCOTT, tenth of Sinton, is variously described on bonds—sometimes as of Sinton and sometimes as of Strickshaws. It is probable that this Laird married first a dau. of Cockburn of Ormiston, who at that time was proprietor of Whits-laid, and according to Mr. Scott it is clear that there was one son only by this marriage and his name was

1. JOHN.

Old Sinton m. again Margaret, dau. of James Riddell of Riddell, and by her had issue:

2. *Robert of Stirches.*
3. *Thomas of Whitchauchbrae.*

There is apparently considerable doubt as to the remaining sons given by Satchells.

XVI. JOHN SCOTT younger of Sinton is entered in the justiciary records of 27th May, 1531, as son and heir of Walter Scott of Sinton. He apparently d. in his father's lifetime leaving issue:

1. WALTER his grandfather's heir.
2. GEORGE.
3. *William,* who had a tack of the lands of Langhope in 1550, and who was probably the first of Huntly.
4. *James,* who had a tack of Dodbank, and was probably Satchell's great-grand-father.
5. *Robert of Shielswood.*

XVII. WALTER SCOTT, eleventh of Sinton, succeeded his grandfather about 1557. He was succeeded by his brother (son according to Satchells, but brother is probably correct owing to the number of generations in a given period),

XVII. GEORGE SCOTT, twelfth of Sinton, who signed the clan bond in 1589 as George of Sinton. According to Satchells he m. Margaret, dau. of John Edmonston, Laird of Ednam, and by her had five sons :

    1. WALTER.   2. *John of Yorkston.*

    3. David.

    4. George, apprenticed to David Brown, saddler, Edinburgh, January, 1610.

    5. James of Kirkhouse, who was at the Carlisle Raid and was father of

        (1) John of Kirkhouse summoned for murder in 1614.

    1. Agnes.

XVIII. WALTER SCOTT, the eldest son, m. Isabel, dau. of Douglas of Whittinghame, and dying July, 1608, left issue :

    1. GEORGE.   2. Archibald (Capt.) d. unm.

    1. Elspeth mentioned with her sisters in he father's testament.

    2. Christian.

    3. Ann said to have m. Captain Gladstaine of Whitlaw.

XIX. GEORGE SCOTT, the eldest son by th marriage, was the fourteenth and last of this famil

designed of Sinton. He m. Mary, dau. of Gladstaines, Laird of Dode, and by her had issue :

1. Walter d. unm.
2. GEORGE of Boonraw.
3. Richard, parson of Ashkirk 1685; d. May,
   1702, aged 82.

George the elder parted with Sinton about 1627,
and it passed into the hands of the Harden family.

XX. GEORGE SCOTT of Boonraw m. a dau.
of Douglas of Garvald, and by her had issue :

1. ARCHIBALD.

XXI. ARCHIBALD SCOTT of Boonraw d.
without succession about 1720, and the representation
of this branch of the family died in him, but the name
" Scott of Sinton " was revived by Francis, a younger
brother of Sir William Scott of Harden, purchasing
this estate in 1627, but as will be seen the property
eventually passed to a representative in the female
line.

Arms (borne by Scott of Boonraw).—Or, two
mullets in chief and a crescent in base azure. Crest.
—A lady richly attired, in her right hand the sun
and in her left hand the moon. Motto.—" Reparabit
Cornua Phœbe."

ﬣeaﬢsﬣaﬡ.

XVIII. JOHN SCOTT of Yorkston, second
son of George, twelfth of Sinton, purchased (1629)
Headshaw and Langhope from the old family of
Headshaw. He died not later than 1649 and left
issue :

1. WILLIAM.

2. Walter of Dryden.

3. *John of Langhope.*

4. Mungo in Dryden.

5. Robert also in Dryden.

XIX. WILLIAM SCOTT of Headshaw m. Jean
Halket, sister of Sir James Halket, and by her had :

1. JOHN.

2. William baptized March, 1648.

1. MARIE.

William Scott of Headshaw witnessed in conjunction with the Lairds of Toderick, Whitslaid,
Sinton, etc., various births and marriages 1688-90.

XX. JOHN SCOTT succeeded his father,
William Scott, in 1688; m. 1682 probably a kins-
woman, Jean Halket, only dau. of Colonel R. Halket.
He seems to have d. s.p. for in 1691 his only sister
Marie was served his heiress. Marie Scott m. Patrick
Porteous, and eventually sold Headshaw, etc., to Sir
Gilbert Elliot.

Langhope.

THIS property belonged the Huntly family till about 1620 when it passed to the old Headshaw family and thence with Headshaw to John Scott of Yorkston.

XIX. JOHN SCOTT of Langhope, described as brother german to William Scott of Headshaw, purchased Langhope from his brother. He m., December, 1653, Margaret, dau. of Robert Scott of Whitslaid, and dying 1666 left issue:

    1. WILLIAM baptized October, 1654.

    1. Elizabeth.

XX. WILLIAM SCOTT of Langhope was duly served heir to his father, but in 1677 disposed of Langhope to Walter Scott, who may or may not have been his brother. Walter m. Janet Scott and d. November, 1685, leaving among others a son and heir John, who sold the estate about 1692 to Adam Scott of Bowhill. Will Scott of Langup, mentioned early in the postral and whose name as William Scott of Langhope appears on three inquests dated 1686, 1693 and 1699, would be the same laird who disposed of his property in 1677 but continued to use the designation.

Huntly.

THIS genealogy is based largely on conjecture, but it is very possible that

XVII.   WILLIAM SCOTT in Huntly, who was upon an inquest in 1592, was third son of John Scott, younger of Sinton.

XVIII.   ROBERT SCOTT of Huntly, probably William's son, attended the Carlisle Raid, and the fact that William, son of John younger of Sinton, had a tack of Langhope reconciles well with Satchells "Robert of Langhope had Outer Huntly for his services."

XIX.   WALTER SCOTT of Huntly was upon an inquest in 1612.

XIX.   JAMES SCOTT of Huntly attended an inquest in 1616, and Mr. Scott of Rodono suggests he may have been a brother of Walter.

XX.   JOHN SCOTT was served heir to his father, James Scott of Huntly, in 1638, and here we lose sight of this family.

Satchells.

XVII. JAMES SCOTT, fourth son of John Scott younger of Sinton, was father of

XVIII. ROBERT SCOTT, who had several charters in connection with the lands of Satchells and Dodbank in Selkirkshire dated 1607 and 1609. He d. about 1629, and was father of

XIX. ROBERT SCOTT of Satchells, who m. Jean, dau. of Sir Robert Scott of Thirlestane. He was father of a large family, of whom the only ones we have any record are :

    1. WILLIAM.

    2. John, whose name appears in a deed dated 1655.

    3. WALTER.

XX. WILLIAM SCOTT of Satchells, together with his brother John, appear to have d. s.p., and the empty succession to the designation devolved on their brother on his return from the wars.

XX. CAPT. WALTER SCOTT of Satchells, one of the younger members of the family b. c. 1613, according to his own statement never was an hour at school. As a youth he joined the first Earl of Buccleuch's regiment and went with the Earl to Holland in 1629, where he tells us he served for the long period of fifty-seven years. He retired about 1686, when he wrote the " True History." It is stated by Dr. Wm. Scott that he m. a young woman by whom he had a daughter whom he called Gustava.

The date of his death is unknown.

Shielswood.

XVII. ROBERT SCOTT of Shielswood, fifth son of John Scott younger of Sinton, was probably father of,

    1. ROBERT of Shielswood.

    2. *Walter of Girnwood.*

XVIII. ROBERT SCOTT of Shielswood is mentioned in various documents (1606-1626). He appears to have had two sons :

    1. WALTER.

    2. Robert.

XIX. WALTER SCOTT of Shielswood, also mentioned in various inquests (1643), m. June, 1636, Margaret Scott, and left two sons and a daughter :

    1. FRANCIS. 2. ROBERT. 1. MARIAN.

XX. FRANCIS SCOTT of Shielswood, b. October, 1638, succeeded his father and d. shortly after obtaining possession of his estates.

XX. ROBERT SCOTT of Shielswood, his younger brother, b. March, 1640, is mentioned on an inquest dated 1669. He also d. s.p.

XX. MARIAN SCOTT, his sister, succeeded, and m. James, son of Adam Scott of Schaws.

Girnwood.

XVIII. WALTER SCOTT of Girnwood, younger brother of Robert Scott of Shielswood, is noted as alive in 1628; he died soon after this date leaving two sons :

1. ROBERT.
2. Walter.

Both minors under the tutory of their uncle Robert of Shielswood.

XIX. ROBERT SCOTT of Girnwood was served heir in April, 1636. He m. June, 1640, Bessie, dau. of Sir Walter Scott of Whitslaid.

Whitslaid.

Scott of Whitslaid·

ACCORDING to Mr. Scott of Rodono it is clear, apart from Satchells' evidence, that old Sinton (XV.) gave up Sinton to his eldest son John, and resided at Whitslaid, which latter he obtained through his marriage with Cockburn. He, however, never gave up his personal designation of Sinton.

At some time he put his second son Robert in possession of Stirches, and the latter, who d. v.p., was always so designed.

Margaret Riddell, old Sinton's second wife, d. at Whitslaid in 1585, the old man having d. between 1557 and 1575.

By his marriage with a Rutherford of Hunthill, Robert of Stirches was father of

XVII. WALTER SCOTT of Whitslaid (The Hawke), who in June, 1575, obtained a charter in which he was designed Walter Scott, son and heir of

Robert Scott of Stirches, second son of Walter Scott of Sinton. He m. a dau. of Douglas of Cavers, and was father of

1. WALTER (Sir) his heir.
2. *Thomas of Toderick.*
3. Robert at the Carlisle Raid.

XVIII. SIR WALTER SCOTT, second Laird of Whitslaid, succeeded his father about 1610. He m. Susannah, dau. of Sir Robert Scott of Thirlestane, but she dying without issue he m. secondly a dau. of Sir John Scott of Newburgh, and by her had three sons and two daughters :

1. ROBERT. 2. WALTER (Sir).
3. THOMAS. 4. George.
1. Isabella m. Francis Scott, fourth son of Walter Scott of Harden.
2. Elizabeth m. Robert Scott of Girnwood.

XIX. ROBERT SCOTT succeeded his father on the latter's death in 1628, and m. Jane, natural dau. to Walter, Earl of Buccleuch, and by her had, possibly among others :

1. Walter baptized January, 1636.
2. Francis baptized June, 1643.
1. Mary.
2. Margaret m. John Scott of Langhope.

Robert Scott was killed at the battle of Marston Moor in 1644, and his sons at any rate appear to have died in infancy as he was succeeded by his brother,

XIX. SIR WALTER SCOTT, fourth Laird of Whitslaid, who did not long survive his predecessor, being killed at the battle of Inverkeithing in 1651. He m. a dau. of Sir Robert Stuart of Ormistone, and by her had several children, of which the sons also must have died in infancy :

1. Robert baptized September, 1647.
2. Walter baptized April, 1649.
1. Jean.

XIX. THOMAS SCOTT, the third son, succeeded his brother in 1651. He m. 1613 Janet, dau. of Walter Scott of Harden, and secondly 1655 Janet Mitchell, and by the latter had issue:

    1. Walter, baptized 1657, presumed d. v.p.
    2. THOMAS.
    1. Marie.

Thomas Scott d. in 1671, and was succeeded by his second son.

XX. THOMAS SCOTT succeeded his father as sixth Laird of Whitslaid, and according to Satchells m. before 1688 Jane, dau. of Sir John Hay of Park, Bart., and by her had issue:

    1. THOMAS.   2. JOHN.   3. Walter.
    4. Robert, a surgeon in Hawick, d. about 1757.
    5. Francis.
    6. William, a physician at Worcester.
    7. James.

Thomas Scott was living in 1688 when Scott's pastoral was written. He was succeeded by his eldest son,

XXI. THOMAS SCOTT, seventh of Whitslaid, who m. Margaret, dau. of Sir John Scott, Bart., of Ancrum, and by her had two daughters:

    1. Elizabeth m. to William, brother to Makdougal of Mackerstoun.
    2. Janet d. unm.

He was succeeded by his brother,

XXI. JOHN SCOTT, eighth and last of Whitslaid, who sold the estates consisting of Whitslaid, Castleside, two large farms called Readfordgreens, Ashkirk, Ashkirkmill, Salanside, Bradley, etc., etc.

Arms.—Or, on a bend azure a star between two crescents of the first, in chief a broken lance gules. Crest.—A hand issuing out of the torse holding a broken spear. Motto.—" Amore Patriæ."

Toderick.

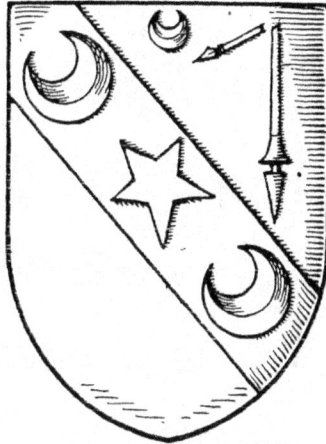

Scott of Toderick.

THIS property was in the possession of the Scotts
for many years prior to the end of the sixteenth
century and a Walter Scott signed the clan bond in
1589. This Walter, however, was probably a cadet of
Harden, and not the father of the Thomas we find as
" of Toderick " in 1637. Compare the arms sketched
above borne by Scott of Toderick subsequent to 1637,
which are obviously derived from Whitslaid, with arms
borne by Scott of Toderick 1622, at the end of Part II.

XVIII. THOMAS SCOTT, younger brother of
Sir Walter Scott, second Laird of Whitslaid, was apparently the founder of this family, and seems to have
settled at Toderick early in the seventeenth century.
He lived till between 1650 and 1656, during which time
we find him and his eldest son referred to as " Thomas
Scott elder and younger of Toderick," respectively; he
left three children :

　　　1. THOMAS.　2. Walter.　1. Janet.

XIX. THOMAS SCOTT, the elder son, succeeded to Toderick before 1656, having m. probably twice, as the fourth son, Robert, only is mentioned as being the son of Thomas Scott and Janet, dau. of Robert Pringle of Clifton. The time between the birth of the other children makes it unlikely that they were all by the same mother. By the first wife he had:

1. WALTER, who succeeded his father.
2. Thomas baptized 1639.
3. *William of Milsington*, baptized November, 1645.

By Janet Pringle he had:

4. Robert baptized October, 1660; d. in Edinburgh in 1752.
1. Marion m. to Dr. Rutherford of Jedburgh.
2. Jane.

XX. WALTER SCOTT succeeded his father before 1691, and m. Elizabeth, dau. of Sir Thomas Ker of Fernielee, by whom he had:

1. THOMAS his successor, and seven daughters:
1. Jane m. William Elliot of Harwood or Hariot.
2. Elizabeth m. William's brother, Henry Elliot of Peel.
3. Nelly m. first John Elliot, another brother, and secondly Rev. Wm. Hume.
4. Janet m. Mr. Purdon of Hawick.
5. Christian m. George Dennison.
6. Margaret m. David Scott of Merrylaws.
7. Violet.

Walter Scott of Toderick d. 1722.

XXI. THOMAS SCOTT succeeded him. He
m. 1708 Mary, dau. of Robert Scott of Scotsbank, and
by her had issue:

1. WALTER.
2. Robert baptized March, 1714, d. young.
3. Thomas baptized February, 1717, went to
   sea in 1740, and was living without issue
   in 1783.
4. John baptized March, 1718, d. young.
5. William baptized November, 1719 (Dr.
   William Scott gives a Patrick and not a
   William, but there is no trace of a Patrick
   in the Parish Register).
1. Janet baptized April, 1710, m. first Mr.
   Howie, surgeon in Selkirk, and secondly
   the Rev. David Brown, minister of
   Selkirk.
2. Elizabeth, living unm. in 1783.

Thomas, sixth and last Laird of Toderick, sold his
estate in 1746. He d. in Selkirk in 1753 and was
buried at Ashkirk.

XXII. WALTER SCOTT served some time in
the Horse Guards; he m. 1732 Jane, only dau. and
heiress of William Robson of High Stokoe, Northumberland, by whom he had:

1. WILLIAM b. 1733.
2. Patrick, a doctor who settled at Douglas,
   I.M., and m. Annas, dau. of Rev. Wm.
   Nelson of Stamfordham, and by her had:
   (1) John Nelson. (2) Walter.
   (3) William.
   (1) Mary m. to J. Best.
3. Walter baptized 14th June, 1739.
1. Isobel.

TODERICK.

XXIII. DR. WILLIAM SCOTT of Stokoe, the eldest son, also a doctor and the compiler of the Pedigree of Scott of Stokoe, from which most of the Whitslaid and Toderick entries are taken, settled in Stamfordham in Northumberland and m. in 1759 Martha, dau. of the Rev. Edward Fenwick, Vicar of Kirkwhelpington, by whom he had, with two children who died in infancy, two sons:

1. WALTER. 2. Edward Fenwick d. s.p.

Dr. William Scott d. November, 1802.

XXIV. DR. WALTER SCOTT, M.D., of Stokoe, J.P., b. August, 1761, m. first Eleanor Walker, who d. s.p., and secondly Mary Bell, by whom he had:

1. WILLIAM ROBSON.
2. Walter John b. October, 1818, living unm. in 1852.
1. Martha Jane m. William Forster of Stamfordham.

Dr. Walter Scott sold Stokoe and d. in February, 1831.

XXV. DR. WILLIAM ROBSON SCOTT b. January, 1811, m. Mary, dau. of Thomas Mason of Doncaster, by whom he had issue:

1. Walter b. 8th August, 1843.
2. William Henry b. 17th July, 1849.
1. Mabel Fenwick. 2. Mary Mason.

Arms.—As of Whitslaid with a crescent for difference. Crest.—The head of a lance proper. Motto.—" Pro aris et focis."

Milsington.

XX. WILLIAM SCOTT, third son of Thomas Scott of Toderick, settled at Milsington about 1670, and m. a dau. of Elliot, Laird of Lariston, and by her had issue:

1. WILLIAM.
2. *Walter*, b. 1682, settled at Girnwood 1712.
3. *Robert*, who settled at Singlie about the same time.
4. James m. June, 1717, Margaret Rea in Hawick, and had a dau., Isobel. He was living as a notary in Hawick in 1726.

Mr. Scott d. 1739 and was buried in Ashkirk church.

XXI. WILLIAM SCOTT in Milsington, b. 1679, m. April, 1731, Elizabeth, dau. of Elliot of Harwood, and by her had issue:

1. WILLIAM.
2. Thomas baptized June, 1735, buried at Ashkirk.
3. Henry baptized October, 1736.
4. Walter baptized April, 1740, buried at Ashkirk.
5. Robert baptized April, 1742, a doctor in Lasswade.
1. Jean.
2. Elizabeth m. her cousin William.
3. Janet.

Mr. Scott d. August, 1744, aged 65.

XXII. WILLIAM SCOTT in Milsington baptized July, 1733, m. 1760 his cousin Betty, second dau. of Walter Scott in Girnwood, and by her had issue :

1. WILLIAM.
2. Walter, tenant in Girnwood (see that Genealogy); d. September, 1837, aged 73. His family were:
    (1) William, tenant in Girnwood.
    (2) JAMES in Milsington and of Allanshaws.
    (3) Walter of Newton m. an Elliot of the family of Elliot of Harwood and had issue,
        (i) Margaret Ann m. Andrew Scott, afterwards of Newton.
    (4) Thomas went to America.
    (5) Henry, tenant in Eilrig, died in Hawick.
3. Henry, who m. and had one son and three daughters, who went to America.
4. Robert, manufacturer in Hawick, d. unm.
5. Thomas went to America, drowned at sea.
1. Jane m. James Richardson, Hawick.
2. Elizabeth m. William Miller.

Mr. Scott d. June, 1797, aged 63.

XXIII. WILLIAM SCOTT, tenant in Milsington, m. 1819 Jessie, dau. of Mr. Arres, farmer, Farmington; d. s.p. April, 1829, aged 68.

XXIV. JAMES SCOTT, the second son of Walter Scott in Girnwood and grandson of William in Milsington, succeeded his uncle to Milsington and lost the farm in 1831. He had a daughter, Mary Anne, m. March, 1861, the Rev. John Thompson, minister of St. John's, Hawick.

Girnwood.

XXI. WALTER SCOTT, second son of William Scott first in Milsington, settled at Girnwood in 1712. He m. August, 1723, Jane, dau. of Philip Scott of Oakwood, by whom he had issue:

    1. William m. his cousin Elizabeth, but d. s.p. and v.p.

    2. ——

    3. Walter. 4. Thomas.

    1. Betty m. her cousin William.

Walter d. January, 1766, aged 84, and his wife September, 1776, aged 74.

XXII. WALTER and THOMAS SCOTT, third and fourth sons, succeeded as joint tenants; both were unmarried. Thomas d. October, 1800, aged 64; Walter d. April, 1818, aged 82.

The Girnwood males being extinct, the above Walter was succeeded by

XXIII. WALTER SCOTT, second son of William Scott, third in Milsington, who had as before mentioned:

    1. WILLIAM. 2. James.

    3. Walter. 4. Thomas. 5. Henry.

He was succeeded by

XXIV. WILLIAM SCOTT, his son, who d. in 1858 and left a son,

XXV. WALTER SCOTT, d. unm. 1892, who succeeded him, and a daughter m. to Mr. Davies, butcher in Hawick, whose daughter has recently purchased the property.

𝕾inglie.

————

THIS genealogy is compiled from information supplied by the late Mr. John Scott of Selkirk and Agnes, dau. of Captain Thomas Scott in Shielswood, and checked to a certain extent from the tombstones in Ashkirk churchyard.

XXI. ROBERT SCOTT b. c. 1688, third son of William Scott of Milsington, settled at Singlie about 1712 and m. Elizabeth Elliot, and dying June, 1768, left issue:

    1. WILLIAM.

    2. *Henry* settled at Over Deloraine.

    1. Margaret m. William Scott in Kirkhope.

    2. Elizabeth.

XXII. WILLIAM SCOTT, baptized March, 1739, succeeded his father in the tenancy of Singlie; he m. Margaret Pott, and dying November, 1811, left issue :

    1. Robert b. 1773, tenant in Todshawhaugh, m. Janet Jardine of Thorlieshope, and by her had :

        (1) William d. young.

        (1) Janet d. young.

        (2) Christian m. Jas. Dickson of Housebyres.

Robert in Todshawhaugh d. July, 1844.

2. James, a doctor in the Army.
3. William, a doctor in the Army.
4. George went to Africa with Mungo Park and d. there.
5. Henry, a hatter in Edinburgh.
6. GIDEON.
7. Thomas, Captain in the Army, and tenant of Shielswood, d. December, 1858, aged 69, and left two daughters, Agnes and Margaret m. to Gideon Thomas Scott, wine merchant, Selkirk.
8. John, a distinguished physician in Edinburgh, who is referred to in very high terms by Mr. W. Riddell-Carr in his Border Memories. Dr. Scott had one son,
    (1) William Henry, also a very distinguished physician, who d. at the early age of 24.
1. Jane m. Elliott of Flat.
2. Elizabeth m. David Henderson of Chapelhope and Abbotrule.
3. Jessie m. Rev. David Scott of Newcastleton.
4. Margaret drowned in the Ettrick 1800.
5. Isabella also drowned in the Ettrick 1800.

XXIII. GIDEON SCOTT, the sixth son, succeeded his father in Singlie, and m. Elizabeth Ballentyne. He d. December, 1839, aged 53, leaving issue :
    1. GIDEON.
    1. Katherine m. Alexander Gibson.

XXIV. GIDEON SCOTT m. Annie Aitcheson. He gave up Singlie and took Hindup, and in about 1879 emigrated to New Zealand; he had issue four sons, of whom two were James and William, and two daughters.

Gilmanscleuch.

THE following information is supplied by the late Mr. John Scott of Lorraine, Selkirk, from a pedigree compiled by his father and his aunt, Mrs. Gibson.

XXII. HENRY SCOTT, baptized March, 1741, second son of Robert Scott of Singlie, settled at Deloraine in 1770, and m. a dau. of Anderson of Reshiegrain, by whom he had a dau. Alison. He m. subsequently December, 1781, Agnes, dau. of John Sibbald, and dying March, 1817, by her left issue:

1. JOHN SIBBALD.
2. *Henry* of Over Kirkhope.
3. James b. c. 1793-4; d. January, 1864.
4. William, M.D., F.R.C.S.E., H.E.I.C.S.
2. Eliza m. Dr. Thos. Anderson of Selkirk.
3. Margaret m. Rev. W. B. Shaw, minister of Roberton and later of Ewes.

Eliza and Margaret were the prototypes of Minna and Brenda in Sir Walter Scott's "The Pirate." Eliza is also "The bonnie lass o' Deloraine" in the Ettrick Shepherd's poem.

XXIII. JOHN SIBBALD SCOTT, tenant in Over Deloraine; b. 1789; m. November, 1822, Christian, dau. of Alexander Scott in Ladhope, d. January, 1864, leaving issue:

1. HENRY ALE, tenant in Gilmanscleuch.
2. *Alexander*, tenant in Ramsaycleuch.
3. *Charles*, tenant in Over Whitlaw.
4. *John* succeeded his father in Deloraine.
1. Arbuthnot.
2. Agnes m. James Gibson, Shaws, Ettrick.
3. Christian m. T. Ballantyne, Whitehope.

XXIV. HENRY ALE SCOTT, the eldest son, tenant in Gilmanscleuch, b. September, 1828, m. Jane Mills of Horsburgh Castle, and dying November, 1881, left issue :

1. JOHN.

1. Jane Purves m. Alexander Scott, tenant in Ladhope.
2. Christina m. Robt. M. Mills, Melbourne, Australia.
3. Lizzie Mills m. Archibald C. Morison, Edinburgh.
4. Georgina Henrietta.
5. Arbuthnot.

XXV. JOHN SCOTT emigrated to Iowa, U.S.A.; b. May, 1863; m. Agnes Grier and has issue :

1. David b. July, 1901.
1. Mildred.

Ramsaycleuch.

XXIV. ALEXANDER SCOTT, tenant in Ramsaycleuch, second son of John Scott, tenant in Over Deloraine; b. April, 1830; m. Helen Scott, Howford; emigrated to Iowa in 1881, and d. October, 1917, leaving eight children:

1. JOHN SIBBALD.

2. William F., b. June, 1864, m. December, 1896, Janet, dau. of Walter Cowan, and has four sons:
     (1) Alexander. (2) Andrew M.
     (3) John F. (4) Walter C.

3. Henry Anderson, b. July, 1876, m. November, 1909, Mary, dau. of John Cowan, Paullina, Iowa, and has two daughters,
     (1) Isabella Helen.
     (2) Jean Elliott.

1. Isabella Michil d. 1907 unm.

2. Jean Elliott m. John Cowan.

3. Wilhelmina Young m. her cousin, John Sibbald Scott.

4. Christina A. m. Thos. H. Aitken.

5. Nelly Janet m. Fred L. Huston.

XXV. JOHN SIBBALD SCOTT b. Septembe 1862, living unm. in 1922.

Residence.—Deloraine Farm, Paullina, Iow U.S.A.

Over Whitlaw.

XXIV. CHARLES SCOTT, tenant in Over Whitlaw, third son of John Scott, tenant in West Deloraine, b. May, 1834, m. 1865 Wilhelmina, dau. of Walter Elliot, Over Kirkhope, and emigrated in 1901 to Iowa. He d. March, 1912, leaving ten children:

1. JOHN SIBBALD.
2. Walter b. March, 1869; d. suddenly in Idaho, U.S.A., February, 1911.
3. Henry b. 1871, a doctor in Chicago, m. 1900 Clara Louise Deitze.
4. Gideon b. June, 1873, m. 1905 Effie, dau. of Andrew Smith, Selkirk, and has issue:
   (1) Margaret Jessie.
   (2) Wilhelmina Elliot.
   Residence.—Keith, Banff.
5. Charles Alexander b. April, 1883; a chemist in Sheldon, Iowa, U.S.A.
1. Margaret, Sheldon, Iowa.
2. Christina Agnes m. Elmer S. Gardner, San Diego, U.S.A.
3. Wilhelmina Elliot m. Dr. George Skene, Willesden, London.
4. Mary Arbuthnott m. Dr. B. C. Stewart, Sioux City, U.S.A.
5. Grace Elliot, nurse, Sheldon, Iowa, U.S.A.

XXV. JOHN SIBBALD SCOTT m. his cousin, Wilhelmina Young, dau. of Alexander Scott of Deloraine Farm, Paullina, Iowa. She d. s.p., and Mr. Scott m. secondly, 1915, Gertrude, dau. of Harley Duckett of Ashville, N.C., and has issue:

1. Walter Elliot.
2. Charles Brooks.
3. John Sibbald.
1. Grace Margaret.
Address.—Sheldon, Iowa, U.S.A.

West Deloraine.

XXIV. JOHN SCOTT, fourth son of John Scott, tenant in West Deloraine, succeeded his father in the tenancy of Over Deloraine, now called West Deloraine. He was b. April, 1836; m. June, 1871, Jane, dau. of John Thomson, Catslackburn; d. December, 1900, leaving issue:

1. John b. 1872; d. January, 1923.
2. James Thomson, M.B., C.M. (Dinnington, Yorkshire), b. September, 1874.
3. WILLIAM.
4. Andrew Thomson, b. January, 1885, emigrated to Manitoba in 1908; m. July, 1917, his cousin, Jean Thomson, and has a daughter, Eileen May.

XXV. WILLIAM SCOTT, M.R.C.V.S., b. October, 1876, settled at Penrith, Cumberland, 1899; m. March, 1904, Alice Watson, dau. of Joseph McCaig, Galashiels, and has issue:

1. John Deloraine b. November, 1904.
2. William Deloraine b. September, 1914.
1. Jean Deloraine.

Over Kirkhope.

XXIII. HENRY SCOTT, Laird of Over Kirkhope and tenant in Crosslie, and a hatter in Edinburgh, second son of Henry Scott of Over Deloraine, b. c. 1790, m. August, 1820, Isabella Martin, and had by her eight children :

1. Henry b. September, 1830, believed to have d. young.
2. JOHN.
3. William Henry b. July, 1836, m. and went to Canada.
1. Elizabeth m. James Alexander.
2. Agnes m. Matthew Whiting.
3. Isabella m. Mr. Mein, dentist, Edinburgh.
4. Janet. 5. Margaret.

Mr. Henry Scott was, it is believed, in partnership with his cousin, Henry Scott, fifth son of William, tenant in Singlie; he eventually succeeded to the business on his cousin's death. He d. August, 1873.

XXIV. JOHN SCOTT, the second son, b. September, 1832, tenant in Crosslie, m. Miss Aitchison, and had three sons and one dau. He gave up the farm in 1881.

1. Matthew. 2. Henry. 3. William.
1. Mary.

Salynside.

XVII. ANDREW SCOTT of Salynside was one of the Water of Ail Scotts at the Carlisle Raid, and is suggested by Rodono to have been a younger brother of Sir Walter Scott of Whitslaid. He was more probably brother to The Hawk and uncle to Sir Walter.

XVIII. THOMAS SCOTT of Salynside, probably son of Andrew, inherited Whitchauchbrae in 1621 from Walter Scott of Whitchauchbrae, who was a near kinsman and possibly first cousin once removed.

Thomas Scott appears to have had two sons :

    1. WILLIAM, who entered into possession of Salynside, and

    2. Andrew, who entered into possession of Whitchauchbrae, both in their father's lifetime.

Thomas disposed of both properties to Sir William Scott of Harden, and died probably about 1636.

XIX. WILLIAM SCOTT of Salynside is heard of at various times 1636-1643, and apparently had two sons :

    1. James, eldest lawful son of William Scott of Salynside.

    2. Thomas "his brother."

Whitchauchbrae.

XVI. THOMAS SCOTT, second son of Walter Scott of Sinton by his second marriage with Margaret Riddell, may or may not have owned Whitchauchbrae, but there is little doubt that he had a son and heir

XVII. WALTER SCOTT of Whitchauchbrae who d. s.p. 1621, and Whitchauchbrae passed into the possession of Thomas Scott of Salynside.

Mr. Scott of Rodono treats this family exhaustively and raises some difficulties which arise chiefly through his (unfounded, I think) assumption that Whitchauchbrae passed from a Thomas to the above Walter and then back to the same Thomas. I think it more probable that the first Thomas referred to by Rodono was the Thomas eventually of Toderick and the second Thomas the son of Andrew of Salynside.

Harden.

Lord Polwarth ❖

SATCHELLS gives a very clear and concise
account of Harden's pedigree from a younger
son of George, sixth Laird of Sinton, but this does not
reconcile with the few facts referred to under Sinton.
It seems quite possible, however, that the founder of
this family did marry twice and to that extent I have
followed Satchells.

The first Sir William bought Mertoun House about
1650, and this became the principal seat of the family
until it was sold recently.   The second Sir William
parted with Harden to his brother, Sir Gideon, and Sir
Gideon's family owned and lived at Harden, but continued to style themselves " of Highchesters," while
Sir William's descendants lived at Mertoun and continued to use the Harden designation.

This explains the statement frequently seen that the Earl of Tarras succeeded to Harden in 1673, which is quite true, but the Earl's family did not succeed to the designation " of Harden " and the headship of the family till 1710.

XV. WILLIAM SCOTT, second son of Robert Scott of Stirches, obtained in 1535 the lands and barony of Harden, Highchesters, Toderick, Wester Essenside, Burnfoot, and Shielswood from his brother, and is the first Laird of Harden so designated. He m. first a daughter of Chisholm of Chisholm, and by her had an only son,

1. WALTER his successor.

He m. secondly a dau. of Kerr of Fernielee and (as suggested by Satchells' book) widow of Riddell of Riddell, and by her had two sons :

2. *Robert of Burnfoot.*

3. *George of Toderick*

William Scott d. probably at Toderick, February, 1561, and was succeeded by his eldest son,

XVI. WALTER SCOTT of Harden, who probably settled at Harden in his father's lifetime. Burke gives no particulars as to marriage of this Laird, and it is possible (from Satchells) that he m. a Riddell, dau. of his stepmother; he d. about 1563, having had two sons :

1. WALTER his heir.

2. William, called " William in the Mott," living in January, 1591, mentioned as one of the Pensioners in the House of Buccleuch.

XVII. WALTER SCOTT, the elder son, succeeded to Harden in 1563; m. March, 1567, Mary,
called the " Flower of Yarrow," dau. of Philip Scott
of Dryhope, and by her had issue :

1. WILLIAM (Sir) his heir.

2. Walter in Essenside m. April, 1614,
   Elspeth, dau. of John Hay of Haystoun,
   and was killed by Simon Scott of Bonnington in 1620, leaving two daughters,
   Jean and Margaret, served heiresses to
   their father in February, 1641.

3. *Hugh of Deuchar.*

4. *Francis*, who bought Sinton in 1627.

5. *George of Castlesyde ?*

1. Margaret m. Sir Gilbert Elliot of Stobs
   (Gibbie wi' the Gowden Garters).

2. Ester m. Elliot of Falnash and secondly
   George Langlands of that ilk.

3. Janet m. Thomas Scott, who succeeded his
   brother to Whitslaid.

4. Isobel m. James Johnstone of Westerhall.

And three other daughters m. to Geddes of
   Kirkurd, Scott of Tushielaw, and Porteous of Hawkshaw.

Auld Watt m. secondly April, 1598, Margaret, dau.
of John Edgar of Wedderlie, and by her had,

8. Margaret m. first, September, 1621, David
   Pringle, younger of Gala; and secondly
   about 1625 Sir William Makdougall of
   Makerstoun.

Auld Watt d. June, 1631, and was succeeded by

XVIII. SIR WILLIAM SCOTT of Harden.
Sir William, a man in great favour with James VI.,
was knighted in his father's lifetime, and possessed of

considerable estates. He m. July, 1611, Agnes, dau. of Sir Gideon Murray of Elibank, and by her had issue :

1. WILLIAM (Sir).
2. GIDEON (Sir), whose line succeeded to Harden.
3. *Walter of Raeburn.*
4. *James of Thirlestane.*
5. *John of Woll.*
1. Elizabeth m. Sir Andrew Kerr of Greenhead.
2. Margaret m. Thomas Kerr of Mersington.
3. Janet m. John Murray of Philiphaugh.
4. Susannah m. Gideon Ogilvie of Hartwoodmyres.

Sir William m. secondly Margaret, dau. of Kerr of Linton, but d. without further issue in 1655.

XIX. SIR WILLIAM SCOTT of Oakwood and later of Harden, the eldest son, knighted 1660, m. Christian, dau. of Robert, sixth Lord Boyd, and d. February, 1699, having had issue :

1. WILLIAM (Sir).
2. ROBERT of Iliston.
1. Christian m. Wm. Kerr of Chatto.
2. Margaret m. Sir Patrick Scott, Bart., of Ancrum.

XX. SIR WILLIAM SCOTT, the elder son, sixth Laird of Harden, m. Jean, dau. of Sir John Nisbet of Dirleton, but dying without issue August, 1707, the estates passed to his brother,

XX. ROBERT SCOTT, seventh of Harden, who m. Jean, dau. of Sir Thomas Kerr of Fernielee. Robert Scott also d. without issue March, 1710, and the estates devolved on his first cousin, twice removed, Walter Scott, great-grandson of

XIX. SIR GIDEON SCOTT of Highchesters, M.P., second son of the first Sir William of Harden. Sir Gideon m. 1643 Margaret, dau. of Sir Thomas Hamilton of Preston, and had issue :

1. WALTER.
2. William m. Jean, dau. of James Kirkaldy, and d. s.p. before 1710.
3. Thomas d. s.p. before 1710.
4. Gideon d. s.p. before 1710.
5. Francis living in 1710.
1. Agnes m. John Riddell, younger of Riddell.
2. Margaret m. James Corbett.
3. Mary.
4. Agnes m. Sir James Grant, Bart.

Sir Gideon d. 1673. His eldest son,

XX. WALTER SCOTT, Earl of Tarras, b. December, 1644, m. February, 1659, Mary, Countess of Buccleuch, and was in consequence created Earl of Tarras for life. The Countess d. s.p. March, 1661, and the Earl m. secondly Helen, dau. of Thomas Hepburne of Humbie, and by her had issue :

1. GIDEON.
2. William b. January, 1682; d. before 1710 s.p.
3. WALTER of Whitfield, who succeeded his nephew to Harden.
4. Thomas b. March, 1681.
5. Francis b. October, 1691; d. before 1710 s.p.
1. Helen. 2. Elizabeth. 3. Mary.
4. Agnes. 5. Ann. 6. Margaret.

The Earl d. April, 1693, when his life peerage expired. He was succeeded in Harden and Highchesters by his eldest son,

XXI. THE HON. GIDEON SCOTT b. October, 1678; m. Anne, dau. of Sir Francis Kinloch, Bart. She d. s.p. He m. secondly February, 1700, Lady Mary Drummond, dau. of John, Earl of Melfort, and d. 1707, having by her had issue:
1. WALTER. 2. JOHN. 1. Mary.

XXII. WALTER SCOTT, the elder son, succeeded his father in 1707 to the estates of Harden and Highchesters, but continued to be known as " of Highchesters " until the death of his cousin Robert in 1710, when he succeeded to Mertoun and the rest of the family estates and became eighth of Harden. He d. s.p. November, 1719, and was succeeded by his brother.

XXII. JOHN SCOTT, ninth Laird of Harden, m. Lady Jean Erskine, dau. of Alexander, fourth Earl of Kellie, and d. 1734, having had by her:
1. Anne m. Thomas Shairp of Houston.
2. Mary. 3. Lilias.
John Scott, dying without male issue, was succeeded by his uncle,

XXI. THE HON. WALTER SCOTT, tenth of Harden, third son of the Earl of Tarras, b. January, 1682; m. first a dau. of Nisbet of Bewlie; she d. s.p. He m. secondly Agnes, dau. of William Scott of Thirlestane, and by her had issue,
1. Christian.
He m. thirdly, February, 1724, Ann, dau. of John Scott of Gorinberrie, and by her had issue:
1. WALTER.
2. John b. February, 1729; d. young.
3. William b. July, 1730; d. young.
4. *Francis of Beechwood.*
2. Jean. 3. Helen. 4. Ann.
He m. fourthly Christian, dau. of Kerr of Frogdean, but had no issue by her.

XXII. WALTER SCOTT, eleventh of
Harden, b. December, 1724; m. April, 1754, Lady
Diana Hume Campbell, third dau. of Hugh, third
Earl of Marchmount. Lady Diana on the death of
her niece, Anne de Jure, Baroness Polwarth, became
de Jure Baroness Polwarth. Walter Scott d. 1793,
having had issue :

    1. Walter d. young. 2. HUGH.

    1. Anne. 2. Diana.

XXIII. HUGH SCOTT, twelfth of Harden,
M.P., claimed and was allowed the Barony of Polwarth
in 1835. His Lordship was b. April, 1758; assumed
the additional name of Hepburne 1820; m. September,
1795, Harriet Bruhl, dau. of Hans Maurice, Count
Bruhl of Martinskirk, and by her had issue :

    1. Charles Walter b. August, 1796.

    2. HENRY FRANCIS, seventh Baron.

    3. William Hugh (Rev.), Rector of Maiden
        Newton, Dorset, b. May, 1801, m. July,
        1833, Eleanor Sophia, dau. of the Rev.
        Charles Baillie-Hamilton, and d. April,
        1868, having by her had issue :
        (1) William George, Comm. R.N.;
           b. February, 1841; d. July, 1881.
        (1) Diana Alicia m. Lieutenant-
           Colonel John A. Digby.
        (2) Charlotte Elizabeth Sophia m.
           Sir George Hugh Wyndham,
           K.C.M.G., C.B., of Rogate
           Lodge, Petersfield.
        (3) Eleanor Blanche Wilhelmina.
        (4) Harriet Diana.
        (5) Alicia Marie.

    3. George William (Rev.), Rector of Kentis-
        beare, Devon, b. August, 1804; d. s.p.
        June, 1830.

4. Francis b. January, 1806, Barrister-at-Law, M.P. for Roxburghshire 1841-7, and for Berwickshire 1847-63; m. July, 1835, Julia Frances Laura, last surviving child of Rev. Charles Boultbee, and d. March, 1884, having by her had issue:
   (1) Georgina Laura.
   (2) Frances Margaret Julia m. Joseph William Baxendale, D.L.

1. Harriet Diana.
2. Maria Amabel m. Major-General George C. D. Lewis, R.E.
3. Elizabeth Anne m. Colonel Charles Wyndham of Rogate, Sussex, M.P.
4. Anne m. Hon. Charles Baillie, Lord Jerviswood.

His Lordship d. December, 1841, and was succeeded by his eldest son,

XXIV. HENRY FRANCIS HEPBURNE-SCOTT, thirteenth of Harden and seventh Baron Polwarth, M.P. Co. Roxburgh 1826-32, a representative lord 1846-67, Lord-Lieutenant, and Sheriff-Principal of Selkirkshire. He was b. January, 1800, and m. November, 1835, Georgina, dau. of George Baillie of Jerviswood and Mellerstain, and sister of the Earl of Haddington, and by her had issue:

1. WALTER HUGH, eighth Baron.
2. *Henry Robert.*   1. Mary Lilias.
2. Helen Georgina.   3. Katherine.
4. Harriet Francis m. Hon. Henry Baillie-Hamilton.

Lord Polwarth d. August, 1867, and was succeeded by his elder son,

XXV. WALTER HUGH HEPBURNE-SCOTT, fourteenth Laird of Harden and eighth Baron Polwarth, Lord-Lieutenant of Co. Selkirk, J.P. and D.L. Co. Roxburgh, J.P. Berwick; b. November, 1838; m. first, January, 1863, Mary, eldest dau. of George, fifth Earl of Aberdeen, and had issue by her:

1. WALTER GEORGE, ninth and present Baron.
2. Henry James b. April, 1866; m. June, 1893, Elizabeth, dau. of the late T. C. Booth of Warlaby, Northallerton.
3. George, M.A. Camb., M.D., b. May, 1871; m. April, 1895, Annie Mary, dau. of J. C. Smith of Newport-on-Tay.
4. Robert b. May, 1873; m. September, 1915, Eliza Margaret, dau. of David Berry Hart, M.D. of Edinburgh.
5. Charles Francis, Hon. Major Scottish Horse, served in South Africa 1902-3 and in Great War; b. August, 1874; m. January, 1905, Elma, dau. of the late Johnson Driver of Maryton, N.B., and has issue:
      (1) Elma Katherine.
1. Georgina Mary. 2. Lilias.
3. Mary Harriet has Kaisar-i-Hind Medal 1st Class.
4. Grisell Katherine. 5. Katherine Grace.

His Lordship m. secondly, January, 1915, Katherine Grisell, dau. of the late Hon. and Rev. John Baillie, Canon of York, brother of George, tenth Earl of Haddington, and d. July, 1920.

XXVI. WALTER GEORGE HEPBURNE-SCOTT, C.B.E., fifteenth Laird of Harden and ninth Baron Polwarth in Scotland, B.A. Camb., J.P. and D.L. Co. Haddington, D.L. Berwick and Selkirk,

J.P. Roxburgh, Lieutenant-Colonel Terr. Force Reserve, Hon. Colonel of 8th Battalion Royal Scots; b. February, 1864; succeeded his father as ninth Baron 1920; m. November, 1888, Edith Frances, eldest dau. of Sir Thomas Fowell Buxton, third Baronet, G.C.M.G., and has issue:

1. WALTER THOMAS, Master of Polwarth, Captain Lothian and Border Horse Yeomanry; b. April, 1890; m. November, 1914, Elspeth Glencairn, dau. of the Right Rev. Archibald Ean Campbell, D.D., D.C.L., Bishop of Glasgow and Galloway, and Helen Anne, his wife, dau. of eighth Viscount Middleton, and has issue:

   (1) Henry Alexander b. November, 1916.
   (2) Francis Michael b. September, 1920.

2. Alexander Noel, Second-Lieutenant Scots Guards; b. October, 1892; killed in action May, 1915.

3. Patrick John b. April, 1899.

1. Helen Victoria m. George Freeland Barbour.

2. Margaret Mary.   3. Edith Christian.

4. Grizel Frances Katherine.

Arms.—Quarterly: 1st and 4th counter-quartered; quarterly, 1st vert, a lion rampant, arg., for Hume; 2nd arg., three papingoes, two and one, vert, for Pepdie; 3rd gu., three piles engrailed, arg. for Polwarth; 4th arg., a cross engrailed, az., for St. Clair of Hormiston; and over all as a surtout, an escutcheon, az., charged with an orange, ensigned with an imperial crown, all ppr. as a coat of augmentation given by

King William III.; 2nd or, two mullets in chief, and a crescent in base az., for Scott, of Boonraw;* 3rd counter-quartered; quarterly; 1st and 4th gu., on a chevron, arg., a rose betwixt two lioncels combatant, of the first for Hepburne; 2nd and 3rd arg., three bay leaves vert, for Foulis. Crests.—For Scott: A lady richly attired holding in her right hand the sun, in her left a half moon. For Lord Polwarth: A man's heart, out of which issues a dexter arm erect grasping a scimitar all ppr. For Hepburne of Humbie: A horse saddled and bridled, beneath a tree, passant. Mottoes.—For Scott, "Reparabit Cornua Phœbe"; for Polwarth, "True to the end" and "Fides probata coronat," and for Humbie, "Keep Trust." The arms given above and as sketched at the head of this genealogy are Lord Polwarth's official arms, but he is also entitled by descent to the old arms of Scott of Harden, namely, or, on a bend azure an étoile between two crescents of the field, in chief, a rose gules, slipped and leaved ppr. and for crest a stag trippant ppr., attired and unguled, or. Motto, "Pacem Amo." These arms have never been marshalled in Lord Polwarth's coat, but I have ventured to suggest in the frontispiece how they might be marshalled if Lord Polwarth so desired. Seat.—Harden, Roxburghshire. Residence.—Humbie House, Humbie, E. Lothian.

---

*Note.—I have purposely described this coat as "Scott of Boonraw" instead of "Scott of Sinton" as there is apparently no evidence that it was ever used by any Scott of Sinton. This coat is, according to tradition, the coat used by the Buccleuch family before the alliance with Inglis of Murdiestoun and was adopted by the Sinton family circa 1670-1700 subsequent to the disposal of Sinton to the Harden family, on the probably erroneous assumptions that Sinton branched from Buccleuch before the Inglis alliance and that Sinton was the senior male family of Scott next after Buccleuch. As already stated the last Laird of Boonraw gave his arms by deed to Harden as his heir in 1700, passing over several intervening families and these arms were registered and adopted by the Laird of Harden in 1820 in lieu of those he was using, under the advice of Mr. Scott of Abbotsford.

J. C. Hepburne-Scott.

XXV. THE HON. HENRY ROBERT HEPBURNE-SCOTT, second son of Henry Francis, seventh Lord Polwarth, Barrister-at-Law, late Captain East Lothian Yeomanry Cavalry, b. January, 1847; m. April, 1880, Lady Ada Home, dau. of the eleventh Earl of Home. He d. March, 1914, leaving issue :

1. JAMES COSPATRICK.
2. Francis William, Lieutenant R.N., b. August, 1886; d. May, 1915, of wounds received in action.
1. Lucy Georgina.
2. Mary Helen Charlotte m. Reginald George Chetwynd-Talbot, C.B.E., Lieutenant-Colonel R.A.F. and Commander R.N.

XXVI. JAMES COSPATRICK HEP-BURNE-SCOTT b. May, 1882, m. October, 1907, Lady Isobel Alice Adelaide Kerr, dau. of ninth Marquess of Lothian, K.T., and has issue :

1. Michael Henry b. January, 1909.
2. Walter Schomberg b. September, 1910.
3. Francis William b. December, 1915.

Residence.—Broomlands, Kelso.

𝔅eechwood.

XXII. FRANCIS SCOTT of Beechwood,
merchant in India, fourth son of the Hon. Walter
Scott and grandson of the Earl of Tarras, b. February, 1732, m. March, 1776, Mary, dau. of Sir Alexander Don, Bart., of Newton, and by her had issue:

1. Walter b. July, 1777; d. April, 1806.
2. ALEXANDER.
3. Francis b. January, 1783; d. November,
   1785.
4. Charles b. April, 1784; d. in Jamaica
   October, 1805.
5. Hugh b. May, 1786, Major H.E.I.C.S.
   and D.A.G. Madras Army; m. Emma
   Harris; d. Bombay May, 1818, leaving
   issue:
   (1) Francis   Henry,   Lieutenant-
       General, b. October, 1817, m.
       first 1839 Grace Maria Poing-
       destre, and had issue:
       (i) Emily Mary Grace m. 1872
           Lieutenant-Colonel Ambrose
           H. Bircham.
       General Scott m. secondly 1867
       Julia Margaret, widow of J. Mac-
       Andrew.
   (1) Mary Jane Anne, who m. June,
       1849, her cousin the Rev. Robert
       Scott,   afterwards   Dean   of
       Rochester.
6. John   b.   August,   1788,   Lieutenant
   H.E.I.C.S., A.A.G. Madras Army; d. in
   India, June, 1818.

7. William b. April, 1791, Midshipman R.N.; d. February, 1807, on board H.M.S. *Isis*.

1. Mary b. July, 1778, m. Rear Admiral Thomas Folliott Baugh, and had with other issue a dau., Mary Harriet, m. to her cousin, the Rev. Robert Scott.

XXIII. THE REV. ALEXANDER SCOTT, the second son, b. April, 1781, Rector of Bootle, Cumberland, m. June, 1807, Agnes, dau. and co-heiress of Colonel Robert Johnston, Hutton Hall, Berwickshire; d. May, 1834, leaving issue:

1. Francis, Vice-Admiral R.N., A.D.C. to Queen Victoria, b. April, 1808; m. Frances Magdalen Harvey; d. s.p. June, 1875.

2. ROBERT.   1. Catherine Hester.

XXIV. THE VERY REV. ROBERT SCOTT, D.D., Dean of Rochester, b. 1811, m. first 1840 his cousin Mary Harriet, dau. of Rear Admiral Thomas Folliott Baugh, and by her had issue:

1. WALTER FOLLIOTT.

1. Mary Agnes d. unm.

He m. secondly June, 1849, his cousin Mary Jane Anne, dau. of Major Hugh Scott, and by her had issue:

2. Emma Katharine Harriet.

3. Lilias Hester Frances.

XXV. REV. WALTER FOLLIOTT SCOTT b. October, 1844; m. April, 1874, Mary Georgina, dau. of the Rev. and Hon. John Baillie, brother of tenth Earl of Haddington.

Residence.—22 Arundel Road, Eastbourne.

Raeburn.

XIX. WALTER SCOTT, third son of the first Sir William Scott of Harden, m. Anne Isabel, dau. of William Makdougall of Makerstoun, and dying before 1688, had issue:

    1. WILLIAM his heir.
    2. *Walter*, known as " Bearded Wat."
    1. Isabel.
    2. Christian.

XX. WILLIAM SCOTT of Raeburn, the elder son, m. Anne, dau. of Sir John Scott of Ancrum, and had:

    1. WALTER. 2. John d. unm.
    1. Isabel m. to Dr. John Rutherford.

Raeburn d. 6th August, 1699, and his widow m. 1702 John Scott of Sinton.

XXI. WALTER SCOTT of Raeburn m. November, 1703, Anne, third dau. of Hugh Scott of Gala, by whom he had one son, WILLIAM, and two daughters, Isobel and Anne.

Raeburn was, according to the Rev. Charles Rogers' Memoirs, killed by one of the Pringles of Crighton October, 1707, but noted as still alive in a sasine dated July, 1710.

XXII. WILLIAM SCOTT, fourth Laird of Raeburn, b. October, 1704, m. 1743 Jean Elliott, and had with one daughter, Anne, m. to Thomas, second son of Robert Scott of Sandyknowe, an only son,

XXIII. WALTER SCOTT, Esquire, of Raeburn, m. 1772 Jean, third dau. of Robert Scott of Sandyknowe, and by her had:

    1. WILLIAM.
    2. Robert b. November, 1774; d. September, 1837.

3. Hugh of Draycott, Derby, b. December, 1777, m. Sarah, dau. of William Jessop of Butterley Hall, Derbyshire, and d. without issue January, 1852.
4. Walter d. unm. 1802.
5. John, Major 8th Bengal N.C., d. unm. June, 1832.
1. Barbara.

XXIV. WILLIAM SCOTT, Esquire, of Raeburn, b. July, 1773; m. May, 1806, Susan, eldest dau. of Alexander Horsbrugh, and d. April, 1855, having had issue:

1. Walter b. September, 1811; lost in H.M.S. *Acorn* 1828.
2. Alexander b. October, 1813; d. in China 1843.
3. ROBERT. 4. *William Hugh.*
1. Violet. 2. Jane.
3. Susan Elizabeth.
4. Barbara m. to W. F. Owen, Esq.
5. Charlotte.
6. Mary m. to J. B. Cole, Esq.
7. Sarah.
8. Anne Rutherford m. to W. T. Cole, Esq.

XXV. ROBERT SCOTT of Raeburn and Lessudden, the third son, b. 5th November, 1817; m. September, 1861, Louisa, dau. of William Campbell of Ederline, and had issue:

1. WALTER.
1. Matilda Wishart. 2. Susan Horsbrugh.
3. Louisa. 4. Violet Georgina Margaret.

XXVI. WALTER SCOTT, Esquire, now of Raeburn and Lessudden, Co. Roxburgh, b. 11th September, 1866, succeeded his father 1897.

M

Draycott.

XXV. WILLIAM HUGH SCOTT, fourth son of William, sixth Laird of Raeburn, obtained the Draycott estates from his uncle Hugh on the latter's death in 1852; b. July, 1822. He m. Sarah, eldest dau. of Alfred Fellows, Esq., and dying 1906, left issue :

1. HUGH.
2. Francis Haliburton b. May, 1870, Captain late 9th K.O.S.B.
1. Susan Lilias. 2. Cicely Violet.

XXVI. LIEUTENANT-COLONEL HUGH SCOTT, J.P., now of Draycott, b. June, 1865.

Residence.—Draycott House, near Derby.

Baillieknowe.

XX. WALTER SCOTT, second son of the first Laird of Raeburn, b. c. 1653, m. Margaret,* dau. of Campbell of Silvercraigs, by whom he had issue :

1. WALTER. 2. *Robert.* 3. *William.*

1. Mary. 2. Christian. 3. Margaret.

Walter Scott was known as " Beardie " owing to a vow not to shave till Stuarts were restored. He was guardian or tutor to his nephew of Raeburn and cousin of Makerstoun, and resided some time at Oakwood and some time at Makerstoun. He d. in 1729.

XXI. WALTER SCOTT, tenant in Baillieknowe, b. October, 1696 ; m. Janet, dau. of Thomas Inglis, surgeon, and had issue by her :

1. Robert baptized March, 1731.

2. William baptized December, 1732.

1. Mary. 2. Janet.

The above are taken from the Parish Register of Stitchel, and the baptisms are witnessed by Walter's brothers, Robert and William, and by Mr. Thomas Inglis. Nothing is known further of this family except that Sir Walter says they went to America.

---

*Beardie's wife is described in the Parish Register as Margaret, not Jean as stated in some genealogies.

Abbotsford.

Scott of Abbotsford.

XXI. ROBERT SCOTT of Sandyknowe, second son of Walter Scott, tutor to Raeburn, b. November, 1699, realized a considerable fortune. He m. July, 1728, Barbara, dau. of Thomas Haliburton of Newmains, and dying 1775, left by her:

1. WALTER.
2. *Thomas.*
3. Robert of Rosebank b. May, 1739; d. June, 1804.
4. John b. September, 1749, accidentally killed.
1. Janet d. at Kelso unm. 1805.
2. Mary d. December, 1805.
3. Jean m. Walter Scott of Raeburn.
4. Barbara m. Mr. Curle, farmer, Yetbyre.

XXII. WALTER SCOTT, W.S., b. May,
1729; m. April, 1758, Anne, dau. of Dr. John Rutherford, by whom he had issue :

1. Robert b. August, 1760; d. an infant.
2. John b. November, 1761 ; d. an infant.
3. Robert b. June, 1763 ; d. an infant.
4. Walter b. August, 1776; d. an infant.
5. Robert, Captain R.N., b. 1767 ; d. unm.
6. John b. 1768; d. unm. May, 1816.
7. WALTER (Sir) first Baronet.
8. Thomas, W.S., b. 1774; m. December,
   1799, Elizabeth, dau. of David McCulloch
   of Ardwell, and dying in Canada,
   February, 1823, by her had :
     (1) Walter, only nephew of Sir
         Walter Scott, b. June, 1807, a
         Lieutenant of Engineers in the
         E.I.C., and rose to the rank of
         General; he d. March, 1876.
     (1) Jessie m. to Colonel Huxley.
     (2) Anne Rutherford.
     (3) Eliza Charlotte m. 1835 Alex-
         ander Peat, C.B.
9. Daniel b. 1775; d. July, 1806.
1. Anne d. an infant.
2. Jean d. an infant.
3. Anne.

Mr. Scott d. April, 1799.

XXIII. SIR WALTER SCOTT of Abbotsford
b. August, 1771 ; created a Baronet 22nd April, 1820 ;
m. December, 1797, Margaret Charlotte, dau. of Jean
Charpentier of Lyons, and by her had :

1. WALTER (second Baronet).
2. Charles b. December, 1805 ; d. unm. at
   Teheran, October, 1841.

1. Charlotte Sophia m. John Gibson Lockhart, LL.D., Advocate.

2. Anne d. unm. June, 1833.

Sir Walter d. 21st September, 1832, and was succeeded by his eldest son,

XXIV. SIR WALTER SCOTT, second Baronet of Abbotsford, Lieutenant-Colonel 15th Hussars, b. October, 1801; m. February, 1825, Jane, dau. of John Jobson of Lochore, and d. without issue 1847, when the Baronetcy became extinct and the estates devolved on his nephew, Walter Scott Lockhart Scott, son of his sister Charlotte, and on his death, without issue, the estates passed to the second Baronet's niece, Charlotte Harriett Jane Hope Scott, and from her to her daughter, the late Mary Monica Constable-Maxwell-Scott, and from her to her son, Walter Joseph Constable-Maxwell-Scott, the present proprietor.

Arms.—Quarterly: 1st and 4th or, two mullets in chief and a crescent in base azure, within an orle of the last for Scott; 2nd and 3rd or, on a bend azure three mascles of the field, in the sinister chief point an oval buckle erect of the 2nd for Haliburton. Crest.—A female figure richly attired, holding in her right hand the sun, and in her left the moon. Motto.—" Reparabit Cornua Phœbe." Seat.—Abbotsford, Melrose, N.B.

Milsington.

XXII. THOMAS SCOTT, second son of Robert Scott of Sandyknowe and Barbara Haliburton, tenant in Woollee farm, b. January, 1731, m. first Anne, dau. of William Scott of Raeburn, and secondly Miss Rutherford of Knowesouth. He was survived by two sons, James and CHARLES, and two daughters, Mary and Anne. James died in Edinburgh unm. and

XXIII. CHARLES SCOTT succeeded to the estate of Knowesouth which belonged to his mother; he m. Esther, dau. of William Elliot, architect of Kelso, and by her had issue:

1. THOMAS.

2. William, M.D., d. in Edinburgh unm.

3. John m. in Australia.

4. Robert m. in U.S.A.

5. Charles. 6. Walter; both d. abroad.

1. Jane m. Mr. Carmichael, writer in Hawick.

2. Mary.

He parted with Knowesouth, and for some time resided at Nisbet Mill, and later (1831) obtained from the Duke of Buccleuch a lease of the farm of Milsington in which he was succeeded by his eldest son,

XXIV. THOMAS SCOTT, b. August, 1815, m. Marion, dau. of Henry Scott, Stelshaw, and by her had issue:

1. CHARLES, who succeeded in his father's tenancy.
2. James m. in Canada.
3. Henry m. in U.S.A.
4. Thomas of Croftheads, b. April, 1867, m. Elizabeth Minto, and by her had issue :
    (1) Thomas b. December, 1907.
    (1) Elizabeth.
5. A fifth son d.
1. Mary m. John Tullie, Highchesters.

XXV. CHARLES SCOTT, Laird of Milsington, b. September, 1857 ; m. Mary Scott, dau. of John Tullie, farmer, Bowanhill, and has issue:

1. THOMAS b. May, 1899.
2. John Charles b. April, 1903.

Mr. Charles Scott has recently purchased the estate of Milsington from the Duke of Buccleuch.

Easter Muirdean.

XXI. WILLIAM SCOTT, third son of Walter Scott, tutor to Raeburn (Beardie) and Margaret Campbell his wife, b. July, 1705, settled as a tenant farmer at Easter Muirdean near Kelso. He was witness together with his brother, Walter, to the baptism of most of the children of Robert Scott of Sandyknowe. He m. February, 1744, Barbara Macdougal, and by her had issue:

1. Walter baptized August, 1745, a Lieutenant on H.M.S. *Barfleur.*

2. James baptized October, 1746, one of the original settlers in Prince of Wales Island, and grandfather of
    (i) Keith Scott mentioned in Sir Walter Scott's journal.

3. Robert baptized September, 1748; d. in the West Indies.

4. George baptized April, 1752; d. at Linthill, Eyemouth, 1826.

5. William baptized May, 1754; drowned at Calcutta.

1. Mary d. unm.

2. Agnes m. Mr. Stuart in Blyth.

3. Barbara d. unm. at Covenheugh, Ayton, 1849.

It has so far been impossible to trace this family further.

Thirlestane.

Scott-Kerr
of Sunlaws

XIX. JAMES SCOTT of Thirlestane, fourth
son of Sir William Scott of Harden and Agnes
Murray, purchased Thirlestane from Sir Andrew Kerr
of Greenhead in 1661; he m. 1659 Agnes, dau. of
Sir Walter Riddell of that ilk, and by her had issue:

  1. WILLIAM. 2. Walter.

  3. John d. before 1710 s.p.

  4. Gideon.

  1. Mary m. to Gideon Scott of Falnash.

  2. and 3. Two other daughters.

XX. WILLIAM SCOTT, second Laird of
Thirlestane, b. February, 1663, m. Christian Don, and
by her had issue :
    1. ALEXANDER baptized April, 1691.
    2. *Walter* baptized December, 1692.
    3. John baptized January, 1694.
    4. Patrick baptized January, 1695.
    5. Andrew baptized August, 1697.
    6. Gideon baptized June, 1699.
    1. Agnes m. the Hon. Walter Scott of
       Harden.
    2. Christian d. young.
    3. Christian. 4. Isabel.

XXI. ALEXANDER SCOTT, the eldest son,
succeeded his father, and m. 1729 Barbara, dau. of
Henry Kerr of Frogdean, and by her had issue:
    1. WILLIAM KERR.
    2. John Kerr b. 1733.
    3. James Kerr b. 1735.
    4. Charles Kerr b. 1740.
    5. Walter Kerr b. 1742.
    1. Barbara Kerr. 2. Christian Kerr.
    3. Ann Kerr. 4. Rebecca Kerr.
    5. Agnes Kerr. 6. Magdalene Kerr.

XXII. WILLIAM KERR SCOTT-KERR of
Thirlestane m. June, 1762, Elizabeth Graeme of Bal-
gowan, Co. Perth, and had issue:
    1. ALEXANDER. 2. ROBERT.
    1. Elizabeth m. Dr. Maclaurin.
    2. Barbara Christian.
    3. Jesse m. Sir Patrick Thriepland, Bart.
  Mr. William Scott assumed, by Royal licence, the
name and arms of Kerr on succeeding to the entailed
estates of Sunlaws and Chatto. He d. May, 1782, and
was succeeded by

XXIII. ALEXANDER SCOTT-KERR of
Sunlaws and Chatto, who d. unm. in Philadelphia in
1790.

XXIII. ROBERT SCOTT-KERR, Esq., of
Sunlaws succeeded his brother. He m. December,
1806, Elizabeth Bell, dau. of David Fyffe of Drum-
geith, and had issue:
1. WILLIAM.
1. Anne. 2. Elizabeth Graeme.
3. Margaret.
4. Rebecca Agnes m. John Lewis Bayly.
5. Madeline.
Mr. Robert Scott-Kerr d. December, 1831.

XXIV. WILLIAM SCOTT-KERR, Esq., of
Sunlaws, the only son, b. October, 1807, m. first
December, 1837, Hannah Charlotte, dau. and heiress
of Henry Scott of Horsleyhill, widow of Sir John J.
Douglas, Bart., and had issue:
1. Elizabeth Mary Charlotte m. July, 1861,
   Sir James Henry Ramsay, Bart., of Banff.
He m. secondly January, 1855, Frances Louisa,
dau. of Robert Fennessy, Esq., of Wilton Place,
London, and by her had issue:
1. ROBERT.
2. William Murray Thriepland of Fingask
   Castle, Perthshire, b. December, 1867,
   succeeded his father's cousin-german,
   Sir Patrick Murray Thriepland, Bart.;
   m. 1899 Eleanor, dau. of Wyndham
   Lewis, and has issue:
   (1) Patrick Wyndham b. May, 1904.
3. Francis Louis b. June, 1868; m. June,
   1894, Sybil Julia, dau. of Horace Abel
   Cockerell, C.S.I., I.C.S., and has issue:
   (1) William Francis b. September,
       1896.
   (2) Robert John Horace b. October,
       1900; d. February, 1919

2. Frances Edith.
3. Jessie Louisa m. James Hunter, Esq., of Anton's Hill, Berwickshire and Medomsley, Durham.
4. Christian Alice m. 26th July, 1883, James W. Fraser-Tyler of Woodhouselee, Midlothian, W.S., and has issue :
5. Susan m. Mr. D. Robertson.
6. Hyacinthe m. Lord Howard of Glossop.
7. Mary Elizabeth m. August, 1911, Henry J. Stevenson, W.S.

Mr. William Scott-Kerr d. May, 1890.

XXV. BRIG.-GENERAL ROBERT SCOTT-KERR, C.B., C.M.G., D.S.O., M.V.O., now of Chatto and Sunlaws, b. November, 1859.

Arms.—Quarterly : 1st and 4th gu., on a chevron, arg., between in chief a crescent and in base a buck's head erased or, three mullets of the field, a border az., for Kerr; 2nd and 3rd, or, on a bend az. a star of six points between two crescents of the field, in the sinister chief a rose gu. stalked and barbed ppr. surmounted of a martlet gules, for Scott. Crests.—1. Kerr, the sun ppr.; motto over, " Regulier et vigoureux. 2. Scott, a stag trippant, armed with ten tynes ppr.; motto over, " Pacem amo." Seat.—Sunlaws, near Kelso, Co. Roxburgh.

Leith.

THE following is compiled from Major Tancred's "Annals of a Border Club," and from supplementary information supplied by members of the family.

XXI. WALTER SCOTT, second son of William Scott, second Laird of Thirlestane (Roxburghshire) and Christian Don; wine merchant in Leith; baptized December, 1692; m. first Martha, dau. of Cunningham of Balbougie, and by her had a son,

    1. THOMAS.

He m. a second time, and by his second wife had a son and a daughter:

    2. Walter, Surgeon 10th Hussars, who d. in 1765.

    1. Euphemia.

XXII. THOMAS SCOTT, b. 1722, was minister at Cavers and afterwards at South Leith; m. Helen Balfour, and dying in 1790, left issue:

    1. Walter b. May, 1752.

    2. John, Surgeon 10th Light Dragoons; b. May, 1758; d. September, 1791.

    3. THOMAS.

    1. Martha Jane.

XXIII. THOMAS SCOTT, minister of Newton, near Edinburgh; b. April, 1764; m. June, 1795, Mary, dau. of Ellis Martin, merchant in Leith; d. July, 1825, leaving issue:

    1. THOMAS.

    2. Ellis Martin b. March, 1801; d. unm. 1827.

3. Walter, Captain H.E.I.C.S.; b. February,
1803; went to India in 1822 as a cadet,
and took with him letters of introduction
from Sir Walter Scott describing him as
cousin;* d. unm. 1871.
4. John b. 1822; m. 1848 Janet, dau. of
Andrew Park, and dying 1902, left issue:
 (1) Thomas. (2) Andrew.
 (3) John m. Edith Wade, and has
 with two daughters, a son,
 (i) John.
 (4) Walter d. young.
 (1) Mary Christina.
 (2) Janet m. Archibald Struthers,
 Toronto.
 (3) Alice. (4) Harriet.
 (5) Cecilia m. James Murray, M.D.
 (6) Helen Louisa. (7) Adeline.
 (8) Margaret m. Archibald Russell.
1. Eliza. 2. Helen. 3. Mary.
4. Cecilia m. Pillans Scarth, W.S.
5. Harriet Matilda Balfour.
6. Jane Essex.
7. Amelia.

XXIV. THOMAS SCOTT b. June, 1799; m.
1829 Jane, dau. of F. Brodie, W.S.; d. 1883, leaving
issue:
1. Thomas b. 1831; d. unm.
2. Frank.
1. Elizabeth m. Richard Mackenzie.
2. Mary Cecilia.

*Capt. Walter Scott would be a fourth cousin to Sir Walter, but
it appears to have been the custom a hundred years ago to describe
anyone with a common ancestor of five or six generations back as
cousin.

Woll.

Scott-Plummer
of Sunderland Hall

XIX. JOHN SCOTT, fifth son of the first Sir
William Scott of Harden, and founder of this family,
bought Woll in 1660.   He m. Agnes, dau. of Robert
Scott of Harwood, and by her had issue :

1. WALTER, who succeeded his father.

2. John, who m. Margaret Scott, and by her
had issue a dau., Agnes, but d. before
1710 without male issue.

3. and 4. Two other sons d. s.p. (male)
before 1710.

5. *Gideon.*

Mr. Scott of Woll resigned Woll to his son on the
latter's marriage in 1694, and d. about 1707.

XX. WALTER SCOTT of Woll m. 1694 Eliza, dau. of Robert Scott of Horsleyhill, and had four sons and two daughters:

1. WILLIAM.
2. Robert baptized February, 1698.
3. John baptized June, 1702.
4. Walter b. July, 1711.
1. Isobel. 2. Jean.

Mr. Walter Scott of Woll d. in 1744.

XXI. WILLIAM SCOTT of Woll, the eldest son, Advocate and Sheriff of Selkirkshire, m. Jean, eldest dau. of Charles Balfour of Broadmeadows, and dying January, 1785, left issue:

1. CHARLES. 2. Andrew.
3. *John of Midgehope*, W.S.

XXII. CHARLES SCOTT of Woll, the eldest, b. 1744, m. February, 1777, Elizabeth, dau. of Wm. Waugh, and by her had five sons and four daughters:

1. WILLIAM.
2. Andrew d. v.p. and s.p.
3. CHARLES BALFOUR succeeded his nephew, Charles Andrew.
4. JOHN, Colonel H.E.I.C.S., succeeded his nephew Charles in 1839. He m. Clementina Shaw, and had by her:
   (1) Clementina m. to J. Durbin, Esq.
   (2) Elizabeth.
   Mr. Durbin parted with Woll to a Mr. Ainslie, and Mr. Ainslie sold it to Mr. Bell, father of Mr. W. Scott Bell, the present owner, in 1863.
5. Gilbert.
1. Barbara. 2. Jean m. to Colonel Dunsmore.
3. Elizabeth. 4. Janet m. James Grieve.

N

XXIII. WILLIAM SCOTT of Woll, Advocate, the eldest son, m. July, 1815, Alicia, dau. of Richard John Uniacke, and dying January, 1820, left two sons:

1. CHARLES ANDREW.
2. Richard d. young.

XXIV. CHARLES ANDREW SCOTT succeeded his father to Woll, but dying unm. 1838 was succeeded by his uncle.

XXIII. CHARLES BALFOUR SCOTT, W.S., third son of Charles Scott of Woll and Elizabeth Waugh, b. 1782, m. November, 1818, Eliza, dau. of the Rev. Alexander Ker, minister of Stobo, leaving one son and four daughters:

1. CHARLES.
1. Catherine m. to Alexander Munro.
2. Elizabeth. 3. Isabella. 4. Barbara.

Mr. C. B. Scott appears to have held the estate a very short time, and on his death March, 1838, he was succeeded by his son,

XXIV. CHARLES SCOTT of Woll. In the following year Mr. Charles Scott succeeded to the estates of Sunderland Hall through his great-grandmother, Jean Balfour, and in terms of the entail resigned Woll to his uncle, Colonel John Scott, to whom refer back. He assumed the name of Scott-Plummer, and m. in 1857 Sophia, dau. of Joseph Goff of Hale Park, Hants, and had issue:

1. CHARLES HENRY.
2. *Joseph Walter.*
1. Jane Eliza m. Robert Lang.
2. Eliza Sophia m. Colonel Sir Philip Trotter.

Mr. Scott-Plummer d. in 1880, and was succeeded by,

XXV. MAJOR CHARLES HENRY SCOTT-PLUMMER of Middlestead and Sunderland Hall, J.P., b. October, 1859; m. August, 1908, Muriel Grace, dau. of Arthur Henry Johnstone-Douglas, D.L., of Lockerbie, and has issue:

    1. CHARLES ANDREW b. February, 1912.
    2. Walter b. March, 1913.
    1. Caroline.   2. Sophia.

Arms (Arms have never been exemplified, but presumably should be as follows).—1st and 4th az., on a chevron between three lions' heads erased or, guttee de sang, as many martlets of the field, for Plummer; 2nd, or, on a bend azure, an étoile between two crescents of the field, and in chief a rose gules stalked and slipped proper, surmounted by an annulet of the third, for Scott; 3rd gu., on a chevron arg. three mullets of the first, in base a stag's head erased or, for Kerr. Crests. —1. A demi-lion rampant arg. in the dexter paw a sprig vert. 2. A stag armed with ten tines, ppr. Mottoes.—1. " Consulto et Audaciter." 2. " Pacem amo."

Charles H. Scott-Plummer.

XXV. LIEUTENANT-COLONEL JOSEPH WALTER SCOTT-PLUMMER, Commanding 3rd Battalion Argyle and Sutherland Highlanders, b. 1861, m. Dorothy Elizabeth Pocklington Senhouse of Nethershall, and dying 1909, left issue:

    1. CHARLES HUMPHREY.
    2. Gavin Joseph b. April, 1908.

XXVI. CHARLES HUMPHREY SCOTT-PLUMMER b. February, 1905.

Teviot Bank.

Colonel ❖
❖ W.A.Scott C.B

XXII. JOHN SCOTT of Midgehope, W.S., third son of William Scott of Woll and Jean Balfour, acquired the estate of Glenormiston. He m. March, 1782, Beatrice, dau. of Thomas Caverhill, and d. 1803, leaving two sons:

    1. WILLIAM.

    2. James of Ellem. No particulars are available of James Scott's birth, marriage or death, but his widow bought Teviot Bank from her nephew, John Scott, in 1854, and left it to her son,

        (1) William John, who sold Teviot Bank in 1860. William J. Scott m. Terese N. Harris, and d., it is believed, s.p. about 1873.

XXIII. WILLIAM SCOTT of Teviot Bank, W.S., b. 1783, purchased Teviot Bank about 1804; he m. first, September, 1808, Miss Jordon of Edinburgh, by whom he had one son,
1. JOHN.

He m. secondly October, 1816, Margaret, dau. of Dr. Andrew Duncan, Professor of Medicine, of Edinburgh, by whom he had two sons and one daughter :
2. ANDREW JAMES.
3. William Charles b. 1820; d. December, 1871.
1. Agnes Beatrice.

XXIV. JOHN SCOTT of Teviot Bank, also a W.S., b. October, 1809, m. October, 1850, Anne, dau. of Henry Singleton of Belpatrick, and d. July, 1867, s.p. He sold Teviot Bank to his uncle's widow, Mrs. James Scott, in 1854. He wrote an exhaustive treatise on the land-owning Scott families in the fourteenth, fifteenth, and sixteenth centuries which was unfortunately never published.

XXIV. DOCTOR ANDREW JAMES SCOTT, eldest son by the second marriage of William Scott of Teviot Bank, b. 1817, m. 1854 Emma, dau. of General Frederick Blundell, C.B., R.A., and d. 1884, leaving issue :
1. WILLIAM AUGUSTUS.
1. Agnes Louisa.
2. Gertrude Elizabeth.
3. Edith Marion m. C. Clark.
4. Emma Letitia Meliora.

XXV. COLONEL WILLIAM AUGUSTUS SCOTT, C.B., b. 1856.
Residence.—3 Down Street, W.1.
Arms of Colonel William Augustus Scott, C.B., as Scott of Woll, the bend invected.

John Rea Scott.

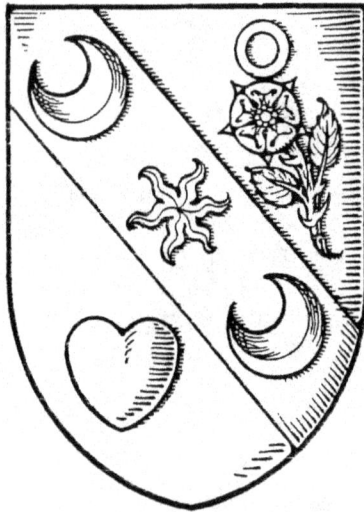

John Rea Scott ❖

XX. GIDEON SCOTT, stated in the records of
the family to be fifth* son of John Scott, first of Woll,
and Agnes Scott, m. 1704 Jean, dau. of William Elliott
of Borthwickbrae by Isobel, dau. of William Scott of
Sinton. This marriage appears to have been a runaway
match, and the couple soon found themselves without
any very definite occupation. The Duke of Buccleuch

---

*There is independent evidence that Gideon was son to John Scott
of Woll but I have been unable to trace the date of his birth or the
existence of brothers beyond those given under Woll.

took pity on them and settled them as tenants in the farm of Ladhope in Yarrow. They had issue :

1. John b. 1706; d. on the coast of Guinea.
2. William, tenant in Kirkhope, b. 1709; m. October, 1761, Margaret, dau. of Robert Scott of Singlie, by whom he had issue :
   (1) Gideon b. December, 1762; d. August, 1841; tenant in Kirkhope and afterwards Laird of Overwells. He left a natural dau., Christian, who d. young.
   (2) Robert b. November, 1769.
   (1) Elizabeth m. Thos. Suter.
3. Walter b. 1712; d. young.
4. Walter b. 1722, m. first Mowbray, secondly Napier, thirdly Williamson.
5. Gideon b. 1724.
6. THOMAS. 7. *Alexander.*
1. Isobel m. James Curle of Moodlaw.
2. Agnes. 3. Betsy.
4. Mary m. John Mair.
5. Anne Jean m. James Pott of Dod.
6. Christian.

XXI. THOMAS SCOTT, sixth son of Gideon in Ladhope; b. December, 1727; m. April, 1768, Ann Douglas, and settled at Morpeth, Northumberland. He left issue :

1. JOHN.
2. William b. May, 1772.
3. George b. November, 1773.
4. Roger b. December, 1776.
1. Dorothy.

Thomas Scott d. at Morpeth June, 1796, and his widow November, 1833, aged 106.

XXII.   JOHN SCOTT, the eldest son, a freeman of Morpeth, b. July, 1770, m. first, October, 1792,
Jane, widow of Thomas Armstrong, by whom he had
one daughter, Eliza, m. to Henry Scott of Whickham,
Durham.   Mrs. Scott d. at Morpeth June, 1822, aged
70, and Mr. Scott m. secondly November, 1822, Jane
Gibb, also of Morpeth, by whom he had issue:

      1. JOHN.   2. *William.*

      3. Henry Thomas b. December, 1833.

      2. Rebecca m. Joseph Lowrey.

Mr. Scott d. at Morpeth July, 1859, and his widow
at Gateshead September, 1871, aged 91 years.

XXIII.   JOHN SCOTT, the eldest son, b. at
Morpeth September, 1823; m. April, 1851, Eliza, dau.
of Peter Fairbairn and granddaughter of William
Fairbairn of Galashiels and Margaret, dau. of John
Scott, younger of Sinton.   He was engaged as a civil
engineer on the Clyde, and d. towards the end of the
nineteenth century, leaving:

      1. JOHN FAIRBAIRN.

      2. Douglas d. unm.

      1. Sarah Fairbairn m. to Edmund Wool-
house of Brixton.

      2. Elizabeth Mary m. to Charles E. H. Rea.

XXIV.   JOHN FAIRBAIRN SCOTT b. May,
1853; m. 1880 Frances Catherine Smith, sister of
Sydney Smith the composer, and by her had issue:

      1. John Fairbairn b. January, 1881; d. June,
1881.

      2. Ronald Oliver Steven b. April, 1882; d.
May, 1882.

      1. Edith Lilian Mary.

Mr. Scott m. secondly Annie Maud, youngest dau. of John Fortune of Belfast, by whom he had two children :

    3. JOHN REA.

    2. Jeanette Fortune.

Mr. Scott was a banker in London, and emigrated to Toronto, where he continued in the same business till his death in September, 1914.

XXV. JOHN REA SCOTT.

Arms.—Or, on a bend azure between in chief a rose gu. leaved and slipped ppr. ensigned of an annulet of the third and in base a heart also gules, an étoile between two crescents of the field. Crest.—A stag trippant ppr. armed with ten tynes and unguled, or, charged on the shoulder with a heart as in the arms. Motto.—" Pacem Amo."

Greenwood.

Keith S. M. Scott ?

XXIII. WILLIAM SCOTT of Killingworth and
later of Crow Hall, Co. Durham, second son of John
Scott and Jane Gibb of Morpeth, b. December, 1825 ;
m. September, 1848, Sarah, dau. of John Rogerson of
Alnwick, and sister of John Rogerson of Croxdale,
Co. Durham, and by her had five sons and five
daughters :

    1. John William b. August, 1853.
    2. JOSEPH ROGERSON.
    3. *Charles Henry.*
    4. Frederick b. April, 1858; d. May, 1859.
    5. Frederick George b. October, 1863, m.
        Minnie, dau. of Matthew Coupland, and
        d. 1922, leaving a daughter Marjory.

1. Mary Jane m. Robert Hedley.

2. Sarah m. Edmond Plotnicki.

3. Louisa.

4. Elizabeth m. Henry Bamber, M.D.

5. Lena m. William Sudbury.

Mrs. Scott d. December, 1866, aged 42, and Mr. Scott m. secondly Ellen, dau. of Waters Richardson, and by her had issue :

6. *Walter Norman.*

7. William Francis b. May, 1873 ; m. Winifred, dau. of George Olerenshaw of Coventry, and has issue,
    (1) Winifred Mary.

6. Ada Violet.

7. Florence Maude.

8. Elizabeth.

Mr. Scott d. October, 1891.

XXIV. JOSEPH ROGERSON SCOTT of Kenton Hall, Northumberland, b. April, 1855; m. March, 1882, Annie, dau. of Richard Latimer, and by her had issue:

1. KEITH STANLEY MALCOLM.

1. Mary m. Captain Alfredo Montaldi.

Mr. Scott d. at Kenton April, 1921, and Mrs. Scott resides with her daughter at Greenwood, Wigton, Cumberland.

XXV. CAPTAIN KEITH STANLEY MALCOLM SCOTT, M.B.E., b. August, 1884 ; m. June, 1910, Rosina Marguerita, dau. of Cavalier V. A. Montaldi of Forest Hall. Captain Scott sold Kenton and purchased Greenwood, a small farm in Cumberland.

Arms (of Mr. Keith Scott).—Quarterly I—IV. The arms of John Rea Scott within a border azure, II—III. Latimer, viz. gules a saltire fleur-de-lysée between four escalops or, crest and motto as John Rea Scott.

Mr. Keith Scott is also entitled to use arms granted to Mr. Jos. R. Scott, viz., or, on a bend azure an étoile between two crescents of the field, on a chief arched of the second, two mullets of the first. Crest.—A female figure vested argent, holding in her dexter hand a crescent and in her sinister hand a mullet, both or. Motto.—" Reparabit Cornua Phœbe." Residence.— 27 Osborne Road, Newcastle-on-Tyne.

The other descendants of William Scott of Crow Hall (with the exception of Charles Henry and Walter Norman and their descendants) also bear the arms of John Rea Scott within a border azure, Marjory Scott charging the border with an annulet and William Francis Scott with a rose, both argent.

Charles Henry Scott.

Lt-Col. C. H. Scott ∴

XXIV. LIEUT.-COL. CHARLES HENRY
SCOTT b. February, 1857, third son of Wm. Scott
and Sarah Rogerson, m. September, 1883, Jane, dau.
of Henry Wilson, and has issue :

    1. CHARLES FREDERICK b. December, 1885.
    2. Wilson b. June, 1890.
    1. Winifred m. Thomas J. Lee.
    2. Gladys m. H. B. Leeson, M.C.
    3. Alice.
    4. Annie m. to Kenneth Jobson, New York.

Arms.—As John Rea Scott, surrounding his arms
with a border invected azure.

Residence.—5 Priors Terrace, Tynemouth.

𝕮𝖆𝖑𝖙𝖊𝖗 𝕹𝖔𝖗𝖒𝖆𝖓 𝕾𝖈𝖔𝖙𝖙.

Walter N. Scott ❖

XXIV. WALTER NORMAN SCOTT b. October, 1871, sixth son of William Scott of Crow Hall, Felling, m. Dora Lydia, dau. of John Robert Carlisle of Newcastle-on-Tyne, and has issue:

    1. WALTER RICHARDSON b. December, 1899.

    2. William Carlisle b. March, 1901.

    1. Dorothy Mary.   2. Mabel Ellen.

Arms.—As John Rea Scott with a border engrailed, azure.

Address.—6 Arlington Street, Hull.

Ladhope.

———

XXI. ALEXANDER SCOTT, seventh son of Gideon Scott in Ladhope and Jean Elliot, succeeded in his father's tenancy; b. May, 1729; m. August, 1782, Christian, dau. of Mr. Scott in Eldinhope, and dying July, 1804, had issue:

1. Gideon b. September, 1783; d. s.p. February, 1844.
2. Walter b. January, 1787; d. s.p. March, 1863.
3. WILLIAM.
4. John, a baker in Edinburgh, b. January, 1795; m. a Miss Buchan of Peebles, and d. s.p.

1. Margaret. 2. Jane.
3. Christian m. John Scott of Over Deloraine.

XXII. WILLIAM SCOTT, the third son, succeeded in the Ladhope tenancy; b. November, 1788; m. 1847 Jean, dau. of Mr. Currie of Howford, and by her had issue:

1. ALEXANDER.
2. Charles William, tweed manufacturer, Galashiels.

1. Henrietta m. Thos. Mitchell of Greengill, Cumberland.

XXIII. ALEXANDER SCOTT, tenant in Ladhope, b. 1847; m. December, 1883, his cousin (once removed) Jane, dau. of Henry Scott of Gilmanscleuch. He took the farm of Whinfell Park, Westmorland, in 1894, and gave up Ladhope in 1897. He has issue :

1. William Henry b. March, 1889; m. February, 1920, Mary Mounsey, Luham, joint tenant in Shap Abbey, Westmorland, with

2. Gideon b. November, 1894.

3. Henry Alexander b. February, 1898.

4. Thomas Mitchell b. August, 1899.

1. Jane Christian.   2. Arbuthnot Sibbald.

Residence.—Whinfell Park, near Penrith.

Gala.

Scott of Gala ∴

XVIII. HUGH SCOTT of Deuchar, third son of Walter Scott, third Laird of Harden, m. Jean, dau. of Sir James Hop-Pringle of Galashiels, March, 1621, and had issue:

1. JAMES his heir.
2. Walter, a Major in the Army.
3. George, progenitor of the Scotts of Auchty-Donald in Aberdeenshire.
4. John, who settled in Italy, where he m. and had issue.
5. David, a surgeon in Edinburgh.
6. Francis, living in 1664.
7. William, living in 1652.

Hugh d. in 1644 or 1645, and was succeeded by his eldest son,

XIX.   JAMES SCOTT, who m. Janet, dau. of
Sir James Murray of Philiphaugh, by whom he had
a son,

XX.   HUGH   SCOTT   of   Gala,   who   m.
Isabella, dau. of Sir Thomas Kerr of Cavers, by
whom he had five sons and three daughters :

1. JAMES (Sir) his heir.
2. Thomas m. April, 1713, Elizabeth Borthwick, and had several children, among
whom
  (1) John, living in 1721.
3. Hugh.
4. Patrick d. young.
5. John, a Colonel in the Guards.
1. Grisel m. John Hop-Pringle of Torsonce.
2. Margaret d. young.
3. Anna m. first 1707 Walter Scott of Raeburn; secondly Henry Makdougall of
Makerstoun, and had issue to both.
She was m. thirdly to —— Home of
Eccles, without issue.

Mr. Scott was succeeded by his eldest son,

XXI.   SIR JAMES SCOTT of Gala, who
m. Euphemia, dau. of Sir William Douglas of Cavers,
by whom he had four sons and two daughters :

1. HUGH his heir.
2. William d. young.
3. John, who was States Doctor at Batavia.
After his return to Scotland he d. without succession anno 1754.
4. Archibald, a Major in the Dutch Service.
1. Catherine.   2. Elizabeth.

Sir James was succeeded by his eldest son,

XXII. HUGH SCOTT of Gala, who m. Elizabeth, dau. of Colonel John Stewart of Stewartfield, by whom he had two sons and eight daughters:

1. James b. September, 1730, who d. young.
2. JOHN b. April, 1732.
1. Elizabeth m. Archibald Douglas of Cavers.
2. Euphemia d. young.
3. Magdalene d. young.
4. Anne.
5. Catherine m. Captain John Douglas of Ederton, a brother of Cavers.
6. Christian b. December, 1737.
7. Isobel d. young.
8. Stewart b. November, 1741.

XXIII. JOHN SCOTT, only surviving son and apparent heir of Hugh of Gala, b. 1732; m. Anne, only dau. of Colonel Sir George Makdougall of Makerstoun; d. 1785, leaving three sons and two daughters:

1. HUGH.
2. George, an Admiral and K.C.B., d. 1841.
3. John d. 1822, leaving three daughters, the eldest of whom, Maria Scott Makdougall, became of Makerstoun.
1. Barbara. 2. Elizabeth.

XXIV. COLONEL HUGH SCOTT of Gala, b. 1764, m. March, 1787, Isabella, dau. of Dr. Munro of Auchenbowie, and d. 1795, leaving an only son,
1. JOHN,

XXV. JOHN SCOTT of Gala, well known as one of Sir Walter Scott's closest personal friends, b. 1790; m. 1820 Madalen, dau. of Sir Archibald Hope, Bart.; d. 1840 leaving issue :

1. HUGH.
2. Archibald (Captain) b. 1827, d. s.p. July, 1870.
1. Elizabeth.   2. Isabella.

XXVI. MAJOR HUGH SCOTT, b. 1822, succeeded to Gala in 1840; m. 1857 Elizabeth Isabella, heiress of Captain Charles Kinnaird Johnstone Gordon, and had issue :

1. JOHN HENRY FRANCIS KINNAIRD.
2. Hugh James Elibank (Scott-Makdougall) late of Makerstoun and heir presumptive to his brother; b. October, 1861; succeeded Miss Scott Makdougall in 1890; assumed the additional name of Makdougall in 1900; m. Agnes, dau. of H. T. Jenkinson of Alverston, and has issue :
   (1) Henry John Alexander b. 1901.
   (1) Barbara Madalen Jean Makdougall m. Sir G. Duckworth-King, Bart.
   (2) Jean Winifred Mary Makdougall m. Philip Frere.
3. Charles Archibald Ramsay, Major South Wales Borderers; b. July, 1863; m. November, 1911, Violet, dau. of J. H. Milligan, and d. 1920.
   1. Madalen Augusta Lavinia m. January, 1896, Lieutenant-General Sir Francis John Davies, K.C.B., K.C.M.G., K.C.V.O., at present Commander-in-Chief Scottish Command.

Mr. Scott d. December, 1877, and was succeeded by his eldest son,

XXVII. JOHN HENRY FRANCIS KINNAIRD SCOTT of Gala, J.P., D.L., b. May, 1859.

Arms.—Quarterly 1st and 4th or, on a bend azure an étoile between two crescents of the field, in the sinister chief point a rose gules stalked and leaved proper for Scott; 2nd and 3rd argent, on a saltire engrailed sable, five escalops or, for Pringle. Crest. —A lady richly attired holding in the dexter hand a rose ppr. Mottoes.—" Prudenter amo "; under the shield, " Sursum." Seat.—Gala House, Galashiels, Co. Selkirk.

Sinton.

Scott of Sinton ❖

XVIII. FRANCIS SCOTT, fourth son of Auld
Watt of Harden and Mary Scott, the " Flower of
Yarrow," m. in 1624 Isabel, dau. of Sir Walter Scott
of Whitslaid, by whom he had :

  1. WILLIAM.

  2. Francis b. February, 1633.

  3. Walter.

  1. Margaret m. William Scott of Tushielaw.

  2. Elspeth. 3. Isabel. 4. Agnes.

  5. Helen. 6. Christian. 7. Grizel.

  Francis Scott bought Sinton in 1627, and d.
between 1646 and 1649.

XIX. WILLIAM SCOTT, the elder son, mentioned in the records of the parish as of Sinton in 1649, m. 14th October, 1647, Jean, dau. of Robert Scott of Headshaw, and by her had:

1. Francis b. June, 1649, presumably d. v.p.
2. William b. April, 1652, presumably d. v.p.
3. JOHN.
1. Grizel.
2. Isobel m. William Elliot of Borthwick-brae.

William Scott d. about 1666-7.

XX. JOHN SCOTT of Sinton, the third son, m. Margaret, dau. of John Murray of Cringletie, and by her had:

1. William b. December, 1688; d. v.p.
2. ALEXANDER b. August, 1690.
1. Jean.
2. Margaret m. her cousin, Wm. Elliot of Borthwickbrae.

John Scott m. secondly, Anne, widow of William Scott of Raeburn, and dau. of Sir John Scott of Ancrum. Mr. Scott d. 1710.

XXI. ALEXANDER SCOTT of Sinton m. 1711 Magdelen, dau. of Sir William Elliot of Stobs, and by her had:

1. JOHN b. 1713.
2. Gilbert b. November, 1717.
3. Alexander b. May, 1719.
1. Elizabeth b. January, 1715.

XXII. JOHN SCOTT, younger of Sinton, m. 1735 Mary, only dau. of Wm. Oliver of Dinlabyre, and left a son Alexander and a dau. Margaret, m. to William Fairbairn,* schoolmaster of Galashiels. John d. v.p.

---

*Uncle to the first Baronet of that name.

XXIII. ALEXANDER SCOTT succeeded his grandfather to Sinton in 1765. He m. Eleanor, dau. of Walter Grieve of Branxholm Park, and by her had:

    1. JOHN.

    1. CATHERINE.   2. Mary.   3. Helen.

XXIV. JOHN SCOTT succeeded his father, but d. without issue, and was succeeded by his sister,

XXIV. CATHERINE SCOTT, who m. 18th March, 1800, John Corse, who took the name of Scott, and this family is represented in the female line by the present Major James Douglas Corse-Scott of Sinton and Satchells.

Arms.—Matriculated by Alexander Scott in 1711, but not rematriculated by the descendants of Catherine Corse-Scott. Or, on a bend azure a star between two crescents of the field, in sinister chief a rose gules barbed and slipped vert, surrounded by a bordure sable. Crest.—A crescent, argent. Motto.—" Crescendo prosim."

————

Castlesyde.

————

XVII. GEORGE SCOTT of Castlesyde, probably a younger son of Walter Scott of Harden, is mentioned in several documents 1592-1629.

XVIII. FRANCIS SCOTT of Castlesyde, probably George's son, succeeded some time between 1629 and 1636.

Burnfoot (In Ail).

FOUR generations of this genealogy (XVII to XX) are authentic and deserve a place in this book. Satchells states that

XVI. ROBERT SCOTT, eldest son by the second marriage of the first Laird of Harden with Riddell's widow, was the ancestor of this family, and although there is no evidence in support of this there is, as far as I know, no evidence against it, and this Robert may quite possibly have been father of

XVII. WILLIAM SCOTT of Burnfoot in Ail, who witnessed the service of Walter Scott of Stirches as heir to his father in May, 1592, and who was doubtless the Laird who was at the Carlisle Raid. William must have died about 1622 and been succeeded by his eldest son,

XVIII. WALTER SCOTT of Burnfoot.

XIX. ROBERT SCOTT of Burnfoot was served heir to his father, Walter, in September, 1641, but it is not clear at what date Walter died. Robert had at least two sons :

1. WALTER his heir.
2. Francis, to whom Satchells addresses one of his dedications.

XX. WALTER SCOTT of Burnfoot succeeded sometime before 1669, and was Laird in 1686, at which time he was also the recipient of an address from Satchells.

Toderick.

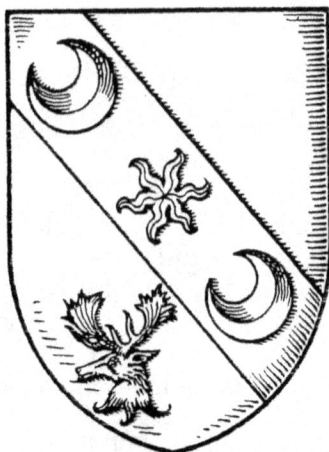

Scott of Todderick
∴   circa 1622

I AM aware that Satchells' statement that a Scott of Toderick was one of the first cadets of Harden, is not given general credence, and certainly some of his pedigrees are so at variance with facts that his whole book must be accepted with reserve, but in this case there is some supporting evidence that the Scott of Toderick, who signed the clan bond, was not of the same family as the Scotts of Toderick, cadets of Whitslaid.

Dr. William Scott, descended from the later Toderick family, in his pedigree of Scott of Stokoe mentions that in 1783 he copied the above arms cut in wood in the Toderick seat in the Kirk at Ashkirk, the arms being dated 1622, whereas the arms given in Nisbet's Heraldry for Toderick descended from Whitslaid are as given in the appropriate place in this book.

XVI. GEORGE SCOTT, third son of William Scott, first Laird of Harden, succeeded to Toderick on the latter's death in 1561. George Scott d. before 1580, and was succeeded by

XVII. WALTER SCOTT of Toderick, who was in all probability his son. This Walter signed the clan bond, and was at the Carlisle Raid.

XVIII. WILLIAM SCOTT, his heir apparent, m. Isabella Livingston, and had a son,

XIX. WALTER SCOTT, b. about 1629, but it is clear that during his father's lifetime his grandfather sold the property to Thomas, brother to Sir Walter Scott of Whitslaid.

Part III.

Balweary.

Scott of Balweary

[112] III. SIR MICHAEL SCOTT, a man of property and power in the County of Fife, flourished in the reign of King William, who succeeded to the crown of Scotland anno 1165.

He m. Margaret, dau. of Duncan Syras of that ilk, by whom he had a son,

    1. DUNCAN his heir.

IV. DUNCAN SCOTT confirmed his father's donation to the monastery of Dunfermline, which was also confirmed by King Alexander II. anno regni 17, i.e., 1231. Duncan had two sons:

    1. SIR MICHAEL his heir.
    2. Gilbert, who is witness in a charter of Alexander, Earl of Buchan, anno 1236.

He was succeeded by his elder son,

V. SIR MICHAEL SCOTT, who had the honour of knighthood conferred upon him by King Alexander II., and was one of the assize. Sir Michael m. the dau. and sole heiress of Sir Richard Balweary, with whom he got the lands and barony of Balweary in the County of Fife, which became the chief title of his family. By her he had a son,

VI. SIR MICHAEL SCOTT* of Balweary, who succeeded him, and was second Baron of Balweary of the name of Scott. Upon the death of his father-in-law, he succeeded to all the possessions of the ancient family of the Balwearys of that ilk. This Sir Michael was a man of extraordinary parts, and made a great figure in his time. Sir Michael of Balweary, with most of the nobility and gentry of Scotland, was compelled to submit to King Edward I. of England anno 1296. He left issue two sons:

    1. SIR HENRY his heir.
    2. Duncan, who was proprietor of lands in Forfarshire, and was also forced to swear allegiance to King Edward I. of England for his lands lying in that county anno 1304. He was progenitor of the Scotts in the North.

Sir Michael d. about the year 1300, and was succeeded by his eldest son,

VII. SIR HENRY SCOTT of Balweary, who was also compelled to submit to King Edward, according to these words in Rymer's collections, dominus Henricus Scott de Fife, miles, fecit homagium Edwardo I. anno 1304.

He d. in the beginning of the reign of King David Bruce, and left issue a son and successor,

---

*In spite of opinion expressed, I believe, by Sir Walter Scott of Abbotsford that this Michael was "The Wizard," I think this is more than doubtful.

VIII. SIR ANDREW SCOTT of Balweary, a great patriot, and always ready to fight in defence of the liberties of his country, but at last lost his life at the taking of Berwick by the Scots anno 1355, leaving issue an infant son,

IX. SIR WILLIAM SCOTT of Balweary, who succeeded him, and got a charter of confirmation from John, Abbot of Dunfermline, domino Willelmo Scot de Balweary, de terris de Balweary, dated 13th June, 1393.

He d. in the end of the reign of King Robert III., and was succeeded by his son,

X. SIR MICHAEL SCOTT of Balweary, who, by an authentic writ still preserved, disposed of the lands of Cambrune and its mill to Sir John Wemyss of that ilk.

Sir Michael was one of the hostages for King James I.'s ransom anno 1424. He left issue a son and a dau.:

    1. SIR WILLIAM.
    1. Margaret m. Sir John Melville of Raith.

He d. in the reign of King James II., and was succeeded by his son,

XI. SIR WILLIAM SCOTT of Balweary, who m. Isabel, dau. of Sir John Moncrief of that ilk. He left issue two sons and one daughter:

    1. SIR WILLIAM.
    2. Alexander of Fingask, who, in a charter under the great seal, is designed frater germanus Willelmi Scott de Balweary, militas, dated 10th April, 1513; but we can give no account of his posterity.
    1. Euphame m. Sir John Arnot of that ilk.

Sir William was succeeded by his eldest son,

XII. SIR WILLIAM SCOTT of Balweary, who m. Janet, dau. of Thomas Lundy of that ilk.

He accompanied King James IV. to the fatal field of Flodden anno 1513, where he was taken prisoner, which obliged him to sell several of his lands to purchase his redemption. By the said Janet Lundy he had two sons:

    1. SIR WILLIAM.

    2. Thomas, who got a charter under the great seal.

He was succeeded by his elder son,

XIII. SIR WILLIAM SCOTT, who, in his father's lifetime, was put in possession of the lands and barony of Innertiel, and was long designed of that title. He m. Isabel, dau. of Patrick, fourth Lord Lindsay of Byres. By the said Isabel Lindsay he had two sons and one daughter:

    1. SIR WILLIAM.

    2. *Andrew*, progenitor of the Scots of Ancrum.

    1. Catherine m. Laurence Mercer of Aldie.

He was succeeded by his elder son,

XIV. SIR WILLIAM SCOTT of Balweary, who, in his father's lifetime, was also designed of the title of Innertiel. He m. Helen, dau. of Sir William Lauder of Hatton. By the said Helen Lauder he had two sons:

    1. Michael, who, in a charter under the great seal, is designed Michael Scott filius senior, et haeres apparens domini Willelmi Scot de Balweary anno 1540; but he d. before his father unm.

    2. SIR WILLIAM.

XV.   SIR WILLIAM SCOTT of Balweary, son
of Sir William, m. Janet, dau. of —— Lindsay of
Dowhill, by whom he had two sons :

    1. JAMES.

    2. Robert, of whom there is no succession.

He was succeeded by his eldest son,

XVI.   SIR JAMES SCOTT of Balweary, who
had the honour of knighthood conferred upon him by
King James VI. at the solemnity of Queen Anne's
coronation anno 1590.

He m. Elizabeth, dau. of Sir Andrew Wardlaw of
Torrie, by whom he had two sons and one daughter :

    1. WILLIAM.

    2. *James*, ancestor of the Scotts of Logie,
       Dunninald, etc., etc.

    1. Janet was m. to Sir John Boswell of
       Balmuto, and had issue.

XVII.   WILLIAM SCOTT, eldest son and
apparent heir of Sir James Scott of Balweary, lived
in the reigns of King James VI. and King Charles I.
Whether William or his father, Sir James, d. first we
cannot ascertain, but

XVIII.   COLONEL WALTER SCOTT of
Balweary succeeded, and was grandson of Sir James.
He betook himself to a military life and rose to the rank
of Colonel, but never married.   He d. in Flanders in
the reign of Charles II., and in him ended the line of
Scotts designed of Balweary.

Arms.—Argent, three lions' heads erased gules.

P

Logie.

Scott of Logie   ❖

XVII. JAMES SCOTT, second son of Sir
James Scott of Balweary and Elizabeth Wardlaw,
purchased Logie, near Montrose. He m. Katherine,
dau. of Orick of Orick, and left a son,

XVIII. JAMES SCOTT of Logie, b. 1593; m.
Margaret Ramsay of Balmain, by whom he had a son,
   1. JAMES.
And marrying secondly Jean Tailyour of Borrowfield,
had five sons and four daughters:
   2. Robert b. 1620. *3. Hercules.*
   4. Patrick of Craig. 5. John.
   6. David of Hedderweek registered arms.

XIX. JAMES SCOTT, the eldest son, b. 1619, m. Margaret Leighton of Montrose, by whom he had a son,

XX. JAMES SCOTT of Logie, who m. 1670 Agnes, dau. of Sir Alexander Falconer, Bart. James left three sons:

    1. JAMES.   2. ALEXANDER.   3. David.

XXI. JAMES SCOTT of Logie, b. 1671, m. Isabella, dau. of Sir Alexander Bannerman, and had issue:

    1. James d. s.p. 1769.
    2. Alexander d. unm.
    3. JOHN succeeded to Logie.
    1. Margaret m. Alexander Mill of Halter, and their son, Robert Hill, succeeded to Logie upon the demise of his uncle John.

XXI. ALEXANDER SCOTT of Baldwie, second son of James Scott and Agnes Falconer, m. Elizabeth Oughterloney, and had, with two daughters, four sons, of whom JOHN, the youngest, alone left issue.

XXII. JOHN SCOTT, b. 1704, m. Margaret Wood, and by her had:

    1. Alexander m. Miss J. Stratton, and d. at Montreal, leaving:
        (1) John d. s.p.
        (1) Jessie.
    2. WILLIAM.
    1. Margaret.

XXIII. WILLIAM SCOTT, the second son, m. 1779 his distant cousin, Janet, dau. of Robert Scott of Dunninald, and by her had issue :

    1. William drowned at sea.

    2. DAVID.

    1. Louisa.

    2. Alexandrina, b. 1786, m. April, 1810, Rev. John Dodgson; d. 1839; had a dau. Louisa, who m. first Robt. Webster, secondly Rev. W. Quekett.

XXIV. DAVID SCOTT, b. 1790, m. 1825 Mary Anne, dau. of William Crawford, M.P., and had issue :

    1. William Henry.   2. David Michael.

Arms.—Argent, a fesse embattled between three lions' heads erased, gules.

Brotherton.

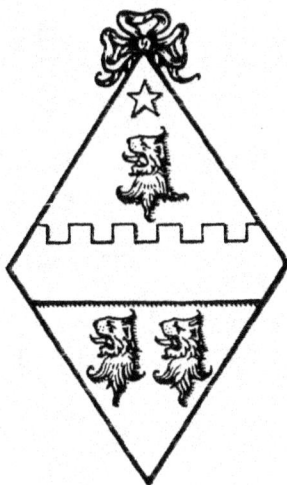

Scott of Brotherton

XIX. HERCULES SCOTT, third son of
James Scott, second of Logie by his second wife,
Jean Tailyour, b. 1621, m. Jane, dau. of Sir James
Oliver of New Grange, and had:

    1. HERCULES.

    2. James of Cornieston, a General in the
       Army.

and five daughters. The elder son,

XX.   HERCULES SCOTT of Brotherton, b. 1659, m. 1707 Helen, dau. of Sir Charles Ramsay, Bart., of Balmain, and d. 1747, leaving issue two sons and six daughters :

1. JAMES.   2. DAVID.
1. Elizabeth m. James Mill of Old Montrose.
2. Jean.   3. Margaret.   4. Helen.
5. Mary.   6. Katherine.

XXI.   JAMES SCOTT of Brotherton, the elder son, b. 1719, d. s.p. 1804.

XXI.   DAVID SCOTT, the second son of Hercules Scott and Helen Ramsay, b. 1725, m. 1774 Wallace, dau. of Archibald Scott of Rossie, and d. 1797, leaving issue with one daughter Helen, four sons :

1. HERCULES, who succeeded to Brotherton.
2. JAMES, who succeeded his brother.
3. Archibald, b. 1779, m. 1824 Anna Maria, dau. of Robert Tulloch, Esq., of Elliston, Roxburghshire; d. 1834, leaving an only son,
    (1) James Robert of Stone o' Morphie.
4. DAVID, who succeeded his brother James to Brotherton.

XXII.   COLONEL HERCULES SCOTT of Brotherton, killed in action Canada 1814, and was succeeded by his brother,

XXII.   JAMES SCOTT of Brotherton, b. 1776, d. 22nd September, 1844, and was succeeded by his brother,

XXII. DAVID SCOTT, Esq., of Brotherton,
J.P. and D.L.; b. 16th June, 1782; m. 15th February,
1813, Mary, dau. of William Seddon, Esq., of Acres
Barn, Co. Lancaster, and by her had issue:

    1. HERCULES.
        1. Wallace Mary m. 1846 Rev. Walter
           Butter.
        2. Helen m. Alexander Porteous.
        3. Isabella.
        4. Penelope Eliza m. Edward W. Dickson.
        5. Emily Augusta m. Joseph St. John Yates.
        6. Flora Alicia m. Rev. Edmund Lane.
        7. Anna Maria m. Captain George S.
           Taylor, R.N.
        8. Diana Octavia m. James Farquhar.
Mr. Scott d. 18th December, 1859.

XXIII. MAJOR HERCULES SCOTT of
Brotherton, J.P. and D.L., b. 14th June, 1823, m.
1847 Anna, dau. of James Moon of Hillside House,
Liverpool, and d. May, 1897, having had issue:

    1. Hercules James b. 1850; d. 1869.
    2. Edward Uchtred b. 1857; d. 1869.
    1. Mary Isabella.   2. Helen.
    3. ANNA KATHERINE, now of Brotherton.
    4. Margaret Rose de Noel.

XXIV. ANNA KATHERINE SCOTT, now
of Brotherton.

Arms.—On a lozenge argent, a fesse embattled
between three lions' heads erased, gu.; a mullet in
chief for difference.

Dunninald.

Scott of Dunninald

XIX. PATRICK SCOTT of Craig, fourth son of James Scott of Logie and Jean Tailyour, his second wife, b. 1623, m. a dau. of David Beattie, Provost of Montrose, and dying in 1690, was succeeded by his son,

XX. PATRICK SCOTT of Rossie, and after the decease of his brothers, of Dunninald and Usan, he m. Margaret, dau. of Sir Archibald Hope, Bart., of Rankeillor (grandson of the famous Sir Thomas Hope, King's Advocate for Scotland, in the reign of Charles II.), and had two sons : Archibald, who d. in 1770, ancestor of Scott of Montrose, and

XXI. ROBERT SCOTT of Dunninald, Advocate, M.P., b. 1705. He represented the Co. of Angus 1732-4, and was a staunch adherent of the house of

Hanover during the rebellion of 1745-6. He m.
1740 Anne, dau. of Brigadier-General John Middleton
of Seaton in Aberdeenshire, and d. December, 1780,
leaving issue :

  1. Archibald m. first Elizabeth Renny,
heiress of Usan, and by her had issue :
    (1) Elizabeth.
    (2) Mary m. John Graham of Esk-
bank.

He m. secondly Margaret Chalmers of
Aberdeen, and by her had two sons:
    (1) Robert d. in London, 1844,
leaving two daughters, one of
whom Isabella Mary m. J. T.
Quekett.
    (2) David b. 1786; of the E.I.S.; d.
s.p. 1831.

Archibald Scott d. 1795.

  2. DAVID.

  1. Diana m. May, 1770, Alexander Shank of
Castlerig.

  2. Janet m. William Scott of Logie.

The younger son,

XXII. DAVID SCOTT of Dunninald, M.P.
for the Co. of Angus and Perth District of Burghs,
Member of Council Bombay, Chairman Hon. E.I.C.;
m. Louisa, widow of Benjamin Jervis and dau. and
co-heiress of William Delagard. She d. March, 1803,
leaving issue :

  1. DAVID.

  1. Diana m. Sir Josias Henry Stracey, Bart.

  2. Louisa m. Major-General Salmond of
Waterfoot.

  3. Amelia Sibbald d. unm. May, 1829.

Mr. Scott d. at Cheltenham, October, 1805. His
brother-in-law,

SIR JAMES SIBBALD, first Baronet of Sil-
wood Park, Berks., son of James Sibbald of London,
was created a baronet 13th December, 1806, with
remainder, in default of male issue, to the nephew
of his wife. He m. May, 1772, Elizabeth, dau. and
co-heiress of William Delagard. She d. April, 1809.
He d. s.p. September, 1819, when the only son and
heir of Mr. David Scott succeeded as

XXIII. SIR DAVID SCOTT, second Baronet
of Dunninald; b. July, 1782; m. March, 1807, Caroline, dau. and co-heiress of Benjamin Grindall, a
lineal descendant of Edmund Grindall, Archbishop
of Canterbury, temp. Queen Elizabeth. By her (who
d. January, 1870) he had issue:
1. JAMES SIBBALD DAVID (third Baronet).
2. Montagu David, M.A. Oxford, Barrister-
at-Law, M.P. for East Sussex 1874-85,
J.P. and D.L. for Sussex, Middlesex,
and Westminster; b. March, 1818; m.
February, 1848, Margaret, only dau. of
James Briggs of Oaklands, Herts.; d.
January, 1900, having by her had a dau.,
(1) Mabel Montagu m. November,
1870, Sir Home Seton Gordon,
eleventh Baronet of Embo.
1. Caroline Louisa m. William James Maxwell.
2. Charlotte Agnes Maria.
3. Ellen Annette.
Sir David was Knight of the Guelphic Hanoverian
Order and M.P. for Yarmouth. He d. June, 1851,
and was succeeded by his eldest son,

XXIV. SIR JAMES SIBBALD DAVID
SCOTT, third Baronet, F.A.S., J.P. and D.L.; b.
June, 1814; m. November, 1844, Harriet Anne, only

dau. of Henry Shank of Castlerig and Gleniston, Co. Fife, and by her had issue :

1. Michael David Sibbald, Lieutenant Royal Aberdeenshire Highlanders Militia; b. December, 1849; d. February, 1884.
2. FRANCIS DAVID SIBBALD (fourth Baronet).
3. Sibbald David Sibbald b. September, 1854; d. May, 1881.
1. Henrietta Caroline Sibbald.
2. Florence Louisa Sibbald m. May, 1873, Lieutenant-Colonel Banks Robinson Greig, late R.A., of the Elms, Biggleswade.
3. Maria Cecilia Sibbald.
4. Lilian Edith Sibbald.

Sir James was formerly a Captain in the Royal Sussex Light Infantry. He d. June, 1885.

XXV. SIR FRANCIS DAVID SIBBALD SCOTT, fourth Baronet, J.P. Co. Berks, Lieutenant R.N. (retired); b. March, 1851; m. November, 1878, Jane Catharine, only surviving dau. of A. A. Pearson of Luce, Co. Dumfries; d. August, 1906, having by her (who d. August, 1918) had issue :

1. FRANCIS MONTAGU SIBBALD, fifth and present Baronet.
1. Ethel Harriet Sibbald m. J. W. Maxwell Johnstone of Melfort, Ceylon.
2. Florence Octavia Sibbald m. William Parkinson Singleton of The Elms, Colwall, near Malvern.
3. Beatrice Ellen Cecilia Sibbald m. Major David Guy Porteous, 90th Punjabis.
4. Constance Mary Sibbald d. young.
5. Evelyn Jane Sibbald m. Maurice Cecil Forsyth Grant, M.C., of Ecclesgreig, Kincardineshire, Captain 9th Seaforth Highlanders.

XXVI. SIR FRANCIS MONTAGU SIB-
BALD SCOTT, fifth Baronet of Dunninald, late
Lieutenant 3rd Battalion Royal Scots Lothian Regiment; b. July, 1885; m. February, 1915, Gladys,
youngest dau. of Captain Thomas Francis Rolt, Coldstream Guards, and widow of the late H. F. Taylor of
Chester, and has issue:

> 1. Elizabeth Catherine Sibbald b. January,
> 1919.

Arms.—Quarterly: 1st and 4th, arg., a fesse
embattled counter embattled between three lions'
heads erased gu.; 2nd and 3rd, gu., on a chevron arg.,
three mullets sa. Crests.—A lion's head erased gu.
Mottoes.—1. " Spe vires augentur." 2. " Tace aut
face." Residence.—7 Hatherly Road, Cheltenham.

Ancrum.

Scott of Ancrum

XIV. ANDREW SCOTT, second son of Sir William of Balweary and Isabel, dau. of Patrick, fifth Lord Lindsay of Byres, got from his father lands in Perthshire, with this express provision, that after the death of this Andrew, these lands should return to the family of Balweary.

He lived in the reign of Queen Mary, was a man of prudence and economy, and acquired the lands of Kirkstile, in the parish of Kinfauns in Perthshire, which became the title of his family. He m. Euphame, dau. of Thomas Blair of Balthycock, by whom he had a son,

XV. ALEXANDER SCOTT of Kirkstyle, who m. Margaret, dau. of Sir Patrick Ogilvie of Inchmartin, by whom he had a son and successor,

XVI. GEORGE SCOTT of Kirkstyle, who m. Catherine, dau. of Hugh Montcrief of Rind, by whom he had a son,

XVII. PATRICK SCOTT, who succeeded him. He lived in the reign of King James VI. and was a man of great application to business. He sold his lands of Kirkstyle in Perthshire, and purchased those of Langshaw in the south country. He afterwards acquired the lands and barony of Ancrum in Roxburghshire, which has since been the chief title of his family. He m. first Elizabeth, dau. of Simson of Monturpie, by whom he had three sons and one daughter :

     1. JOHN his heir.
     1. James d. s.p.
     3. Francis d. s.p.
     1. Agnes m. William Douglas of Ardit, and was mother of the late Sir Robert Douglas of Glenbervie, Bart.

He m. secondly Cicely, dau. of Sir Robert Drury of Rugham in the Kingdom of England, widow of Doctor George Douglas, grandfather of the said Robert Douglas of Glenbervie, and by her he had a dau. Cicely m. Charles Kerr of Abbotrule, by whom she had a dau. m. to John Scott of Gorinberrie. He d. in the reign of King Charles I., and was succeeded by his son,

XVIII. SIR JOHN SCOTT of Ancrum, who got a charter under the great seal of the lands and barony of Ancrum, etc., etc., dated anno 1670. He was by King Charles II. created a Baronet by his royal patent to him and his heirs male, dated anno 1671.

He m. first Elizabeth, dau. of Francis Scott of Mangerton, by whom he had five sons and five daughters:

1. PATRICK his heir.
2. Charles of Palace Hill, who m. Margaret, sister of John, fifth Lord Rutherford, and had several children, including John Scott of Belford, who m. Marion, dau. of A. Baillie of Ashiestiel, and had one dau., Agnes.
3. John, who, being bred a merchant, settled in New York, where he m. and had a numerous issue.
4. Andrew, also bred a merchant, but without surviving issue.
5. William, bred to the law and an advocate, also without succession.

1. Elizabeth m. Sir William Elliot, second Baronet of Stobs, without issue.
2. Anne m. first William Scott of Raeburn; secondly 1702 John Scott of Sinton, and had issue to the former.
3. Cicely m. Wm. Ainslie of Blackhill, and had issue.
4. Jean m. John Murray of Bowhill.
5. Elizabeth m. John Erskine of Shielfield, and had issue.

Sir John m. secondly Elizabeth, dau. of Sir William Bennet of Grubbet, by whom he had two daughters:

6. Margaret m. first Thomas Scott of Whitslaid; secondly Sir David Murray of Stenhope, and had issue to both.
7. Christian m. Sir Thomas Calder of Muirton, Bart., and had issue.

He m. thirdly April, 1708, Barbara, dau. of Walter Ker of Littledean, by whom he had no issue. He d. anno 1712, and was succeeded by his eldest son,

XIX. SIR PATRICK SCOTT, Knight and second Baronet of Ancrum, Advocate 1676, M.P. Roxburghshire 1685-93, a man of great knowledge, singular honour and integrity. He m. first Anne, dau. of William Wallace of Helington, with whom he got a considerable fortune, but by her had no surviving issue.

He m. secondly Margaret, dau. of Sir William Scott of Harden, by whom he had two sons and four daughters :

1. JOHN his heir.

2. William, who was bred to the law and an advocate before the Court of Session. He m. first Anne, dau. of Captain Benjamin Barton; secondly Elisabeth, dau. of William Ainslie of Blackhill, but had no issue by either.

1. Christian m. John Pringle of Whitebank, and had issue.

2. Elizabeth m. George Douglas of Friarshaw, and had issue.

3. Anna.

4. Jean m. David Muirhead of Linhouse, and had issue.

5. Margaret d. unm.

He d. anno 1734, and was succeeded by his eldest son,

XX. SIR JOHN SCOTT, third Baronet of Ancrum, who m. Christian, dau. of William Nisbet of

Dirleton, by whom he had four sons and one daughter:

1. Patrick, who was an officer in the Army, but d. unm. September, 1742.

2. WILLIAM, who became his father's heir.

3. John baptized May, 1729, who, in right of his mother, succeeded to the estate of Craigintinnie, and m. December, 1756, Margaret, dau. of Chambres Lewis, Esq., Collector of His Majesty's customs at Leith, by whom he had issue a son, JOHN, who succeeded his uncle.

4. Walter baptized November, 1733; no succession.

1. Christian baptized October, 1730; d. October, 1788.

He d. anno 1748, and was succeeded by his son,

XXI. SIR WILLIAM SCOTT, fourth Baronet of Ancrum, d. s.p. June, 1769.

XXII. SIR JOHN SCOTT of Craigintinnie, b. 1757, succeeded his uncle; m. July, 1792, Harriet, dau. of William Graham of Gartmore, and by her had issue two sons, SIR JOHN, who succeeded him, and SIR WILLIAM, who succeeded his brother, and four daughters.

XXIII. SIR JOHN SCOTT, sixth Baronet, succeeded his father in 1812 at the age of 14, but was drowned in the Mediterranean when serving as Midshipman on H.M.S. *Rhine*.

XXIII. SIR WILLIAM SCOTT, seventh
Baronet of Ancrum, b. July, 1803, m. 1828 Elizabeth,
dau. of David Anderson, Esq., of Balgay in Forfar, by
whom he had:

    1. WILLIAM.

    2. John, Captain in the Army; d. unm.
       February, 1859.

    3. Harry Warren b. August, 1833, m. Cecilia
       Louisa, dau. of —— Burnaby, Esq., and
       widow of the Rev. Charles Cavendish
       Bentinck; d. s.p. 1889.

    4. Arthur d. unm. November, 1874.

    1. Elizabeth m. April, 1871, Lieutenant-
       Colonel Charles Lennox Tredcroft.

    2. Harriet m. May, 1879, Colonel Dulier,
       C.B.

    3. Louisa m. February, 1871, Sir Robert
       William Duff, P.C., K.C.M.G., Governor
       of New South Wales.

XXIV. SIR WILLIAM MONTEATH-
SCOTT of Ancrum, b. 1829, m. January, 1861,
Amelia, dau. of Sir Thomas Monteath Douglas,
K.C.B., and dying May, 1902, left one dau.,

XXV. CONSTANCE EMILY MONTEATH-
SCOTT, now of Ancrum.

Arms.—On a lozenge argent three lions' heads
erased gu., a mullet for difference.

Part IV.

___

Arkleton.

Scott-Elliot ❖
❖ of Arkleton

THE earliest record we have of this family in the male line is

WALTER SCOTT, who purchased Bonchester in 1632. He d. in 1653, and was succeeded by his second son,

THOMAS SCOTT of Bonchester. Thomas Scott d. in 1680, leaving three sons, WALTER, *George* and John, and two daughters, Christian and Janet. The eldest son,

WALTER SCOTT, third of Bonchester, b. December, 1650, m. Jane Turnbull, and d. February, 1733, having had three sons, WALTER, James and *John*, and a daughter Janet. The eldest son,

WALTER SCOTT of Bonchester, m. 1726 Helen, sister to the Rev. Wm. Turnbull, minister of Abbotrule, and d. 1743, leaving issue :

1. Walter d. young.
2. Thomas of Bonchester b. September, 1729, who sold the estate, and d. at Bowhill, leaving an only daughter,
    (1) Dora m. Dr. Lorrain of Glasgow.
3. Adam b. May, 1731, went to the West Indies; m. Mrs. Thorpe and had a dau. m. a Mr. Buchanan.
4. WILLIAM. 5. Walter b. October, 1741.
1. Agnes. 2. Janet m. John Rutherford.
3. Helen.

THE REV. WILLIAM SCOTT, the fourth son, minister of Southdean, b. July, 1735, m. Sybil, dau. of John Hewitson of Lockholm, Westmorland, and d. May, 1809, leaving issue :

1. Walter, who left two sons, William and John, both d. s.p.
2. John, father of
    (1) William. (2) Rev. Charles.
    (3) Adam.
    (1) Margaret. (2) Sybil. (3) Ann.
    (4) Elizabeth. (5) Mary. All d. s.p.
3. Thomas d. s.p. 4. ADAM. 5. Robert.
1. Ann m. first —— Reid and second Charles Baxter.

ADAM SCOTT, the fourth son, b. 1777, m. August, 1807, Margaret, sister and heir of Robert Elliot of Arkleton. He assumed the name and arms of Elliot in addition to his own. He d. 1821, leaving issue:

1. WILLIAM.
1. Cassandra m. John Rutherford, W.S.

WILLIAM SCOTT-ELLIOT of Arkleton, J.P., b. March, 1811, m. March, 1848, Margaret, dau. of L. A. Wallace, and d. May, 1901, having had issue:

1. WILLIAM.
2. Lewis Alexander, b. March, 1858, m. first 1901 Laura, dau. of Colonel Hastings, U.S. Army. She d. s.p. 1903. He m. secondly July, 1908, Princess Eydua, dau. of H.H. Prince Arthur Odescalchi of Hungary, and had issue:
    (1) Ninian Balthazar. (2) Eydua Helen Margaret.
3. Adam b. February, 1860, Colonel Q.O. Cameron Highlanders; m. February, 1906, Marjorie, dau. of Lewis Evans, and had issue:
    (1) Aline Margaret.
    (2) Isabel Louisa.
1. Louisa Isabel.
2. Isabel m. Edward A. Baxter of Kincaldrum.
3. Margaret. 4. Mary.

WILLIAM SCOTT-ELLIOT of Arkleton, Langholm, J.P., b. March, 1849, m. October, 1893, Maude Louisa, dau. of Robt. Boyle Travers of Farsid, Co. Cork, and d. September, 1919, leaving issue,
1. WALTER TRAVERS.

CAPTAIN WALTER TRAVERS SCOTT-ELLIOT of Arkleton, b. October, 1895, Captain Sp. Res. Coldstream Guards.

Arms.—Quarterly: 1st and 4th grand quarters, quarterly (1) and (4) Gu., on a bend indented or a flute of the first (Elliot) (2) and (3) Arg., issuing from the sinister side a dexter arm, vested, the hand grasping the trunk of an oak tree eradicated and broken at the trunk ppr., accompanied by a crescent in the sinister chief and a mullet in the dexter flank both gu. (Armstrong) 2nd and 3rd grand quarters; or, on a bend azure between two tents of the last a mullet between two crescents of the field (Scott). Crest.—A demi-chevalier in complete armour holding in his right hand a sword erect ppr. Motto.—" Pro rege et limite." Seat.—Arkleton, near Langholm, N.B.

Ashtrees.

———

ALTHOUGH there is no proof available there are several reasons for suspecting that

JOHN SCOTT, who m. Helen, dau. and heiress of Thos. Oliver of Ashtrees, was of the Bonchester family and possibly third son of Walter Scott, third of Bonchester, and Jane Turnbull, his wife. By Helen Oliver John Scott left issue:

     1. ADAM. 2. *Thomas of Peel.*

ADAM SCOTT of Ashtrees, the eldest son, who succeeded to Ashtrees, was father of

JOHN SCOTT of Ashtrees and tenant in Wood-house; he m. a Miss Rae, and had issue among others,

     1. ADAM.

Mr. John Scott's executors sold Ashtrees to his cousin, Thomas Scott of Peel, from whom it eventually passed to the latter's brother, John Scott of Riccalton.

ADAM SCOTT, Esq., J.P., of Tullich, Loch Carron, farmed a large tract of land in West Rosshire; he was b. 1790, and m. Janet, dau. of James Hall, Sciberscross, Sutherlandshire, and dying 1865, left among other children :

1. JOHN.
2. James, b. 1828, went to Australia 1852; d. 1880.
3. *Henry Hall.*
4. Thomas b. 1836; d. 1907 Kingsburgh, Skye.
1. Margaret. Residence.—8 Doune Terrace, Edinburgh.
2. Anne. Residence.—8 Doune Terrace, Edinburgh.
3. Jessie m. John Reid, Newkelso, Loch Carron.
4. Esther m. Tom Purves, Rhifail, Sutherland.

Several other daughters d. unm.

JOHN SCOTT, Drynoch, Skye, the eldest son, b. 1823, m. first 1856, Margaret, dau. of Andrew Ross, and had issue,

Mr. Scott m. secondly Jane, dau. of Sheriff Fraser, and had issue:

1. ADAM.
2. Thomas Fraser.
3. John Elliot.
4. Fraser Fowler, Captain R.A.

ADAM SCOTT, b. 1858, m. Jean Charlotte, dau. of Tom Purves, Rhifail, Sutherlandshire; d. 1922, leaving issue one son and two daughters:

1. JOHN.   1. Esther.   2. Jessie Hall.

JOHN SCOTT b. 1910.

Residence.—8 Doune Terrace, Edinburgh.

Alnham.

SIR HENRY HALL SCOTT, third son of Adam Scott of Tullich, Loch Carron, m. Henrietta, dau. of George Gaukroger, Esq., J.P., and dying 1911, left issue:

1. ADAM.
2. George Henry Hall (Captain) b. 1881; killed in action, Great War 1916.
1. Margaret Christabel m. Brigadier-General J. F. Riddell.
2. Janet Mary m. first Captain R. S. Hebeler, and secondly Mr. R. Daud.

ADAM SCOTT, the elder son, the north-country owner, trainer, and amateur steeplechase rider, b. 1875, m. 1910 Mary, second dau. of Major-General G. C. Lambert, J.P.

Residence.—Alnham, Whittingham, Northumberland.

Peel.

Robson-Scott
of Ashtrees :

THOMAS SCOTT of Peel and tenant in Letham, second son of John Scott and Helen Oliver, b. 1737, m. Esther Turnbull, and had issue :

1. Thomas of Peel and Newton d. unm.
2. John of Riccalton and Ashtrees and joint tenant with his brother in Letham, also d. unm.
1. Helen m. Thomas Elliot in Kiandean (son of Elliot of Harwood) and is now represented by Mr. W. E. Boog-Scott (elder brother of Mr. J. E. Boog-Scott of Peel).

2. Esther m. James Robson, Belford and
   Chatto, by whom she had two sons, James
   Robson-Scott of Ashtrees and Thomas
   Robson-Scott of Newton. The latter has
   four sons living, two of whom being
   Mr. J. A. Robson-Scott of Newton and
   Mr. T. W. Robson-Scott of Letham;
   former's only son is Major J. S. Robson-
   Scott of Ashtrees, co-representative with
   Mr. Boog-Scott of Thomas Scott of Peel.

Arms (of Major J. S. Robson-Scott).—Or, on a
bend azure a mullet between two crescents of the first,
on a chief gules, a stag trippant, also of the first
between two boars' heads couped argent. Crest.—A
stag trippant proper. Motto.—" Patriam Amo." Residence of Major Robson-Scott.—Blandford, Dorset.

ffalla.

THIS family is also very possibly a branch of the Bonchester family, although there is now no definite tradition as to its descent. There are several reasons for assuming that

GEORGE SCOTT, second son of Thomas Scott, second of Bonchester, was father of

ALEXANDER SCOTT, miller in Rulewater and tenant in Roughheugh Mill, from whom downwards the pedigree may be taken as authentic as far as it goes. The miller left two sons:

1. GEORGE. 2. *Robert.*

GEORGE SCOTT, the elder son, tenant in Falla, b. 1724, m. Elizabeth Borthwick, and dying 1815, left issue:

1. Alexander d. young.
2. John m. his cousin Euphemia, dau. of Robert Scott in Roughheugh Mill, and had issue:
   (1) Robert. (2) George. (3) John.
   (1) Ann m. to Mr. D. Clarke.
   (2) Betsy.
   All d. s.p. as far as we can tell.
3. Thomas b. 1761; d. at Falla 1849.
4. ALEXANDER. 1. Elizabeth.

ALEXANDER SCOTT of Falla, the fourth son, was a Bailie of Jedburgh, and also a draper in that town. He was of an inventive turn of mind, and spent a considerable amount of money on new kinds of explosives. He m. Isabella Rutherfurd and obtained possession of Falla through this marriage. He became factor to the Earl of Hopetown, and d. December, 1835, having had issue:

1. George b. 1786; in the Admiralty Office; d. unm. 1825.
2. William, b. 1788, m. Charlotte, dau. of Robert Leslie, and dying 1820, left issue:
    (1) William Ferguson d. at sea 1819, aged 1 year.
    (1) Charlotte Eliza m. R. H. Ramas.
3. JOHN.
4. Thomas b. 1805; d. young.
5. Adam d. young.
1. Isabella.   2. Elizabeth.
3. Alice.   4. Ann.

On Mr. Alexander Scott's death Isabella, Elizabeth and Ann, his daughters, became joint proprietors, and on the death of the last of these, Falla passed to their nephew.

JOHN SCOTT, the third son, also a factor to the Earl of Hopetown, m. 1829 Harriet Henderson, and d. June, 1860, leaving issue:

1. ALEXANDER.   1. Jessie Harriet.

ALEXANDER SCOTT of Falla, the only son, b. 1835, succeeded to Falla on the death of his last surviving aunt; m. Marion Isabella, dau. of Charles Robert Somervail of London, and dying 1887, left issue:

1. JOHN ALEXANDER.
2. Charles Robert b. 1877; d. 1894.
1. Marion Elizabeth.
2. Harriet Rutherfurd m. Robert Laing.
3. Agnes Emily.

JOHN ALEXANDER SCOTT of Falla and tenant in Mossburnford; b. 1873; m. Alice, dau. of George Douglas, Upper Hindhope, and dying 1920, left issue :

1. ALEXANDER GEORGE.
2. Charles Douglas b. 1908.
3. John Robert b. 1910.
1. Aheila Marion Isabella.
2. Jean Harriet.

ALEXANDER GEORGE SCOTT b. 1905.

Residence.—Falla, Jedburgh, N.B.

Kinning Hall.

R OBERT SCOTT, younger brotĥer to George
Scott, tenant in Falla, and after his father
tenant in Roughheugh Mill, Hawick, left four children:

1. ALEXANDER.
2. Thomas of Little Cot, who m. but left no
   issue.
1. Euphemia m. her cousin John, brother to
   Falla.
2. Alice m. Briggs of Middlesnows.

ALEXANDER SCOTT of Kinning Hall m.
Margaret Bell, and was buried at Bedrule, leaving
issue:

1. ROBERT. 2. William.
1. Marky m. William Hobkirk.
2. Ann.
3. Mary m. John Scott in Barnhills.

ROBERT SCOTT of Kinning Hall and tenant
in Falnash, b. 1817, m. Mary Purdom, sister of

Thomas Purdom, Town Clerk, Hawick, and dying
1897, left issue:

1. Alexander d. young.
2. ALEXANDER.
3. Robert m. Kate Worth, and has issue:
    (1) Robert. (2) Alexander.
    (3) William.
    (1) Mary m. Frank Bradley.
    (2) Annie m. —— MacMinchen.
    (3) Louise. (4) Rita.
4. William.
5. Walter Purdom, tenant in Falnash.
6. Thomas m. Ada M. Fox, and has issue:
    (1) Malcolm. (2) Walter.
    (1) Jean.
1. Mary. 2. Margaret.
3. Agnes m. Alexander Nicol.
4. Annie.

ALEXANDER SCOTT of Kinning Hall, and
later tenant in Venchen, Yetholm, m. first Agnes, dau.
of Robert Hobkirk of South Burn, Dumfriesshire, and
secondly her sister, Georgina Isabella Grierson.

Residence.—Venchen, Yetholm, N.B.

Clonmell.

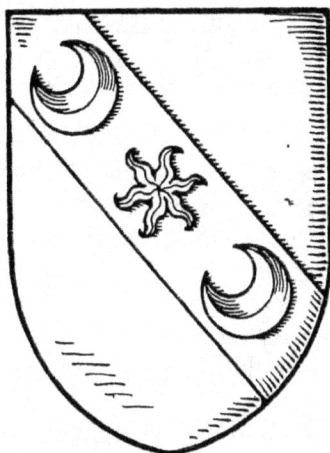

The Earl
of Clonmell

NOTHING is known definitely as to this family's descent from Buccleuch, but it must be presumed that when the arms were granted there was at least a tradition in the family that they were connected with the Border Scotts.

THOMAS SCOTT of Urlings, Co. Tipperary, was, according to Burke, the first known member of this genealogy. He m. Rachel, dau. of Mark Prim of Johnswell, and had issue,

JOHN SCOTT, Solicitor-General and Attorney-General, created Baron Earlsfort, Viscount Clonmell and Earl of Clonmell; b. June, 1739; m. first 1768

R

Catherine Anna Maria, widow of Philip Roe, and
sister of Francis Mathew, first Earl of Llandaff. She
d. s.p. He m. secondly June, 1779, Margaret, dau. of
Patrick Lawless and niece of first Lord Cloncurry.
She d. November, 1829, having had issue:

    1. THOMAS.
    1. Charlotte m. 14th March, 1814, John,
       third Earl of Beauchamp.
  Lord Clonmell d. 23rd May, 1798. His only son,

THOMAS SCOTT, second Earl of Clonmell, b.
August, 1783, m. February, 1805, Henrietta Louisa,
dau. of George, second Earl of Brooke and Warwick,
and by her had issue:

    1. JOHN HENRY.
    2. Charles Grantham, Colonel in the Army;
       b. March, 1818; m. March, 1843, Frances
       Maria, dau. of Ralph William Grey of
       Backworth, Northumberland. He d.
       January, 1885, leaving issue:
          (1) BEAUCHAMP HENRY JOHN, sixth
            Earl.
          (2) Louis Guy b. April, 1850; m.
            February, 1885, Inna Georgiana,
            dau. of Colonel the Hon. Lewis
            Richard Watson Milles; d. April,
            1900, leaving issue,
            (i) Inna Vera Evelyn m. Feb.,
               1908, Brevet Lieutenant-
               Colonel Stuart Hay, D.S.O.,
               Cameron Highlanders.
          (3) Dudley Alexander Charles, heir
            presumptive (51 Chester Square,
            S.W.) b. May, 1853; m. August,
            1909, Rose Clare, dau. of George
            Cutting of New York.
          (1) Evelyn Mary.
          (2) Jessie Louisa.

(3) Annie Henrietta m. October, 1880, Frederick Wm. Fane, son of Colonel John Wm. Fane of Wormsley, Co. Oxford.

1. Harriet Margaret m. June, 1827, Edward Lord Mostyn.

2. Louisa Augusta m. December, 1828, John Slater Harrison of Shelswell Park, Oxon.

3. Charlotte Rachel m. April, 1830, Henry Arbuthnot, second son of the Rt. Hon. Charles Arbuthnot.

4. Caroline Sophia. 5. Sophia Louisa.

6. Frances Mary. 7. Augusta Anne.

His Lordship d. 18th January, 1838, and was succeeded by his elder son,

JOHN HENRY SCOTT, third Earl of Clonmell, b. January, 1817, m. April, 1838, the Hon. Anne De Burgh, eldest dau. and co-heir of Ulysses, second Lord Downes, by whom he had issue:

1. JOHN HENRY REGINALD, fourth Earl.

2. THOMAS CHARLES, fifth Earl.

3. Francis Ulysses b. April, 1850; d. August, 1861.

1. Maria Henrietta m. July, 1864, Captain the Hon. George Fitzclarance, late Captain R.N.

2. Annette Louisa m. February, 1870, Percy Robert O'Connor La Touche of Harristown, Co. Kildare.

3. Rachael Mary m. May, 1866, Llewellyn Traherne Bassett Saunderson of Dromkeen House, Co. Cavan.

4. Edith Caroline Sophia m. July, 1874, fifth Viscount Monck.

The Earl d. 7th February, 1866, and was succeeded by his eldest son,

JOHN HENRY REGINALD SCOTT, fourth Earl of Clonmell, D.L., late Lieutenant 1st Life Guards; b. March, 1839; d. unm. June, 1891, and was succeeded by his brother,

THOMAS CHARLES SCOTT, fifth Earl of Clonmell, D.L., Co. Kildare, Lieutenant-Colonel Rifle Brigade; b. August, 1840; m. February, 1875, Agnes, dau. of Robert Godfrey Day. His Lordship d. 18th June, 1896, s.p., when the title devolved upon his cousin,

BEAUCHAMP HENRY JOHN SCOTT, 6th Earl of Clonmell, formerly Captain Scots Fusilier Guards; b. December, 1847; m. March, 1875, Lucy Maria, dau. of Anthony Willson of Rauceby Hall, M.P., leaving issue,

      1. RUPERT CHARLES, seventh and present Earl.

The Earl d. 2nd February, 1898, and was succeeded by his son,

RUPERT CHARLES SCOTT, seventh Earl of Clonmell, Viscount Clonmell and Baron Earlsfort, Co. Tipperary in Ireland, Captain Territorial Force Reserve R.H.A., late Captain Warwickshire R.H.A.; b. November, 1877; succeeded his father as Earl 1898; m. August, 1901, Rachel Estelle, eldest dau. of the late Samuel Berridge of Toft Hill, Rugby, and has issue:

      1. Moira Estelle Norah Frances b. August, 1902.
      2. Shiela Mary b. October, 1906.

Arms.—Or, on a bend azure, an étoile between two crescents arg. Crest.—A buck trippant ppr. Motto.—" Fear to transgress." Seat.—Eathorpe Hall, Leamington. Town Residence, 20 Hertford Street, W.

Craigmuie.

Goldie-Scott
of Craigmuie

R OBERT SCOTT, who m. in 1723 Margaret
Ruddach in the parish of Grange, Banffshire,
is the earliest name we have of this family. He was
father of

THE REV. ROBERT SCOTT of Haddington,
who m. Margaret Sheriff, and by her had, possibly
among others,

DR. WILLIAM SCOTT, private physician to
H.H. The Rajah of Travancore, who m. Helen,
eldest surviving co-heiress of Thomas Goldie of
Craigmuie, and by her had issue:
    1. Robert Conway d. young.
    2. William. 3. THOMAS GOLDIE.

4. Patrick George, a Major-General in the Army, m. 1860 Elizabeth MacLeod, dau. of James Stewart of Cairnsmon, and d. 1894, leaving:
> (1) William (Dr.), 15 Claremont Crescent, Edinburgh.
> (2) James Stewart.
> (1) Helen.
> (2) Elizabeth MacLeod.
> (3) Margaret. (4) Mary.

5. Robert Francis (Rev.), Rector of Farnborough.

1. Helen Mary.

THOMAS GOLDIE SCOTT of Craigmuie, Surgeon-Major 79th Highlanders, b. 1820, m. 1862 his cousin, Frances Elizabeth Lever, and d. 1874, leaving issue:

1. William Robert Lesingus b. 1862; d. 1886.

2. ARCHIBALD MURGATROYD GOLDIE.

3. Thomas Goldie, M.B., C.M., M.R.C.S., b. 1866, m. 1908 Evelyn Fayrer Lilley, and has issue:
> (1) Thomas Robert b. 1909.
> (2) Darcy Lever b. 1911.
> (3) Percival John b. 1913.

4. Darcy Ashton Lever b. 1871; d. 1890.

5. Robert Conway b. 1873; d. 1874.

1. Helen Mary Dorothy b. 1868; d. 1881.

2. Frances Emilia Foley Lever b. 1869; m. 1896 Rev. Henry Hooke Bartram, M.A., and has issue.

3. Mary Stephana b. 1872; m. 6th August, 1910, John Robinetta Scruby.

Dr. Thomas Goldie Scott d. 1874, and was succeeded in Craigmuie by his widow, who d. 1904.

ARCHIBALD MURGATROYD GOLDIE
GOLDIE-SCOTT of Craigmuie, b. March, 1863,
succeeded his mother. He m. 1885 Ellen Gertrude,
fourth dau. of the late Rev. Michael Simpson, Vicar of
Towlaw, Co. Durham, and has issue:
    1. Dorothy Lever. 2. Cecil Mary.

Arms.—1st and 4th or, on a bend between two
griffins' heads erased az., a mullet between two crescents of the first; 2nd and 3rd arg., a chevron gu.
between three trefoils slipped vert.; on a shield of
pretence arg. two bends sable, the upper engrailed
(for Lever). Crests.—1. A stag trippant ppr. 2. A
garb or. Mottoes.—1. " Fideliter amo." 2. " Quid
utilius." Seat.—Craigmuie, Moniaive, Thornhill,
N.B.

Glendowran.

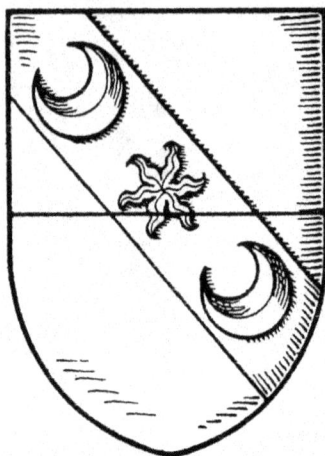

Sir
J.S.A. Murray Scott

SIR WALTER of Kirkurd received in 1458 a charter of Glendowran and other lands in Lanark. These lands are said to have been held by a cadet branch from the chief of the family for 300 years till 1773. His descendant,

JOHN SCOTT, portioner of Glendowran, brother of Wm. of Glendowran, who d. s.p. 1770, left a son,

WALTER SCOTT, father of

JOHN SCOTT of Glendowran, which he inherited from his great-uncle William in 1770, and sold it in 1773. He m. Jean French, and had issue:
　　1. John d. s.p.
　　2. DAVID his heir.　3. *George*.
　　1. Elizabeth d. s.p.　2. Wilhelmina.

DAVID SCOTT of Lawfield, Fifeshire, b. July, 1783, m. July, 1816, Margaret Donaldson, and d. August, 1862, leaving issue:

1. JOHN. 2. David Donaldson.
3. Alexander Mackenzie d. s.p.
1. Jane m. Henry Craig.
2. Maria Georgina.

JOHN SCOTT of Chandos Street, Cavendish Square, W., M.D., b. 1817, m. April, 1846, Alicia Lucy, dau. of George St. Vincent Thomas Nelson Murray, D.L., and d. July, 1890, leaving issue:

1. John Edward Arthur Murray (Sir), Bart., K.C.B., of Castle House, Lisburn, Co. Antrim; b. February, 1847; d. s.p. January, 1912.
2. DOUGLAS ALEXANDER.
3. Edward Maude (Rev.), b. September, 1850, m. August, 1885, Ida Marion, dau. of George Fenwick of Crag Head, Bournemouth, and has issue:
    (1) Alexander Malcolm b. Dec., 1896.
    (1) Kathleen Margaret.
    (2) Brida Madeline.
    (3) Ruth Millicent.
4. Donald Malcolm b. May, 1852; m. August, 1898, Anne Elizabeth, dau. of late Rev. Walter Mayhard, and has issue,
    (1) Alice Katherine.
5. Walter Montagu b. October, 1867; d. August, 1920.
1. Alice Florence. Residence.—Stow-on-the-Wold, Gloucestershire.
2. Mary Katherine Teesdale.

MAJOR-GENERAL DOUGLAS ALEX-
ANDER SCOTT, C.B., C.V.O., D.S.O., F.G.S.,
late R.E.; b. December, 1848; m. January, 1894, Mary,
dau. of Captain Christopher Baldock Cardew, and has
issue:

    1. IAN DOUGLAS MURRAY b. August, 1905.
    1. Cynthia Mary m. William V. Cardew.
    2. Lucy Murray.

    Arms granted 1864 to descendants of David Scott
of Lawfield.—Per fess, arg. and az., on a bend an
étoile between two crescents counterchanged. Crest.
—A stag trippant ppr. Motto.—" Fidus et fortis."
Residence.—36 St. Margaret's Road, Oxford.

Welwyn.

GEORGE SCOTT of Glendowran, third son of John Scott of Glendowran and Jean French, purchased Glendowran from his brother David. He m. Emily, dau. of General Graham of Arcot, and by her had issue:

1. ALEXANDER DE COURCY, General R.E.
2. Frederick Beaufort, C.M.G.
3. Ankerville b.   ; d. July, 1903.
4. *Lothian Kerr.*

GENERAL ALEXANDER DE COURCY SCOTT, R.E., b. 1837; m. 1862 Rosalind, dau. of Henry Dumbleton of Thornhill Park, Hants.; d. leaving issue:

1. Arthur de Courcy, Colonel, b. 1866; d. 1917 in action.
2. CECIL GRAHAM.
3. Alick Lauriston b. 1873.
1. Rose Isabel b. 1863; d. 1880.
2. Alice D. b. 1868; m. J. George, Ithaca.

CECIL GRAHAM SCOTT b. 1867.

Residence.—

ffarnborough.

LIEUT.-COL. LOTHIAN KERR SCOTT, C.B., R.E., fourth son of George Scott of Glendowran; b. May, 1841; m. February, 1869, Agatha Harriet, dau. of G. A. Anstey, and d. July, 1919, leaving issue :

    1. LOTHIAN GRAEME.

    2. Herbert Stewart Lauriston, M.C., Major.

LOTHIAN GRAEME SCOTT b. 1879.

Residence.—Forest Lodge, Farnborough, Hants.

Hartwoodmyres.

THIS property was owned by Scotts from 1573 to 1695, but it is not possible to give a connected pedigree. Walter of Hartwoodmyres in 1573 was son to William Scott of Tushielaw, but this Walter would afterwards be the Sir Walter of Tushielaw, and it is not clear what relation, if any, he was to

WILLIAM SCOTT of Hartwoodmyres in 1589, who was one of the rescuers of Kinmont Will in 1596. In 1627

ROBERT SCOTT of Hartwoodmyres was one of the commissioners left by the Earl of Buccleuch to administer his affairs when he left for Holland. In 1667

WILLIAM SCOTT of Hartwoodmyres was commissioner for the King's Bounty.

Headshaw.

Scott of Headshaw

THIS family is known as the old family of Headshaw as distinct from the comparatively modern
branch of Sinton in Part II. There is apparently
nothing to give any hint as to its origin.

WALTER SCOTT of Headshaw was in possession before 1486. He must have had at least six
sons :

    1. PHILIP his heir.
    2. David. 3. *Simon.* 4. Robert.
    5. Walter. 6. Thomas.

PHILIP SCOTT succeeded his father before
1510, and was father of

WALTER SCOTT of Headshaw, mentioned in
1564; m. a dau. of Sir William Scott of Kirkurd, and
had two sons, ROBERT his heir, and a second son, who
was father of Robert Scott of Easter Groundiston.

ROBERT SCOTT of Headshaw succeeded
before 1593, at which date he received a crown
charter. He had issue:
    1. ROBERT. 2. Francis.

ROBERT SCOTT, the eldest son, younger of
Headshaw, apparently never succeeded, the family
having become impoverished and the property disposed of to John Scott of Yorkston, son of the Laird
of Sinton.

Arms.—Or, on a bend azure an étoile between two
crescents of the first, within a bordure quarterly arg.
and of the second.

Dryhope.

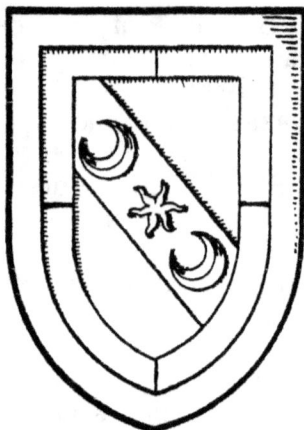

Scott of Dryhope

SIMON SCOTT of Dryhope is stated by Satchells to have been a brother of Adam Scott of Tushielaw, but I believe this statement is entirely unsupported and have therefore, in view of the arms that are on record to Dryhope, placed this genealogy after Headshaw. He had several sons, all mentioned as brothers to the elder Philip:

      1. PHILIP. 2. *Simon*. 3. Andrew.
      4. Adam. 5. Walter.

PHILIP SCOTT of Dryhope is mentioned in several documents, and is noted principally for being the father of Mary, " The Flower of Yarrow." He was followed by his son,

PHILIP SCOTT of Dryhope, Laird of Dryhope from about 1618 to 1625, after which we find his son,

WILLIAM SCOTT of Dryhope. Although William was definitely Philip's son, it is only probable that

ROBERT SCOTT of Dryhope in 1640 was son to William.

WALTER SCOTT of Dryhope in 1669 was possibly brother to Robert, and

PHILIP SCOTT, the last Laird of Dryhope, was definitely brother to Walter.

Arms.—The arms of Headshaw within a bordure gules.

𝔐ountbenger.

SIMON SCOTT of Mountbenger was second son of Simon Scott, the first of Dryhope, and was father to

ROBERT SCOTT of Mountbenger, who was father of

WALTER SCOTT of Mountbenger, who was father of

JOHN SCOTT of Catslackknow, who was father of the REV. JAMES SCOTT of Ancrum, and also probably father of William Scott of Catslackknow, Pensioner to the House of Buccleuch (one of the nine-and-twenty knights of fame in the " Lay ").

THE REV. JAMES SCOTT of Ancrum was, according to Satchells, father of

JAMES SCOTT of Bristo, " a worthy and much respected generous gentleman " living in 1688.

James Robert Scott.

WALTER SCOTT—b. 1712; d. 1748—is the first
member of this family of whom we have any
knowledge; he is believed to have come from Roxburgh, and to have been descended from one of the
Scott families sprung from Buccleuch. By Jennet
Carlyle, his wife, he left issue,

ROBERT SCOTT b. 1736; d. 1824. Mr.
Robert Scott m. Mary McMichael, and left issue,

ROBERT SCOTT b. 1780; d. 1861. By his
marriage with Jean Lindsay, the second Mr. Robert
Scott left issue :
1. WILLIAM. 2. *John Lindsay.*
3. Robert of Castle Dykes d. s.p.
4. *Walter.* 5. *James.*
1. Mary. 2. Jane.

WILLIAM SCOTT, M.D., b. 1819, m. first
Rachel, dau. of James Wilkin of Tinwald Downs,
Dumfries, and by her had issue :
1. James d. young. 2. ROBERT.
1. Rachel Amy.
Dr. Scott m. secondly a Mrs. Pike, but d. July,
1887, without further issue.

ROBERT SCOTT b. June, 1842; d. July, 1893;
m. first Mary, dau. of John Morin of Allanton, Dumfriesshire, and secondly Mary, dau. of John Bennet
of London, and by the latter had issue,

JAMES ROBERT SCOTT b. September, 1876,
a merchant in Glasgow. Mr. J. R. Scott m. April,
1908, Emily Florence, dau. of Robt. McIntyre,
merchant in Glasgow, and has issue :
1. John Robert b. March, 1909.
2. Walter Douglas Campbell b. June, 1919.
3. Henry Francis Morin b. June, 1922.
Address.—5 Albert Gate, Dowanhill, Glasgow W.

Mollance.

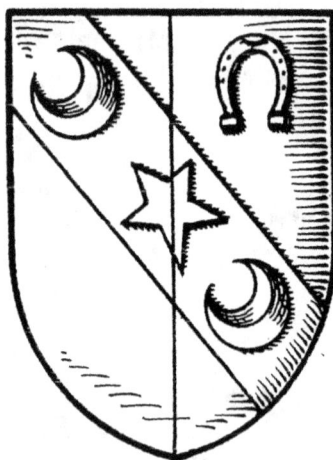

Scott of Mollance

JOHN LINDSAY SCOTT of Mollance, second son of Robert Scott and Jean Lindsay of Dumfries, m. Mary, dau. of Charles Gillam, and by her had issue :

      1. Robin d. young.

      2. CHARLES NORMAN LINDSAY.

      3. Ernest d. young.

      4. Lindsay. 5. John.

      1. Edith. 2. Constance.

CHARLES NORMAN LINDSAY TOLLE-MACHE-SCOTT, Esq., of Bosworth Park, Leicester, D.L.; b. 1852; m. February, 1882, Lady Agnes Mary Tollemache, second dau. of William, Lord Huntingtower, and granddaughter of the eighth Earl of Dysart. Mr. Scott assumed the name of Tollemache in addition to his own, and has issue,

1. Winifrede Agatha Tollemache (Tolle-mache-Scott) heir presumptive to the Dysart Earldom, m. Major Owain Edward Greaves.

Arms.—Parted per pale, or and azure, on a bend a mullet between two crescents all counter-changed, in the sinister chief a horseshoe of the first. Crest.—A stag trippant gules, attired and unguled or, charged on the shoulder with a horseshoe also or. Motto.—" Amo." Seat.—Bosworth Park, Leicester.

Charles Walker Scott.

WALTER SCOTT, fourth son of Robert Scott and Jean Lindsay of Dumfries, m. first a Miss Walker, by whom he had issue :

1. CHARLES WALKER.
2. Walter Henry m. a Miss Penfold.
1. Fanny m. T. C. Carthew.
2. Mary m. Dr. Murray.

Mr. Walter Scott m. secondly E—— Gordon, and had issue :

3. Frederick m. E—— Wilson.
4. Frank d. unm.
3. Ada m. Colonel Pearce.
4. Ethel m. Colonel King.   5. Lily.

Mr. Scott d. 1899.

CHARLES WALKER SCOTT m. —— Lorimer, and has issue.

Walter Scott.

JAMES SCOTT, fifth son of Robert Scott and Jean Lindsay of Dumfries, m. Jessie Irvine, and dying 1902 left issue:

1. Robert (Dr.) d. unm. 1896.
2. WALTER.
3. Arthur, b. 1837, m. A—— Patterson, and has issue.
4. James, Colonel in the Indian Medical Service.
5. Francis.
1. Jane. 2. Mary m. Thomas McGowan.

WALTER SCOTT m. G—— Rutherford.

Lilliesleaf.

THIS family's ancestors were tenants of Selkirk
Corn Mills early in the seventeenth century,
and, according to tradition, were descended from the
Scotts of Sinton. They removed from Selkirk to
Boose Mill on Ail Water, and at the same time
farmed Dimple Knowe adjoining Satchells. From
Boose Mill they removed to a mill on Rule Water
just below Wells House.

The first member of whom we have any individual
knowledge is

JOHN SCOTT who, when a young man, went
to Hummelknowe Mill on Slitrig as miller. John
Scott subsequently married the tenant of the mill,
who was a widow named Henderson, by whom he left
issue, possibly among others, one son,

JOHN SCOTT, who m. a Miss Deans, and lived
all his life at Hummelknowe Mill, and d. there leaving issue a son,

WALTER SCOTT, who lived first at Hummelknowe Mill and in 1859 with his family left and went
to Ormiston, near Hawick. He left issue,

WILLIAM SCOTT, Esq., J.P., b. April, 1848;
m. Mary, eldest dau. of Thomas Bailey, Gatley,
Cheshire, and has issue,
    1. WALTER NICHOL b. March, 1887.

Residence.—Cheviot View, Lilliesleaf, Roxburghshire.

London and Cambridge.

WILLIAM SCOTT, a freeman of the Town of Cambridge, is the first known member of this family; they claim descent from the Border Scotts, and the members of the family have for several generations used the crest and coat of arms of the Buccleuchs. William Scott, b.c. 1742, m. at Cambridge, October, 1768, Elizabeth Edwards, and dying c. 1816 left issue:

1. WILLIAM.
2. John b. November, 1776.
3. George Henry b. March, 1778.
4. Thomas b. June, 1779.
5. Samuel, Surgeon 6th Dragoon Guards, b. July, 1780; d. unm. in Edinburgh August, 1825.
6. Christopher Somergill b. June, 1782.
7. Edward Forlow, Captain R.N.; b. October, 1784; d. July, 1857, at Herne Bay, Kent.
8. Octavius, Captain R.M.; b. June, 1787; m. September, 1812, Mary, dau. of Thomas Edwards, and d. at Great Mongeham, August, 1837.
9. Charles b. December, 1788.
1. Elizabeth m. —— Derisley of Croxton, near Thetford.
2. Catherine m. Rev. Wm. Butcher, M.A.
3. Sarah.   4. Harriet.

WILLIAM SCOTT, M.A., of Stubbington House, County of Southampton, and of Tottenham, London, b. March, 1774, m. Harriet, dau. of Wm. Coleman of Edmonton, and dying October, 1827, left issue :

1. WILLIAM.

2. Henry b. November, 1805; d. September, 1817.

3. Edward, Lieutenant R.N., b. March, 1811; d. October, 1839.

1. Harriet Eliza m. Charles Hooper.

2. Mary. 3. Louisa.

WILLIAM SCOTT, M.A., of Tottenham, London, b. August, 1801, m. June, 1837, Marianne, dau. of James Michael Fitzgerald of Cork, and d. September, 1879, leaving issue :

1. WILLIAM FITZGERALD.

2. Morris George, Captain Mercantile Marine; b. September, 1844; drowned at sea August, 1897.

3. George, Midshipman R.N.; b. May, 1865; drowned at sea September, 1879.

1. Ada Eliza. 2. Mary Amy. 3. Edith.

WILLIAM FITZGERALD SCOTT of Stifford, Essex, b. April, 1841, m. May, 1865, Sarah, dau. of Joseph Deeley, and d. December, 1896, leaving issue :

1. MORRIS FITZGERALD.

1. Mary Amy Sarah.

2. Gertrude Anne.

3. Agnes Ada. 4. Edith Maud.

5. Louisa Josephine.

LIEUTENANT-COLONEL MORRIS FITZ-
GERALD SCOTT, late commanding 40th Battalion
Royal Fusiliers and 2nd Battalion London Regiment,
life member Royal United Service Institution ; b. May,
1870 ; m. October, 1909, Lilian, dau. of Walter Scott
of " Mostyn," Tadworth, Surrey, and has issue :

1. WILLIAM MORRIS FITZGERALD b. July,
   1912.
2. David John b. December, 1917.
1. Lilian Mary.   2. Lettice Margaret.

Residence.—68 Birdhurst Road, South Croydon.

𝕸alleny.

Scott of Malleny.

T HIS branch was settled at Irvine, Ayrshire, in
the sixteenth century. After their migration to
Midlothian about 1600 they were recognized as kins-
men of the Buccleuchs, who appointed them at various
times executors of their wills and tutors to their
children.

HEW SCOTT of Scotsloch, Irvine, d. 1618, and
is said to have married Margaret Wallace, and by
her had issue :

1. LAURENCE.
2. James of Scotsloch, J.P.; m. first Agnes
   Blair, and by her had a dau. m. to
   Thomas Cunningham; he m. secondly
   Lillias Scott, by whom he left on his
   death in 1634 three daughters :
     (1) Agnes m. Captain Bryce Blair.
     (2) Margaret m. (1645) John Eleis.
     (3) Lillias m. Hugh Boyd.
1. Margaret d. unm.
2. Janet m. John Blair, and had issue.
3. Susanne m. James (brother to John) Blair,
   and had issue.

LAURENCE SCOTT, J.P., apprenticed before
1592 to Robert Scott of Knightspottie, Rector of
Chancery; sold Scotsloch to his brother and bought
Harperrig 1605, Bavelaw 1628, Bonnington 1629,
Clerkington 1634, and other lands in Midlothian.
He m. Elizabeth, dau. of William Pringle of Edin-
burgh, and d. in December, 1637, leaving issue :

1. WILLIAM.
2. *James.*   3. *Laurence.*
1. Marion m. James Scott of Vogrie, uncle
   to Sir John Scott of Scotstarvit, and had
   issue.
2. Margaret m. William Wallace of Shewal-
   ton, and had issue.
3. Agnes m. Patrick Kinloch, and had issue.
4. Joanna m. James Clerk.
5. Alison m. Peter Houston.

SIR WILLIAM SCOTT succeeded to Clerkington and other lands.   He was knighted in 1641,
appointed a judge of the Court of Session with the
title of Lord Clerkington 1649, and d. December,
1659, having m. first, October, 1621, Katherine, dau.
of John Morison of Preston Grange, and by her had:

1. Sir Laurence m. Helen, dau. of Sir John
   Dalmahoy, having had three daughters:
      (1) Euphame m. George Winrain.
      (2) Helen m. Robert Kennedy.
      (3) Margaret.
2. William of Clonbeith m. Margaret Kerr,
   but d. s.p.
3. Walter succeeded to Clonbeith, but also
   d. s.p.
1. Bessie.
2. Katherine m. 1633 Hugh Montgomerie,
   and had issue.

Lord Clerkington m. secondly Barbara, another
dau. of Sir John Dalmahoy, by whom he had:

4. JOHN.
5. Francis b. November, 1642; d. young.
6. Alexander d. in infancy.
7. James m. Margaret Boyd.
8. David d. in infancy.
9. Robert m. Barbara Martin.
3. Barbara m. 1663 Sir Wm. Drummond of
   Hawthorndean, and had issue.
4. Agnes m. 1671 Thomas Ogilvie of
   Shannalie.
5. Margaret m. 1678 Sir Alexander Home,
   Bart., of Renton.
6. Mary m. 1681 Robert Montray of
   Roscobie.

JOHN SCOTT, fourth son of Lord Clerkington, obtained in patrimony the barony of Malleny, Midlothian. He m. Anne, dau. of Sir John Thomas Nicholson of Cockburnspath, and had issue:

    1. THOMAS.   2. *William.*
    1. Barbara m. Charles Scott of Bavelaw.
    2. Susanna m. Sir William Calderwood of Polton, afterwards Lord Polton.
    3. Another daughter.

John Scott d. 1709, and was succeeded by his son,

THOMAS SCOTT of Malleny, who m. Isabel, dau. of Sir John Lauder, Bart., and had with two daughters, Anna and Janet, a son and successor,

JOHN SCOTT of Malleny; m. August, 1742, Susan, dau. of Lord William Hay of Newhall, and had issue:

    1. John, younger, of Malleny, d. September, 1791.
    2. THOMAS.
    3. James commanded a ship in India, and d. there.
    4. Alexander, a Major in the Army.
    5. Archibald; killed in action.
    6. FRANCIS CARTERET.
    7. Hamilton; killed in action.
    8. George, Lieutenant-Colonel in the Army.
    1. Margaret.   2. Jane.
    3. Susan.   4. Molly.

Mr. Scott d. between 1791 and 1803, and was succeeded by his eldest surviving son,

THOMAS SCOTT, Esq., of Malleny, a general officer who served with distinction in the campaign under Prince Ferdinand in Holland; in the American War and in India; b. December, 1746; d. unm. about 1842, and was succeeded by his nephew, Carteret George, son of

FRANCIS CARTERET SCOTT, sixth son of John Scott of Malleny and Susan Hay, who m. 1801 Charlotte Elizabeth, eldest dau. of Major-General George Cunningham, and had six sons and five daughters :

1. Thomas b. 1802; d. 1832.
2. CARTERET GEORGE, late of Malleny.
3. George of Jamaica.
4. Alexander, a Captain in the Army; m. Julianne, dau. of —— Cockburn, Esq., Judge in the E.I.C.S., and had issue eight children, of whom survive :
    (1) Henry. (1) Jane.
5. John, an officer in the Army.
6. Stair Primrose bred to the law.
1. Isabella Frances m. George Nisbet of Cairnhill.
2. Charlotte d. 1814.
3. Jane.
4. Charlotte Elizabeth.
5. Lavinia Cockburn.

CARTERET GEORGE SCOTT, Esq., of Malleny, J.P. and D.L.; late Captain H.E.I.C.S.; m. first 1830 Charlotte, dau. of Colonel M'Dougal and grand-niece of George, Marquess of Tweeddale; and secondly 1833 Emily, dau. of Admiral Francis Holmes Coffin, R.N., of the ancient family of Coffin of Devon, and had issue :

1. FRANCIS CUNNINGHAM.
2. George.

Mr. Scott d. 1875, and was succeeded by his eldest son,

MAJOR-GENERAL SIR FRANCIS CUN-
NINGHAM SCOTT, K.C.B., K.C.M.G., J.P. for
Midlothian and Suffolk; b. 1834; m. 1859 Mary
Olivia, dau. of the Rev. E. J. Ward, Rector of East
Clandon, and had issue:

1. CARTERET CUNNINGHAM.
1. Florence Emily Cunningham m. Alexander Ward, J.P.
2. Ethel Mary Cunningham m. 1910
   Captain William Gardiner.

Sir Francis parted with Malleny to Lord Rose-
bery in 1882.

CARTERET CUNNINGHAM SCOTT, b.
1862, m. first 1885 Anna, dau. of Major R. Low, Co.
Limerick, and secondly 1917 Mary Helen, dau. of
Captain A. W. Chitty, C.I.E., late Indian Navy.

Arms.—Or, on a bend az. a star between two
crescents of the first, in base an arrow bendways ppr.
feathered and barbed arg. Crest.—A stag lodged
ppr. Motto.—"Amo probos." Address.—C/o Bank
of Scotland, E.C.2.

T

Blair of Blair.

Blair of Blair ❖

WILLIAM SCOTT, who assumed the surname of
Blair, second son of John Scott of Malleny
and Anne Nicholson, m. first Magdalene, dau. and
heiress of William Blair of Blair, and had one son,

    1. WILLIAM BLAIR OF BLAIR.

  Wm. Scott m. secondly Catherine, dau. of
Alexander Tait, and had five sons and six daughters,
all of the name of Blair:

    2. HAMILTON.

    3. Alexander,   Surveyor   of   Customs,
       Glasgow.

    4. John, an officer in the Army, killed at
       Minden, 1759.

    5. Thomas, an officer in the Army, killed at
       Vald, 1747.

    6. William, an officer in the Army.

1. Anne m. David Blair of Adamton.
2. Magdalene m. Sir William Maxwell, Bart.
3. Janet m. Alexander Tait.
4. Barbara m. William Fullarton.
5. Catherine d. unm.
6. Mary m. Sir John Sinclair, Bart.

William Blair d. c. 1715.

WILLIAM BLAIR OF BLAIR d. unm. 1732, and was succeeded by his half-brother,

MAJOR HAMILTON BLAIR OF BLAIR. He m. Jane, dau. of Sydenham Williams of Herringston, and dying 1782 left (with two daughters, Agatha m. to Lieutenant-General Avarne, and Jane m. to Robert Williams of Cerne Abbas, Dorset) an only son,

WILLIAM BLAIR OF BLAIR, M.P. He m. Madelene, daughter of John Fordyce, Esq., of Ayton, Berwickshire, and by her had issue:
1. Hamilton, Captain R.N.; d. May, 1816.
2. John Charles, Captain R.N.; d. July, 1836.
3. WILLIAM FORDYCE.
4. Henry Melville, Lieutenant R.N.; d. July, 1837.
5. Augustus, Captain in the Army; d. June, 1857.
1. Catherine m. Matthew Fortescue.
2. Madelene m. Alexander Scott.
3. Louisa m. Colonel Jackson.
4. Elizabeth. 5. Charlotte.
6. Jane Gordon.
7. Georgina m. James Hamilton.

Colonel Blair d. 21st October, 1841.

CAPTAIN WILLIAM FORDYCE BLAIR OF BLAIR, R.N., b. September 1805, m. July, 1840, Caroline Isabella, dau. of John Sprot of London, and d. December, 1888, leaving:

    1. William Augustus b. June, 1843; d. May, 1861.
    2. FREDERICK GORDON.
    1. Mary m. John Cuninghame.
    2. Caroline Madelina m. Sir Chas. Fairlie-Cuninghame, Bart.
    3. Adelaide Gordon.

COLONEL FREDERICK GORDON BLAIR OF BLAIR, C.B., C.M.G., A.D.C. to King George 1914-1921; b. November, 1852, m. June, 1880, Mary Elizabeth, dau. of William Baird of Elie, and has issue,

    1. Cecilia Magdaline.

Arms.—Quarterly: 1st and 4th arg., on a saltire sa. nine mascles of the field, 2nd and 3rd the arms of Scott of Malleny. Crest and motto as Scott of Malleny. Seat.—Blair, near Dalry.

Bonnington.

JAMES SCOTT, second son of Laurence Scott of Harperrig, obtained Bonnington from his father. He m. 1630 Violet, dau. of Robert Pringle, W.S., and had by her:

1. William, who d. v.p. having m. Elizabeth Elliot, and left an only child,
   (1) Margaret m. James Cockburn.
2. ROBERT.
1. Violet m. James Douglas of Cliftonhall.
2. Elizabeth m. John Maitland.
3. Marion m. John Lumsden.
4. Jean m. (1673) James Park.

James Scott m. secondly Margaret, dau. of William Elliot of Stobs, and by her had:

3. GILBERT. 4. Charles.
5. James, last male of this family.
5. Catherine. 6. Barbara.

ROBERT SCOTT, the second son, succeeded to Bonnington, and m. Barbara, dau. of Sir Alexander Dalmahoy, and had an only daughter,

1. Margaret.

GILBERT SCOTT succeeded to Bonnington, which was appraised from him by the creditors of his brother Charles.

𝔅𝔞𝔟𝔢𝔩𝔞𝔴.

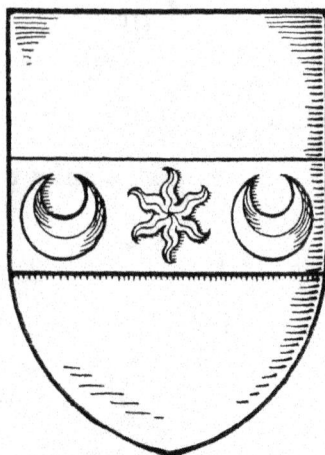

Scott⁹ of Bavelaw.

L AURENCE SCOTT, third son of Laurence
Scott of Harperrig, obtained Bavelaw from his
father, and m. Margaret, dau. of Stephen Boyd of
Temple, by whom he had :

1. LAURENCE.
1. Elizabeth m. 1622 Sir William Binning.
2. Marion. 3. Ann.
4. Margaret m. Hugh Wallace, W.S., 1665.
5. Barbara. 6. Janet.

Laurence Scott m. secondly 1650 Katherine, dau.
of James Binning, by whom he had :

2. WILLIAM. 3. CHARLES.
4. Hew b. 1658. 5. David b. 1660.
7. Katherine.
8. Barbara·m. Sir Roger Hog.
9. Eupham.
10. Christian m. Sir Alexander Brand.
11. Marion.

12. Janet m. Michael Lumsden.
13. Anna.
14. Agnes m. Adam Fullerton, W.S., of Bartonholm.

LAURENCE SCOTT, the eldest son, succeeded to Bavelaw; b. 1643; m. January, 1670, Margaret, only child of John Maxwell, but d. s.p. 1679.

WILLIAM SCOTT succeeded his half-brother, but d. unm. March, 1690, aged 42. During his elder brother's lifetime he recorded his arms with a bordure counter componée, but this matriculation would lapse on his death.

CHARLES SCOTT succeeded to Bavelaw on his brother's death, and m. Barbara, dau. of his cousin, John Scott of Malleny, and dying December, 1701, left issue :

    1. JOHN. 2. WILLIAM.
    3. Laurence b. 1695, merchant in Glasgow; m. and left issue :
        (1) Charles, a merchant in Glasgow.
        (1) Barbara.

JOHN SCOTT, the eldest son, succeeded to Bavelaw on his father's death, but d. unm. July, 1703.

WILLIAM SCOTT of Bavelaw, the second son of Charles and Barbara Scott, m. November, 1721, Mary, dau. of William Foulis of Woodhall; d. September, 1741, leaving issue :

    1. WILLIAM.
    2. Charles d. in infancy.
    3. LAURENCE. 4. CHARLES. 5. David.
    1. Barbara.
    2. Mary m. Andrew Home.
    3. Margaret.

WILLIAM SCOTT succeeded to Bavelaw in 1741, but d. unm. 1747.

LAURENCE SCOTT, b. 1736, succeeded him, but also d. unm. 1755.

CHARLES SCOTT succeeded his brother; b. April, 1738; m. 1762 Frances, dau. of John Vicaradge. He sold Bavelaw in 1774, and d. circa 1784, leaving issue, among others :
1. William.
   1. Primrose, maid of honour to Queen Charlotte, and close personal friend of Walter, fifth Duke of Buccleuch (d. unm.)

LIEUT.-COLONEL WILLIAM SCOTT b. January, 1763; Lieutenant-Colonel 23rd Bengal N.I.; Ambassador to Persia; formed an alliance with a Persian princess, who died leaving a daughter, which daughter m. a Captain Richardson, whose son, also Captain Richardson, Connaught Rangers, m. his cousin, Grace Scott. Colonel Scott subsequently m. December, 1800, Henrietta, dau. of Lieutenant-Colonel Robson, Deputy Governor of St. Helena, and d. at sea May, 1808, leaving issue :
1. Francis Charles b. January, 1802, Colonel Madras N.I., Governor of the Straits Settlements; m. Mary Fenning, and d. at Rothesay 1866, leaving issue :
   (1) Samuel b. 1850; m. a Miss Scott of Glasgow, and d. in America 1889.
   (1) Grace m. Captain Richardson (above).
2. Henry Emanuel.
3. Montagu b. (p.h.) 1808; a doctor in Canada; m. and left issue among others,
   (1) William —— Sawyerville, U.S.A.

HENRY EMANUEL SCOTT, a civil engineer, b. at Cawnpore, December, 1804, m. November, 1841, Mary Anne Kilby, and d. at Karachi, Scinde, in 1860, leaving issue :
1. Henry George b. 1843; d. s.p. 1871.
2. Arthur Percy Hall b. 1846; d. s.p. 1879.
3. CHARLES.
4. Laurence b. 1858.
1. Caroline m. John Harding of Rockfield, Monmouthshire.
2. Laura m. G. C. Kilby, Calcutta.
3. Rosamond m. R. Lidderdale, Surgeon-General, Bengal.
4. Alice m. Sandford Kilby, Calcutta.

COMMANDER CHARLES SCOTT, H.M. Indian Marine, and late Chief Constable of Sheffield; b. February, 1855; m. Evelina, dau. of John Williams, and has issue :
1. CHARLES MONTAGU LAURENCE, Commander R.N., b. 1882; m. Helen, dau. of John Harvey, and has issue,
    (1) Lalage.
2. Henry Ioan, Commander R.N., b. September, 1885.
3. Victor Wynne b. and d. May, 1887.
4. Richard, Captain Cheshire Regiment, b. December, 1888.
5. Evelyn b. November, 1890.
1. Irene. 2. Laura.
3. Aileen m. Lieutenant Roome, R.N.
4. Beryl m. Lieutenant Bullock.

Arms (not recently recorded).—Or, on a fesse azure, a mullet of six points between two crescents of the field. Crest.—A hand holding a scroll of paper. Motto.—" Facundia Felix." Residence.—4 Holyrood Terrace, The Hoe, Plymouth.

Newark.

JAMES of Newark about whose origin nothing is known, apparently left Newark to his son and became a Magistrate in Selkirk c. 1603-7.

JOHN SCOTT of Newark settled at Newark in his father's lifetime, m. Agnes Simpson, and appears to have had three sons:

    1. JAMES.

    2. Robert burgess in Selkirk.

    3. *Walter in Broadhaugh.*

John d. January, 1622.

JAMES was served heir to his father, December, 1626, having m. December, 1605, Grisel, dau. of James Murray of Philiphaugh. He apparently parted with Newark to the Buccleuch family and is probably subsequently identical with James Scott, Merchant Burgess in Selkirk.

Harwood.

Scott of Harwood.

WALTER SCOTT in Broadhaugh, third son of
John Scott of Newark: m. Agnes, dau. of
Turnbull of Minto; he acquired Arkleton and Meikle-
dalehope, and was almost certainly identical with
Walter Scott mentioned in documents in the possession
of Mr. Scott Bell of Woll as having left several
daughters, one of whom married Maxwell of Broom-
holm, and a son

ROBERT SCOTT of Harwood. Robert Scott
m. Beatrice Gladstaines "of the ancient family of
Gladstaines," and by her had issue:

1. WALTER. 2. Francis of Greenhill.
3. William. 4. Robert.
5. *Gideon of Falnash.*
1. Agnes m. John Scott of Woll.

WALTER SCOTT of Harwood registered his arms at Lyon Office about 1672. He married Christian, dau. of Sir Andrew Ker, and had issue several sons and a dau. Elizabeth m. to Gilbert Elliot of Woolie. The family was ruined by the extravagance of the Laird's wife, and the estate was sold. The eldest son,

ROBERT SCOTT of Harwood, and the latter's son,

ROBERT SCOTT, Younger, of Harwood, were both alive in 1738, but nothing is known of any other descendants of Walter, the last actual proprietor of Harwood.

Arms.—Or, an oak tree vert, surmounted by a bend azure charged with a mullet between two crescents of the field. Crest.—A stag's head erased ppr. Motto.—" Ardenter Amo."

Falnash.

Scott Bell of Woll

GIDEON SCOTT of Falnash, fifth son of Robert Scott of Harwood and Beatrice Gladstaines, purchased Falnash from his brother. He m. Mary, dau. of James Scott of Thirlestane, and had issue:

    1. ROBERT.

    1. Agnes m. Robert Scott of Burnhead.

    2. Beatrice m. Walter Scott of Crumhaugh.

    3. Christian m. —— Johnstone.

    4. Mary.

ROBERT SCOTT of Falnash m. Violet, dau. of Thomas Rutherford of Edgerston, and dying in 1734, left issue :

    1. GIDEON. 2. THOMAS.

    3. James, minister of Perth, m. Beatrice, dau. of Thomas Mercer of Pinhall, and d. 1818, leaving issue :

        (1) Thomas. (2) Robert.
        (3) James. (1) Violet.
        (2) Elizabeth. (3) Susan.
        All d. unm.

    4. ROBERT. 1. Susannah.

GIDEON SCOTT succeeded his father to Falnash in 1734, but d. s.p. 1759.

THOMAS SCOTT succeeded his brother, and sold the estate to the Duke of Buccleuch. He d. in 1779.

ROBERT SCOTT, fourth son of Robert Scott of Falnash and Violet Rutherford, m. Elizabeth, dau. of Robert Howieson of Orchard, and eventually became " of Orchard." He d. in 1813, leaving issue :

    1. Margaret m. Dr. Andrew Wilson, M.D., Kelso.

    2. Violet m. William Bell, farmer, whose son purchased the estate of Woll from Mr. Ainslie in 1863, and who was father of

WILLIAM SCOTT BELL, now of Woll.

Arms (granted 1855 to Mr. W. S. Bell's father). —Or, an oak tree vert surmounted by a fesse azure charged with an étoile between two crescents of the field between three bells of the third, the star being charged with a crescent gules for difference. Crest.— A stag's head erased ppr. Motto.—" Ardenter Amo." Seat.—The Woll, Hawick, N.B.

𝕎𝔥𝔦𝔱𝔢𝔥𝔞𝔲𝔤𝔥.

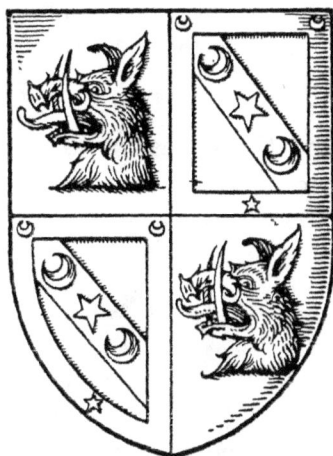

Scott Chisholm ⋄
⋄   of Stirches

JOHN SCOTT of Borthwick is said to have been descended in some way from Buccleuch, but how, is not quite clear. This John appears to have had two sons; John, who succeeded him, and —— father of Walter Scott, the first designed of Whitehaugh.

JOHN SCOTT, second of Borthwick, is principally noted for having fasted eighty days.

WALTER SCOTT, the first designed of Whitehaugh, grandson of John Scott of Borthwick, was apparently ancestor of Walter Scott, a shepherd living in 1688, and the steps of descent are given by Satchells as follows :

ROBERT SCOTT of Whitehaugh, son of the above, was father of

WALTER SCOTT of Whitehaugh, who was father of

WILLIAM SCOTT of Whitehaugh and Thomas in Wester Groundiston, a pensioner to the House of Buccleuch.

ADAM SCOTT was son to William and father of

WALTER SCOTT, a " shepherd swain " living in Satchells' time.　So far this pedigree must be accepted with the greatest reserve, but in 1697 the property is inherited or purchased by

WILLIAM SCOTT of Whitehaugh, who m. in 1705 Ann, dau. of Dr. John Rutherford of Knowesouth.　William Scott d. s.p. 1751, and was succeeded, we are told by Major Tancred, by his sister, Isobel, and on her death in 1759 by her second cousin,

JOHN SCOTT of Whitehaugh; the relationship is, however, not quite clear.　Mr. Scott m. Margaret, the eldest dau. and co-heiress of Walter Scott of Newton, by whom he had three surviving sons and three surviving daughters.

WALTER SCOTT of Whitehaugh, the eldest, was educated as a surgeon, and practised as such for many years.　He d. unm. 1841, and was succeeded by

JAMES SCOTT of Whitehaugh, the third brother, who for a long time resided at Whitslaid. He d. unm. October, 1852.

AGNES SCOTT, one of the three daughters, m. Adam Stavert of Hoscote.

ELIZABETH, another daughter, m. Gilbert Chisholm of Stirches, and this family is now represented by Mr. Scott-Chisholm of Stirches.

Arms.—Of Scott-Chisholm, gules, a boar's head and neck couped argent; quartered with or, on a bend azure a mullet argent between two crescents of the field, a bordure of the second charged with as many crescents in chief and a mullet in base of the former. Crest.—A dexter arm in armour, embowed from the shoulder, the hand holding a scimitar in bend all proper. Motto.—" Vi et Virtute." Seat.—Stirches, near Hawick, N.B.

Willsboro'.

Scott
of Willsborough

THE earliest extant record at Willsboro' is the
Ordination paper of

REV. GIDEON SCOTT, M.A., to priest's orders
by the Rt. Rev. Dr. Wiseman, B.P., of Dromore, Co.
Antrim, and is dated 1685. He acted as Chaplain in
King William's Army in 1688, and purchased the
Willsboro' estate 1696; m. Jane, dau. of Robert
McNeil, Esq., of Ballintoy, and d. 1724, leaving issue:

  1. WILLIAM.

  1. Anne. 2. Jane.

WILLIAM SCOTT, Esq., a lawyer, b. 1704, for many years Recorder and M.P. for the City of Londonderry. He was Prime Sergeant and elevated eventually to the Bench as a Baron of the Exchequer. He m. Hannah, dau. of Thomas Gledstanes, and d. in 1772, having had issue:

1. Thomas, Recorder of Derry, d. 1770.
2. JAMES. 3. Anthony d. 1770.

JAMES SCOTT, Esq., of Willsboro', b. 1745, m. 1779 Catharine Elizabeth, dau. of James Leslie, D.D., Bishop of Limerick, and by her had issue:

1. William d. 1803-4.
2. THOMAS.
3. Edward, Major in the Army, d. 1821.
4. Richard m. the eldest dau. of Colonel Sankey of Fort Frederick, Co. Cavan; d. 1856.
5. *George* (Rev.).
6. Charles m. Jane, dau. of Mr. Farrell of Larne, and d. at Trincomalee, in the Island of Ceylon, where he was many years Judge and Magistrate.
7. *James Leslie Montgomery.*
1. Joice m. Robert Ogilby, Esq., of Pellipar, Co. Derry.
2. Hannah. 3. Maryanne Martha.
4. Jane.

Mr. Scott d. 1820, and was succeeded by his second son,

THOMAS SCOTT, Esq., of Willsboro', J.P. and D.L., High Sheriff, formerly Lieutenant Bengal Army, afterwards Brigade-Major of Yeomanry in Ireland; b. October, 1783; m. first, December, 1823, Hannah, widow of John Campbell, Esq., of Newtownlimavady; secondly 1827 Anne (d. 1840), third dau. of

Rev. Edward Lucas of Rathconnel, Co. Monaghan; and thirdly 1844 Katharine Elizabeth, eldest dau. of Rev. Thomas Richardson of Somerset, Co. Londonderry. By his second wife he left issue:

    1. James d. 1846.   2. WILLIAM EDWARD.

    3. THOMAS LUCAS.

    4. Charles Stewart (Right Hon. Sir), G.C.B., G.C.M.G.; b. March, 1838; m. 1875 Christian Crawfurd, dau. of the late James Macknight, W.S., of Edinburgh, and has issue:

        (1) Charles Edward Stewart m. 1906 Margaret Mary, dau. of Rev. W. Percy.

        (1) Vera Helen.   (2) Alice Maud.

        (3) Margaret Aimee m. Sir Herbert Wm. Davis-Goff, Bart.

        (4) Marie Christian m. John Henry Warre.

        (5) Eileen Agnes m. Henry Bowger Sparke of Gunthorpe Hall, Norfolk.

    1. Elizabeth m. Rev. John Lyle of Knocktarna, Co. Derry.

    2. Hannah m. Rev. Edward Bowen, Archdeacon of Raphoe, and d. 1884.

    3. Annette.

By his third wife he left issue:

    5. Henry Richardson b. August, 1850; m. Elizabeth, dau. of W. Gage of Co. Derry, and d. 1875.

    4. Hatton Thomasina m. 1872 Right Rev. H. S. O'Hara, Bishop of Cashel.

    5. Katherine Emily d. 1855.

    6. Jane Barbara d. 1850.

Major Scott d. January, 1872.

WILLIAM EDWARD SCOTT, Esq., of Willsboro', J.P., D.L., High Sheriff; b. January, 1833; m. 1861 Catherine Georgina, dau. of the Ven. Alexander Stuart, Archdeacon of Ross, and by her had issue:

1. Thomas George Stuart d. 1868.
1. Katherine Elizabeth m. Edward Loftus son of the late Chas. P. Phillips of Berkeley Cottage, Herts.
2. Anne Frances Emily.

Mr. Scott d. 1913, and was succeeded by his nephew, son of his brother,

REV. THOMAS LUCAS SCOTT, b. August, 1834; m. February, 1864, Frances Maria, dau. of Ven. John Russell, Archdeacon of Clogher, and had issue:

1. Thomas Arthur b. 1865; d. 1891.
2. JOHN RUSSELL.
3. William Lucas b. July, 1870; m. 1909 Mabel, dau. of Rev. George Kirkpatrick.
1. Frances Elizabeth m. Rev. Leslie A. Handy.
2. Mary Monica. 3. Norah Leslie.
4. Agnes Geraldine.
5. Kathleen Varena Storey.

JOHN RUSSELL SCOTT, Esq., of Willsboro', J.P. and D.L., High Sheriff; b. April, 1866; m. 1905 Amina Gertrude, dau. of Rev. Robert Walmsley, Vicar of Aspull, near Wigan.

Arms.—Or, on a bend az. a star between two crescents of the field, within a bordure engrailed pean. Crest.—An escallop sable charged with a trefoil or. Motto.—" Perge." Seat.—Willsborough, Co. Londonderry.

Note.—These arms are registered in Dublin, and all male descendants of the grantee have right in arms.

Hartley.

R EV. GEORGE SCOTT, fifth son of James
    Scott of Willsborough, Rector of Banagher, m.
1823 Elizabeth J. Richardson, and left issue:

    1. James Bedell, Rev., b. 1827; d. 1897.

    2. Charles Stewart, Captain H.E.I.C., R.E..
       killed at Oudh 1857.

    3. George.

    1. Maria m. Rev. J. Y. Rutledge, D.D.,
       Rector of Armagh.

    2. Katherine.

GEORGE SCOTT b. November, 1830; m. 1857 Annie, dau. of Rev. John Colthurst, and d. August, 1910, leaving issue:

1. George Colthurst d. young.
2. CHARLES VICTOR GEORGE.
3. William Ernest Richard (Rev.) M.A., b. November, 1874; m. June, 1903, Ada Creed, dau. of Sir James Creed Meredith, LL.D., Dublin, and has issue:
    (1) George Colthurst b. December, 1905.
    (2) James Creed Meredith b. May, 1910.
    (3) Charles Fitzmaurice b. October, 1912.
    (4) Ernest Archbold b. October, 1916.
    (1) Vivienne Meredith.
    (2) Nellie Howe Meredith.
    Address.—Ardtrea Rectory, Stewartstown, Co. Tyrone.
4. George Colthurst d. young.
1. Charlotte Elizabeth.
2. Edie. 3. Helen.
4. Georgina m. Francis Albert Gibson.
5. Caroline Colthurst m. Dr. Joseph Worthington.
6. Mabel Colthurst m. Owen H. Weeks.
7. Marguerite.

CHARLES VICTOR GEORGE SCOTT, C.E., I.S.E., b. August, 1872; m. August, 1914, Violet, dau. of Richard Levinge, and has issue:

1. RICHARD LEVINGE b. 1915.
1. Dorothy Mabel.

Arms.—As Scott of Willsboro'. Address.—Tedburn, Hartley, Plymouth.

George Scott.

REV. JAMES LESLIE MONTGOMERY SCOTT, Chancellor of Down, seventh son of James Scott of Willsboro'; b. 1795; m. 1823 Elizabeth, dau. of Rev. Edward Lucas of Co. Monaghan, and d. 1885, leaving issue:

1. JAMES EDWARD, M.D.
2. Theophilus Leslie, Major-General, b. 1831; m. first Jane, dau. of Wm. Alley, and has issue:
   (1) Edward Lucas.
   (2) Francis Leslie.
   (3) Harold. (4) Arthur.

General Scott m. secondly 1884 Louisa, dau. of Robert Wm. Parsons, but had no further issue.

3. Richard Leslie (Rev.) Rector of Little Parndon, Essex; m. Isabella, dau. of Wm. Charley of Seymour Hill, Co. Antrim, and d. 1901.

4. Horatio, M.D., m. Anne, dau. of Rev. Wm. Steele of Raphoe; d. 1895 leaving issue:

    (1) Horace, M.D.
    (1) Elizabeth m. J. Seaman.
    (2) Dorothea m. Colonel Birch.
    (3) Maud.

5. Francis Montgomery (Rev.) m. Anne, dau. of Thos. Agmondesham Vesey, and d. 1899, having had issue:

    (1) Francis Lucas Clements m. 1907 Alice, dau. of Theophilus Lucas Clements of Rathkenny.

6. Lucas Clements, Lieutenant 88th Connaught Rangers; d. in Indian Mutiny.

7. Walter Henry (Rev.) m. 1874 Katherine, dau. of Samuel Galbraith of Clanabogan, Co. Tyrone.

JAMES EDWARD SCOTT, M.D., b. 1824; m. Martha, dau. of George Johnston, Esq.; m. secondly 1873 Dorothea, dau. of Rev. John F. Gordon. By his first wife he had a son,

GEORGE SCOTT.

Arms as Scott of Willsboro'.

THE PENSIONERS

———

ALTHOUGH not in any sense a genealogy, I think room should be found for an extract of Satchells " Belanden," recording the names of the " four-and-twenty gentlemen " whom Buccleuch kept at his call, and who received various " rooms " or small estates for their services.　The date referred to must be approximately 1580-1620.　Only those marked with an asterisk have I been able to place in the body of this work, and it should be noted that Satchells is probably wrong in stating that Scotstarvit sprung from Hassendene.

" Walter Scott of North House, the first gentleman descended from the family; in a former age Robert Scott of Allanmouth; David Scott of Stobiescot,* brother to Sir Walter Scott of Gaudilands; David Scott of Raes-know, one of the house of Allanhaugh; Robert Scott of Clack, the land of Fennick for his service; William Scott in Hawick* called William in the Mott, brother to Walter Scott of Hardin, possessed these lands without the West-port for his service; John Scott of Monks-tower, brother to old William Scott of Altoun; Robert Scott of Easter-groundiston,* brother-son to Robert Scott of Head-shaw;* James Scott of Altoun-Crofts, Raes-knowe and Allanmouth, were all of the Family of Allan-haugh.　Thomas Scott in Westergroundiston,* brother to William Scott of Whitehaugh,* descended of

the ancient Family of Buccleuch; John Scott in
Drinkston, descended of the ancient Family of
Robertoun; William Scott in Lies, alias Milma,
called William Scott of Catslac-know, descended
from the ancient Family of Dryhope; Robert Scott in
Clarilaw descended from the ancient house of
Hassendene; William Scott of Totchahaugh, from the
aforesaid family of Bortoheugh; Andrew Scott of
Totchahill, from the family of Robertoun; John Scott
in Stowslie; Scott of Whames, descended from the
North-house; Scott of Castlehill, was of that kind;
Walter Scott of Chappel-hill, he was half-brother to
the Laird of Chisholm; Robert Scott of Howford* had
the lands of Cowdhouse for his service; Robert Scott
of Satchells* had Southinrig for his service; Robert
Scott of Langup* had the lands of Outterhuntly for his
service for several ages; there was one William Scott
commonly called Cut-at-the-black, he had the lands of
Nether Delorain for his service; Walter Gledstanes
had Whitelaw. These twenty-four were all of the
names of Scott, except Walter Gledstanes of Whitelaw, who was nearly related to my Lord. Now I
come to Sir Walter Scott of Buccleuch, who was
grandfather to Walter, the good Lord of Buccleuch.
These twenty-three Pensioners, all of his own name
of Scott, and Walter Gledstanes of Whitelaw, a near
cousin of my Lords, as aforesaid; they were ready
upon all occasions, when his Honour pleased cause
to advertise them. It was known to many in the
country better than it is to me, that the rents of these
lands, which the Lairds and Lords of Buccleuch did
freely bestow upon their friends, will amount above
twelve or fourteen thousand marks a year. This I
have thought good to let the reader see, the benefits
which the younger brethren of the name had by their
Chief, when he was but a Baron and Knight, they
were esteemed with more respect than they have been
since."

In 1589 a bond was signed called the clan bond, a copy of which is in the possession of Lord Napier, wherein the various Lairds of the name of Scott bound themselves together for their mutual protection. The following is a list of those who signed the bond :

Walter of Buccleuch.
Walter of Goldielands.
Walter of Eidshaw.*
George of Sinton.
Robert of Haining.
Walter of Howpasley.
Symon of Bonitoun.
Robert of Thirlestane.
Robert of Oakwood.
John of Dryhope.
Walter of Whitslaid.
Walter of Harden.
Walter of Blindhaugh.
William of Burnfoot.
Robert of Burnfoot.
William of Glack.
Walter of Toderick.
Robert of Burnhead.
Robert of Crumgillis.
John of Deuchar.
William in Huntly.
Adam of Todshawhaugh.

Philip of Dryhope.
Symon of Dryhope.
Walter in Ladhope.
James of Gilmanscleuch.
Robert of Altoun.
William of Hartwood-
   myres.
Robert of Hassendene.
William of Howford.
Arthur of Gamescleuch.
William in Mountbenger.
John in Kirkhouse.
John in Dringstone.
William of Allanhaugh.
William of Whithaugh-
   brae.
John in Ormiston.
Walter of Catslack.
John in Commonside.
James, brother to Sir
   Walter of Tushielaw.

* Headshaw.

THE RESCUE OF KINMONT
1596

BELOW will be found Satchells' list of the Clansmen who rode with their Chief to the rescue of William Armstrong from Carlisle Castle, with references, where known, to the pages on which they appear in this book.

20. Robert Scott of Headshaw . . 239
21. Walter Scott of Harden . . 132
22. —— Scott of Commonside . . —
23. Robert Scott of Satchells . . 107
24. William Scott of Burnfoot in Ail . 185
25. Robert Scott of Burnfoot in Teviot . 36
26. Walter Scott of Goldielands (uncertain whether the old man or his son) 11
27. Robert Scott of Howfoord . . 294
28. John Scott of Roberton . . 91
29. —— Scott, brother probably to Walter Scott of Howpasley . 44
30. —— Scott, brother to William Scott of Allanhaugh (or more possibly Willie himself) . . . 16
31. William Scott in Clack . . —
32. Adam Scott of Altoun . . 42
33. Robert Scott of Hassendene . . 35

APPENDIX I

ROYAL DESCENT

THE claim to Royal Blood, especially by those not closely related to any of the old nobility, is rightly looked upon with a great deal of scepticism by the general public, and a few words on this subject may not be out of place here.

The descent of the Buccleuch family from Princess Mary of Scotland is as authentic as any genealogical or historical fact connected with Scottish history, but the truth of the participation in this connection by other members of the Scott family must rest on the reliability of their respective descents from Buccleuch.

The descent of Wicked Wat from the early kings of Scotland and England, showing also the Norman blood of Bruce, is given as follows and may be taken as authentic.

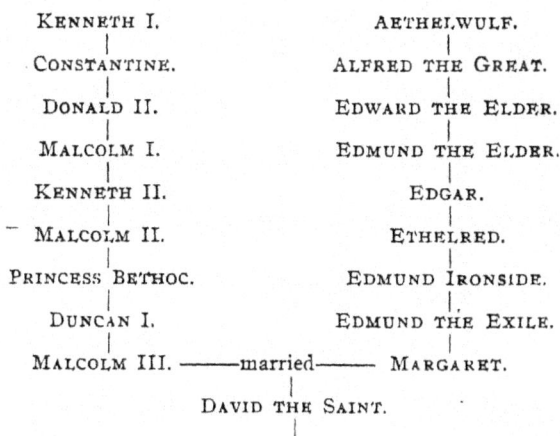

```
KENNETH I.                    AETHELWULF.
     |                            |
CONSTANTINE.                ALFRED THE GREAT.
     |                            |
DONALD II.                  EDWARD THE ELDER.
     |                            |
MALCOLM I.                  EDMUND THE ELDER.
     |                            |
KENNETH II.                    EDGAR.
     |                            |
MALCOLM II.                   ETHELRED.
     |                            |
PRINCESS BETHOC.            EDMUND IRONSIDE.
     |                            |
DUNCAN I.                   EDMUND THE EXILE.
     |                            |
MALCOLM III. ——married—— MARGARET.
                  |
           DAVID THE SAINT.
                  |
```

HENRY, EARL OF HUNTINGDON.

DAVID, EARL OF HUNTINGDON.

ISOBEL.
(Married to Robert de Brus being fourth in descent from
Robert de Brus who came over with the Conqueror.   )

ROBERT BRUCE, LORD OF ANNANDALE.

ROBERT BRUCE, EARL OF CARRICK.

ROBERT I.
(Robert the Bruce.)

PRINCESS MARJORIE OF SCOTLAND.
(Married Walter Stewart.)

ROBERT II.

ROBERT III.

PRINCESS MARY OF SCOTLAND.
(Married George Douglas, Earl of Angus.)

WILLIAM DOUGLAS, EARL OF ANGUS.

GEORGE DOUGLAS, EARL OF ANGUS.

LADY JANE DOUGLAS.
(Married David Scott, Younger of Buccleuch.)

SIR WALTER SCOTT, EIGHTH OF BUCCLEUCH.

WICKED WAT.

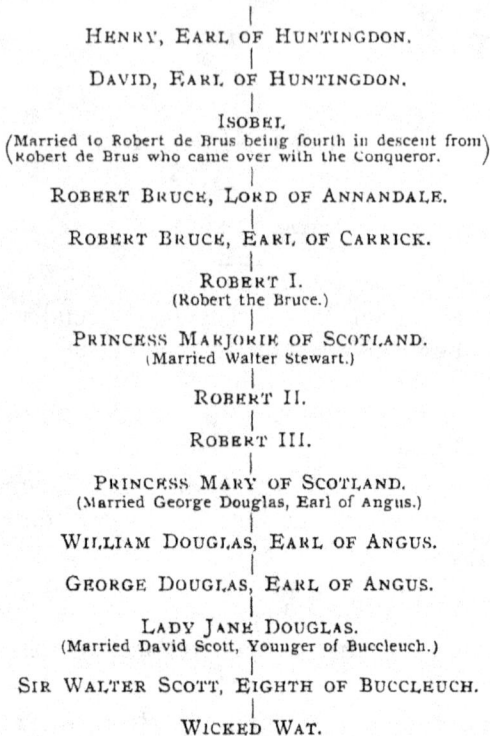

The reader will be able to see for himself which families mentioned in this book can claim descent from Wicked Wat, but attention might be drawn to the following points.

The descendants of Anna, Duchess of Buccleuch and Monmouth, descended directly through Buccleuch, also pick up the Stuart blood through the marriage with Monmouth.

The Harden family* from Walter, eleventh Laird, is descended through Anna of Gorinberrie, also Mr. Macmillan-Scott and others of his family through Sir Walter Scott of Goldielands.

---

*The present Lord Polwarth's family can trace Royal descent independently of the marriage of David Scott and Lady Jane Douglas, and this probably applies to many other families mentioned in this work, as most of the principal families of Scotland intermarried at some time or other with the Stuarts or Bruces.

The whole of the Napier family, including the senior branch, the Scott-Elliots, are descended from Margaret of Buccleuch, aunt of the first Lord Scott.

The modern Sinton family and (via Elliot of Borthwickbrae) the descendants of Gideon Scott in Ladhope are descended from a sister of the above Margaret through the old Headshaw family, and this connection is supported by Satchells'

> " Robert of Headshaw himself would gang,
> He was his Honour's cousin german."

There are also several branches of Scott in Singlie who are connected through the Ladhope family, and there must be many in addition of the name of Scott descended from Wicked Wat, legitimately or otherwise, through the male or female line, particulars of whose descent have been lost.

APPENDIX II

SHORTLY after this book was in the printer's hands, and after most of it was in type, there came into my hands, through the kindness of Colonel W. A. Scott, representative of Teviot Bank, a manuscript work by his uncle, John Scott of Teviot Bank, and afterwards of Rodono, entitled " A Genealogical Memoir of the Scotts of Thirlestane with Genealogical Notes of Other Families of the Name of Scott."

This treatise is comprised in six volumes, of which the first is confined to a discussion on the origin of the present Napier family. The remaining volumes deal with other families living in the fifteenth and sixteenth centuries, and their probable connection with the parent stem of Buccleuch is dealt with at great length and with extensive references.

The Lord Lyon King of Arms has kindly consented, with Colonel Scott's concurrence, to take

x

permanent charge of Mr. John Scott's MS., and eventually I intend to place a typed copy of the whole work in the Lyon Office, and also with the Society of Antiquaries of Scotland.

Mr. Scott's work appears to me to be of exceptional historical value, and from that point of view far surpasses the small work which I have attempted, but the cost of printing, which Mr. Scott obviously intended undertaking when his death in 1867 intervened, may make its publication prohibitive as a financial success. I take this opportunity of intimating that I will gladly subscribe in a small way towards this cost should any public spirited gentleman decide to undertake it. I feel sure Colonel Scott will willingly give his consent.

Without destroying a large quantity of linotype and otherwise incurring considerable expense and delay it has been impossible to revise my book to bring in anything like all the extra matter contained in Rodono's work, as I should have preferred to have done, but I have made several references to Mr. Scott of Rodono, principally under Davington and Sinton, slightly rearranged Tushielaw and Howpasley, and added one or two brief pedigrees taken from Rodono's work such as Shielswood, Girnwood, and Salynside.

As I have already mentioned (page 99) Mr. Scott of Rodono states in his memoirs that the ancestry of Robert Scott of Sinton (XIV), as here given, is absolutely fictitious, but at the same time he states that there is no reason to doubt the truth of the tradition that the family sprung from Buccleuch, in fact "from no other source could any family of the name —— have sprung and at once attained such importance than directly from the House of Branxholm."

Mr. Scott gives his reasons for placing Robert of Sinton as a son of John Scott of Weltoun, No. XI in the Roberton Genealogy, but I think that this is nearly as problematical as Satchells' version, and in any case this book was too far advanced to make possible such a rearrangement as Rodono's version would entail.

It will be noted that the genealogies of Sinton, Whitslaid, and Harden from Robert of Sinton downwards differ materially from those given by Douglas and Burke, particularly as to whether Harden or Whitslaid was the senior family, and it should be mentioned that these genealogies were compiled and arranged independently of Rodono's work and that Rodono concurs in almost every detail.

Mr. Scott of Rodono also concurs with me with regard to the two distinct families of Toderick, but suggests that the first family descended from "William in the Mott" and not from his uncle George, whom he classes among Satchells' myths, having decided, as probably many other readers have done, that Satchells is extremely reliable as to tradition but very unreliable as to detail.

Mr. Scott makes no attempt to trace his pedigrees down to modern times, dealing only with old controversial points, and with families of which all trace has been lost. Without wishing to suggest that my work can be considered on the same plane as the late Mr. John Scott's, it might be possible at some future date to combine the two, and I should be glad to render assistance to anyone who would care to undertake this work.

The following additional genealogies and notes are culled from Rodono's work and condensed* into a similar form to the remainder of this book.

Page 9. GORINBERRIE.

JOHN SCOTT (XIX) of Gorinberrie had, besides his eldest son Francis, two other sons:

    2. David, living in 1670.
    3. Robert, living in 1676.
John Scott d. May, 1668.

---

*Mr. Scott of Rodono averages several pages to each individual dealt with.

FRANCIS SCOTT (XX) of Gorinberrie d. 1689.

Page 16. ALLANHAUGH.

XV. WILLIAM SCOTT of Allanhaugh, who served on an Inquest of Service in May, 1592, was almost certainly eldest son and heir of William No. XIV in this genealogy, and

XVI. JOHN SCOTT of Allanhaugh, living in 1643, was probably a son of the second William.

Page 43. HOWPASLEY.

Rodono discusses at some length the question of Howpasley's descent from Buccleuch.

He states that the fact that Walter Scott of Howpasley was in 1509 tutor to Wicked Wat is proof positive that he was the nearest male relative (in the paternal line) then (1509) living over twenty-five years of age, and from this he considers that the descent of Howpasley as usually accepted and as here given is conclusive except that Alexander was probably the elder brother of James of Hassendene.

It is probable that William, undoubted brother german of David (XII), younger of Buccleuch, was dead in 1509, and was not the William of Foulshiels mentioned in a charter dated 1532 (the latter being possibly identical with Sir William of Kirkurd), and that Robert of Allanhaugh, if a brother of David (XII), as is most probable, was also dead in 1509, and his sons minors or at any rate under twenty-five.

Page 46. TUSHIELAW.

The statement that William Scott of Tushielaw (XVII) married a daughter of Robert Scott of Thirlestane is an obvious error, and it is possible that William (XIV) is the Laird intended.

Page 51. HORSLEYHILL.

According to Rodono, Captain Robert Scott (XXI) was followed by Captain Francis James Scott who left an only child, a daughter married to her cousin Sir John (?) Douglas. Whilst John (XXII) is evidently an error for Francis James the remainder of the genealogy is, I think, correct as given by me, Henry being undoubtedly the last male of this line.

Page 88. GILMANSCLEUCH.

Mr. Scott of Rodono states that James Scott (XIV) was more probably of the Roberton family, and refers again to the mythical existence of John (or Sir John) Scott of Thirlestane. There is, how-ever, little doubt that Rodono is wrong in disputing the existence of John Scott of Thirlestane, and James Scott, first of Gilmanscleuch, is referred to definitely in contemporary documents as eldest son of John Scott of Thirlestane by his second marriage with Marian Douglas.

James had issue, besides Robert his heir, three younger sons of whom William and Andrew were two.

Schaws.

XVI. ADAM SCOTT of Schaws (page 88) had apparently at least four sons:

1. JAMES.
2. Adam in Deloraine, who afterwards pur-chased North Bowhill.
3. —— of Grassyard.
4. Francis, a shepherd mentioned in the Postral.

XVII. JAMES SCOTT m. Marian Scott of Shielswood and became " of Shielswood," and by her had issue more than one son as

XVIII. WALTER SCOTT is designed (1705) eldest lawful son of James.

Page 131. HARDEN.

The Christian name of William of Harden's (XV) second wife was Elizabeth.

Page 173. GALA.

In Mr. Scott's Genealogy of Gala he quotes, among others, two interesting charters dated 1649 and 1757 from which it appears that James (XIX) had at least one other son besides Hugh, and that in 1757 there was in life a considerable number of male descendants of Hugh Scott of Deuchar in addition to the issue of Hugh (XX) and their issue.

Howfoord.

RODONO does not even suggest a possible origin for this family, but the following brief pedigree should be given.

ROBERT SCOTT of Howfoord, living in 1558, was probably the father of

ROBERT SCOTT of Howfoord, who assisted at the rescue of William Armstrong in 1596.

WILLIAM SCOTT of Howfoord, so designed in 1607, was probably the younger Robert's son. He died not later than 1621, when his son,

WALTER SCOTT of Howfoord, witnessed several documents. Walter parted with Howfoord to Sir William Scott of Harden, but was represented in 1686 by Scott of Coudhouse.

Langshaw.

PATRICK SCOTT of Eddrington obtained a Crown Charter of Langshaw in 1653. From the fact that Satchells states that Langshaw " is of kin to me," and from the Christian names, it would seem possible that this family is a branch of Thirlestane, but there is no reliable evidence on the point. In the same charter Patrick's wife is mentioned as Elizabeth Scott and his eldest lawful son as

JOHN SCOTT of Langshaw.

FRANCIS SCOTT of Langshaw, younger brother of John Scott of Langshaw, obtained Crown Charters in 1674 and 1690.

WALTER SCOTT of Langshaw was served heir to his father Francis in 1695.

THOMAS SCOTT of Langshaw was served heir to his father Francis and brother Walter.

In the course of compiling this work it has been suggested to me that the pedigrees are lacking very much in value through my not having given references for each fact stated, with which criticism I am compelled to agree.

Most of the modern pedigrees are obviously taken direct out of Burke and similar works corrected to date when possible by the family, and I am very glad to be able to state that to a very large extent Mr. Scott of Rodono's work supplies the references desirable to establish the steps in my skeleton pedigrees between 1500 and 1700.

INDEX.

Confined to estates and farms owned or tenanted by members of The Family and surnames (and titles) of families allied by marriage.

In some few cases where the surname of allied families occurs frequently, the designation is also given (e.g. Stobs), and in these cases the name and designation are indexed separately and as a rule the designation will more readily locate an individual than the surname.

The name " Scott " is not indexed, but compounds of it are indexed under the first name only. Any member of the Scott family not traceable under a designation may possibly be found under the maiden name of either wife or mother.

Places such as Nether Ancrum, West Deloraine, Easter Muirdean, are indexed under the principal part of the name.

Y

INDEX.

Corrections and Additions.

Page xviii, line 16. For 'when' read 'where'.

,, 23, line 2. For 'second' read 'third'.

,, 31, ,, 13-14. Omit 'Philadelphia'.

,, 77. This should have been titled "Owen Napier."

,, 120, ,, 21. (2) Gideon, tenant in Middlemoss, m. Barbara Armstrong; d. c. 1835, aged 38.

,, 25. (3) —— m. William Dove, who succeeded his father-in-law in Todshawhaugh.

,, 183, ,, 1. For 'elder' read 'eldest.'

,, 32. For 'Alexander' read 'ALEXANDER.'

,, 192, ,, 19. For 'Scots' read 'Scotts'.

,, 195, ,, 14. For 'Robert Hill' read 'Robert Mill'.

,, 228. Lady Moira Scott m. Major H. S. Combe, D.S.O.

,, 295. Too late for alteration it was noticed that Patrick Scott of Langshaw was almost certainly Patrick Scott first of Ancrum (page 206), but possibly through there being no record of Satchells' paternal grandmother, or great-grandmother, it is not easy to trace any near relation between Francis, who would be 'of Lang-shaw' in 1686, and the author of "The True History."

CORRECTIONS AND ADDITIONS.

Page 195, line 32. James Scott, the eldest son (not John), succeeded to Logie and married Margaret, daughter of James Scott, of Comieston, but d.s.p. and, *both* the younger sons having predeceased him, he was succeeded by Robert, son of Margaret, his eldest sister, and Alexander Myln of Hatton, who assumed the name of Scott and became Robert Scott, seventh of Logie. James had three or four other sisters, one at least of whom was married.

,, **196.** Arms here given are the arms of Logie which, according to Scottish practice, would pass to Robert Myln with the property and not to the heir-male. David Scott (XXIV) registered 14/12/1824 as heir-male, the Logie arms, charging the fess with a chess rook.

,, **197.** For 'Cornieston' read 'Comieston'.

,, **213.** Colonel Adam Scott-Elliot, d. December, 1921.

,, **215.** John Scott, of Ashtrees, m. secondly, Betty Rutherford and d. 1779. He left issue besides Adam and Thomas :—
  1. Helen.
  2. Janet, m. James Chisholm.
  3. Margaret, m.———
  4. Betty, m.———
One of the two latter married William Brewhouse. Adam, Thomas and Helen were children of first marriage. I have no evidence as to the others.

,, **220, line 8.** Roughheugh is probably a mistake for Doveshaugh.

,, **229.** This family continues to use the old spelling of Scot.

,, **230, line 1.** For 'Major-General' read 'General'.

,, **230, ,, 3.** For 'Cairnsmon' read 'Cairnsmore'.

,, **230, ,, 6.** Dr. Wm. Scot was b. 1862.

Archibald Murgatroyd was the eldest son and Wm. Robert was b. 1864. Thomas Goldie, the third son, m. secondly, Alice Phillips, and has issue :—
  4. Norton.

,, **231.** Dorothy Lever m. Major Wm. Miles Logan-Home of Edrom, and Cecil Mary m. Lieut.-Com. John Uniacke Penrose-Fitzgerald.

,, **248.** It has been suggested that John in Hummelknowe may have been a son of Alexander, miller in Rulewater. (Page 220).

,, **253, line 26.** Marion, m. secondly, Richard Lauder of Holtoun.

,, **255.** For 'Sir John Thomas Nicholson of Cockburnspath' read 'Sir Thomas Nicolson, King's Advocate'.

,, **258, line 3.** For 'Nicholson' read 'Nicolson.'

,, **270, ,, 26.** For '1863' read '1871'.

,, **292.** XVII. WALTER SCOTT of Allanhaugh is noted as proprietor in 1678.

,, **294, line 9.** For 'page 173 Gala' read 'page 178 Gala'.

,, **307, ,, 21.** For 'almost certainly' read 'certainly' (Lyon Register).

CORRECTIONS AND ADDITIONS.

There are several spelling mistakes in both the body of the book and the index—e.g., Huntley—which do not necessitate individual attention.

Page 10.		John Scott of Gorinberrie had a third daughter, m. to John Elliot of Whithaugh (Unthank tombstone).
,,	12.	Sir Walter Scott (XVI) of Goldielands was knighted in 1619. It is possible that the knighthood attributed to his father 'the Laird's Wat' is an error.
,,	24.	The bordure indented has been accidentally omitted from the description of the Gordon quartering.
,,	26, line 15.	Charles Scott m. Isabella Scott.
,,	44.	Howpasley does not now belong to the Napier family.
,,	57.	William, third son of Francis, was tenant in Holm before becoming 'of Beattock.'

Francis, his brother, was tenant in Nether Davington and m. Barbara Armstrong of Hardenside, Dumfries, and besides Agnes had other children :—
1. Francis, d. in East Indies, s.p.
2. Margaret, m. John Scoon, Canonbie.
3. Ellen, m. John Scoon, cousin of above.
4. Barbara, m. John Martin, of Closegap.

Francis, of Davington, d. 1706.
Robert Scott of Davington, m. Mary McAlpine.

,,	58.	Susanna, third daughter of James Scott of Davington, m. John Stewart.
,,	119, line 5.	William Scott was tenant in Girnwood in December, 1767 and must have survived his father by at least sixteen months.
,,	121, ,, 34.	'Hindup' now commonly called 'Hindhope'.
,,	132, ,, 26.	After 'Wedderlie' add 'and relict of Spottiswoode of that Ilk.'
,,	133, ,, 29.	Lady Scott m. secondly Sir William Scott of Thirlestane.
,,	135, ,, 19.	For '2. Mary. 3. Lilias' read '2. Mary Lilias'.
,,	135, ,, 34.	Helen m. Geo. Brown of Elliston.
,,	136, ,, 5.	For 'de Jure' read 'de jure'.
,,	138, ,, 29.	Hon. Grisell Katherine m. Arthur Sutton.
,,	139, ,, 23.	Add '2nd Lieut. 8th Royal Scots'.
,,	143.	The Rev. W. F. Scott, d. Jan. 1924.
,,	144, line 22.	The sasine stating Raeburn was alive in 1710 is incorrect.
,,	151, ,, 9.	For 'mother' read 'Uncle Capt. Rutherford'.
,,	161, ,, 32.	For '1863' read '1871'.
,,	171.	Mrs. J. R. Scott d. May, 1924.
,,	178, line 17.	For '1707' read '1703'.
,,	183.	William Scott of Sinton, d. July, 1661.

www.ingramcontent.com/pod-product-compliance
Lightning Source LLC
Chambersburg PA
CBHW071835270326
41929CB00013B/2004